On my way to victory with the Le Mans Replica in the 2-litre class of the Production Sports Car race at Silverstone in May, 1952 (T. C. March).

Roy Salvadori

Racing Driver

Roy Salvadori
Racing Driver

Roy Salvadori
&
Anthony Pritchard

PSL
Patrick Stephens, Wellingborough

First published in 1985

British Library Cataloguing in Publication Data

Salvadori, Roy
Roy Salvadori.
1. Salvadori, Roy 2. Automobile racing drivers – Biography
I. Title II. Pritchard, Anthony
796.7′2′0924 GV1032.S/

ISBN 0-85059-634-3

Patrick Stephens Limited is part of the Thorsons Publishing Group

Photoset in 11 on 12 pt Plantin by J&L Composition Ltd, Filey, North Yorks. Printed in Great Britain on 115 gsm Fineblade coated cartridge, and bound, by The Garden City Press, Letchworth, Herts, for the publishers, Patrick Stephens Limited, Denington Estate, Wellingborough, Northants, NN8 2QD.

Contents

Foreword by Sir Jack Brabham

For three years Roy and I drove together in the Cooper team, years during which Cooper battled in sports car racing with the rival Lotus Elevens, dominated Formula Two during its first three seasons and began to play a serious role in Grand Prix racing. They were years during which Roy and I formed a close working relationship, scrapping furiously on the track while good friends in the pits and at the Cooper works. While Roy did much to promote Cooper business interests, I worked intensively on the cars and we both brought the team a good measure of racing success.

My drive with Rob Walker's 1.9-litre Cooper-Climax at Monaco in 1957 represented a turning point in Cooper history and from then onwards the team competed regularly in Formula One. During 1957–58 the Coopers improved in speed and reliability and we achieved more and more success. Roy was already an established Grand Prix driver, with experience with the works Connaught team and three years' racing with the Gilby Maserati 250F behind him. Roy used the benefit of this experience to smooth the way for Cooper in International events and life was much easier for the team abroad that it might otherwise have been. Roy was also an immensely versatile driver who could rapidly switch from car to car and achieve success in many different categories of racing.

Roy and I enjoyed racing together so much that we both planned to join the Aston Martin Formula One team for 1959. At first it seemed that the Aston DBR4 would prove a very serious contender for International success, but then we heard that Coventry-Climax would be making available that year a new 2.5-litre engine. We were confident that this new and more powerful engine could achieve consistent success for Cooper and transform its prospects in Grand Prix racing. Roy felt committed to going to Aston Martin and I stayed with Cooper. The result is history.

Despite this parting of the ways, we remained good friends and Roy raced with me in Australia in 1961. I am delighted to write this foreword, and I am sure that this book will enthrall enthusiasts for racing as it used to be in our day.

Jack Brabham
October 1984

Co-author's note

As a racing driver Roy always attracted great publicity, partly because of the sheer press-on bravado and flamboyance of his driving, partly because he had more than his fair share of bad accidents, but above all because he was very successful and very versatile.

In the 1950s he cut a dashing image, a tall slim figure in blue overalls, most closely associated with the beautifully prepared Gilby Engineering Maserati 250F Grand Prix car and the works Aston Martin team. Roy and his contemporaries entertained the motor racing public, but they also provided inspiration for a generation of schoolboys. Roy did what thousands dreamed they would do one day and, indirectly, helped the likes of me battle through their 'O' and 'A' levels in the knowledge that there was something better in the future.

Many never had the chance to try their hand at motor racing and they are probably the lucky ones, because they can still think and talk of what might have been. For my part, three years of racing, sprinting and hill-climbing with a Lawrencetune Morgan Plus Four served to convince me that the skill and courage were never there and that I should restrict my driving of fast cars to the road and at speeds within my limited ability!

While writing this book with Roy, it has been a topic of conversation on many occasions, at business meetings, in flying clubs and the local pub, and I have been constantly surprised at the number of middle-aged men, with no interest at all in motor racing today, who were spectators at Goodwood and Silverstone in the 1950s, and remember vividly Roy's exploits with the 250F and Aston Martin sports cars.

I think that the seed of an idea for this book was first sown in September 1954 when a schoolfriend and myself asked Roy for his autograph in the paddock at the Crystal Palace. Thirty years later here it is.

Anthony Pritchard,
Bourne End, Bucks. October 1984

Introduction

Flat out through the night, braking very late, accelerating hard but smoothly from the corners, changing up at 5,500 rpm to conserve the engine, anxious that the gearbox – the Achilles' heel of the DBR1 – would last the distance, straining to hear any unusual noise. Past the pits and grandstands – a stream of dazzling lights – pulling 140 mph in fifth gear, round the right-hander just after the pits at 5,300 rpm in fifth, down to third on the crash 'box for the Esses, the latest possible braking for the darkness of Tertre-Rouge. Gradually the revs rise until I see 6,000 rpm – about 167 mph – on the tachometer; flat out through the kink, waiting, waiting, then hard, very hard on the brakes, heeling and toeing down through the 'box to second for Mulsanne, that slow, tight, right-hander taken at about 40 mph, a quick look across to the signalling point on my right, accelerating through the gears to a full 5,600 rpm in fifth on the straight before heavy braking and changing down to third gear for the first part of Indianapolis; a short burst of power, brake and down into second gear for the second part of the corner which tightens up, another short burst in second to Arnage, accelerating up to fourth and 5,100 rpm for White House, then into top and past the pits again.

Uneasy whether slower cars will cross my line at the corners, but settling down into a relaxed concentration on the long Mulsanne straight. Worrying whether the car will last, as I have never finished Le Mans before in my racing career. Peering through the mist that masks the Sarthe circuit in the early hours of the morning, the gentle breaking of dawn, the soft early morning sunshine and the unvarying rhythm of consistent lap times as I claw back valuable seconds on the leading Ferrari. The spectator enclosures increasingly crowded, the circuit occupied by fewer and fewer cars as Sunday morning edges towards the afternoon. The short breaks in the pits while Shelby is at the wheel, time for a coffee and a rest, but my mind still in the cockpit of the DBR1. During the final stages of the race I can only sit in the pits and watch, full of anxiety and hope, as Carroll Shelby gently steers the DBR1 to the chequered flag. The last lap that seems it will never end, the chequered flag and, almost unbelievably, Carroll's lap of honour with the winning car. Afterwards, anti-climax, the pain of my feet burned on the DBR1's exhaust, the so-welcome sleep back at La Chartre.

Le Mans, 1959

Chapter 1

Climbing the ladder

I started life with the dubious advantage that my mother's maiden name was Ferrari – a common enough name in Italy. My parents Gino and Zelinda had left their native Lucca in Tuscany to settle eventually at Dovercourt near Harwich in 1920. My father was a great jack-of-all-trades, sometimes successful and sometimes not so successful, and he used his large property with its spacious grounds for his various business activities. His great speciality was the manufacture of ice cream and it was probably one of his more successful enterprises. All day, all weekend – and sometimes all night – the manufacturing went on. He distributed his ice cream throughout South-East England and he used an adaption of a famous slogan, 'Stop me and buy too'. There were many complaints from neighbours about the noise and my father would always listen very courteously, say very little and round off the meeting by presenting the complainant with a large tub of ice cream and a promise to try to cut down on the noise. My father was always trying something new and later he had businesses in London.

My parents had four children and I, the second eldest, was born in 1922. We were all educated at a convent boarding school in Brentwood. Some years later my father disposed of the Dovercourt property and moved to London. I worked with my father in whatever happened to be the family business at the time, including a refrigeration leasing business and the manufacture of alabaster and plaster models that were the product of my father's last and most successful business venture. During the war my father carried on business in London, but my mother evacuated herself to Nottingham where she opened a successful restaurant. She now lives in Enfield, aged 90, and is still as sweet and generous as ever.

Like so many teenagers I was obsessed by motor cycles and motor cycle racing. I was already well versed in the art of breaking bones on these lethal machines and because my own Rudge TT Ulster was being repaired after a previous stunt, I borrowed a friend's BMW transverse twin one evening in 1940 to see a girlfriend who lived in Hatfield. I was riding near Hatfield on my way back to London with the very dim light that was all that was permitted in wartime when I came to a fork in the road. It was a fork that I knew very well, but I was confused because a house seemed to have appeared in the middle. In fact the house was one of those pill boxes that were being erected all over the country at the time. As I thought that I was going to hit it, I slammed the bike down on its side, something that I had done before when I had been in trouble. One of the cylinder heads dug into the road, the bike rebounded off the road and pinned me to the concrete side of the pill box. I lost consciousness, the first of many such occasions in my life, and suffered very serious injuries that included a broken femur. The result was many months spent in hospital, some of the time in the company of three German airmen who had been shot down in a Heinkel and a Polish airman whose main aim in life was to carry on the war against his German enemies. Several unsuccessful attempts were made to set my badly-broken femur and eventually the doctors decided that the only solution was a stainless steel plate. It was almost a year before I could walk properly again and my leg still gives me problems. As a result of the accident I missed military service – I was classed Grade Four, the lowest grade.

During the war I continued to ride motor cycles, but I soon turned to cars. I started my own business manufacturing and wholesaling plaster and alabaster models and it was during this time that I started motor racing. In about 1947 I bought a car hire business in Leytonstone and we specialised in the supply of Daimler and Rolls-Royce cars for weddings and funerals. I bit off more than I could chew because the cars were rather old – due to their lack of reliability we sometimes had difficulty in being punctual, and customers were often refusing to pay. It was difficult to work out whether or not their complaints were genuine or whether they were just trying it on. Thanks to the help of Irish racing driver Joe Kelly I managed to sell the business, but what the purchaser was really after was the Hackney Carriage licences and not my dilapidated fleet of cars. He moved the business to Harlesden while I used the spacious premises at Leytonstone for the sale of cars, mainly the seven-seater limousines which I knew so well.

Later, in partnership with William Mansfield, I took offices at 48 Fitzroy Street. We had garage accommodation in the mews at the back of the premises and continued to run a successful business, buying and selling the larger cars. I was talked into buying a Riley Sprite two-seater; I liked dealing in this sort of car and I became more and more involved in the sporting side of the motor trade. William Mansfield decided to buy a business in Broxbourne and I came to an arrangement to share an office in the same block with OM and Brooklands expert Dick Oats. Because Dick had a garage in Penzance he was rarely there, but when he was there we did nothing but talk motor racing, and he gave me a good grounding in the ins and outs of Brooklands racing which had gone for ever.

In 1952 I opened a garage showroom, Elmbridge Motors, on the Kingston by-pass, and this soon flourished. Although we had space for only 24 cars, I obtained a total of 12 agencies and distributorships including the Lancia distributorship for Surrey and agencies for Aston Martin, Jaguar, MG and Wolseley amongst others. Because of the limitations of space we needed a very rapid turnover to get through our allocation of cars without too many problems, and in this Mario Tozzi-Condivi, who came to work with me in the business as a director/sales manager, proved an invaluable aid. He plays an important role in my story as years later I sold Elmbridge Motors to the Chipstead Group, of which he was a director, and he proved a vital link in the sale of Cooper Cars to Chipstead and my appointment as racing manager. Elmbridge Motors was ideally placed for me to combine business and motor racing, as Goodwood was only 45 minutes away and Silverstone an hour and a quarter – if I was really trying. When practice was on the Friday for a Saturday meeting I could slip away, practice and return to the business the same day.

1946

In the spring of 1946 I saw an R-type MG advertised and from the advertisement I thought that it was a sports car. It was owned by R.J. Symonds and I went to see it at Enfield. When I saw the MG, I discovered that it was a Zoller-supercharged 746 cc single-seater with a pre-selector gearbox and wishbone and torsion bar independent suspension front and rear. It looked superb, it sounded even better and it did not take much for me to convince myself that if MG made good sports cars, then their single-seaters must be even better. A deal was soon concluded and I paid around £500 for the MG, just about all the money that I could afford at the time. William Mansfield, who was then an engineer with the JAP motor cycle engine company, helped me with the MG and I entered it at the first post-war British motor race meeting held at Gransden Lodge Airfield on June 15 1946. I drove in the race for 750 cc racing cars, finishing second to Issigonis with the Lightweight Special – there were only three starters and two finishers. The MG was not without its problems and after a few events I decided to sell it. I cannot remember who bought the MG, but it ended up with Duncan Hamilton.

I had been thoroughly bitten by the motor racing bug and I looked for a car that was both faster and more reliable. Arnolds of Manchester were advertising the very famous ex-Dobbs 2-litre Riley single-seater with offset body and I bought this for £750. Before I competed with the Riley, I sent it for a checkover to Monaco Motors at Watford, that famous company whose directors were Peter Monkhouse, Ian Connell and John Wyer. When I received their bill I was horrified, and it was only then that I realised just how expensive motor racing was.

I ran the Riley at the West Court Speed Trials at Finchhampstead on September 15 and I set the fastest time of the day, beating Allard and ERA opposition. *Motor Sport* commented, 'First came in the 1½–3-litre-racing-car-class. Salvadori, with the black, ex-Dobbs, ex-Fernihough, ex-Bellvue Garage 2-litre Riley, wearing ordinary clothes (and a crash-hat on his second run) clocked 23.40 sec, and then got that down to 23.32 sec, a fine show. He learned his record time from Marcus Chambers on his return, shook hands with Cooper, and was decently modest about the whole thing. . .'

For me the significance of that report is the reference to John Cooper. 500 cc racing cars were just beginning to make their mark and the Cooper-JAP driven by Eric Brandon and John Cooper took the first two places in the class for racing

My first run at the 1946 Finchampstead Speed Trials with the ex-Dobbs Riley 2-litre (The Motor).

cars up to 1,100 cc. That meeting with John Cooper at West Court marked the beginning of a long and happy friendship with the Coopers that stretched throughout my motor racing career and afterwards.

Whilst I had found the Riley fast and reliable, above all competition driving in those days was immense fun, but of course it was very expensive and something that most of us could only afford occasionally during the year. I had just as much enjoyment from preparing and polishing the Riley in its garage at Stoke Newington, starting it up and showing it to friends, as I did from competing with it. At the end of the year I sold this car to Joe Kelly.

1947

By now I hankered after something faster and I looked at the Alfa Romeo Monoposto which Kenneth Evans was selling. The Monoposto, designed by Jano, was the most famous Alfa Romeo racing car and featured eight cylinders cast in two blocks of four with integral cylinder heads and blocks. There was a 3-speed gearbox with the gate between the driver's legs, but with the lever cranked to the left of the steering wheel and drive to the rear wheels by means of two prop-shafts enclosed in torque tubes running from a single differential behind the gearbox. This car had been driven to victory by Nuvolari in the 1935 German Grand Prix and it had been sold to Austin Dobson with a 2.9-litre engine developing around 215 bhp. Evans, who had looked after the car meticulously, had been racing it since 1937. As soon as I saw the Monoposto I was hooked and in partnership with Mansfield I bought it for £2,000.

The Monoposto was a fantastic car, but I must admit that I never got the measure of it and it was quite a frightening car to drive. Evans warned me that it weaved at speed, but I had no appreciation of just how bad weaving could be until I raced the Monoposto on the narrow Chimay road circuit where it occupied all the road. It was more powerful than anything that I had driven previously and it took me a while to get used to both the performance and the rather difficult gear-change. It was very nicely balanced, with reasonable brakes and almost solid suspension. It must be remembered that almost all powerful cars of this era were rather a handful, very difficult to control in the wet and frightening to most drivers except the Fangios of this world. We had very little mechanical trouble with the Monoposto apart from gearbox trouble at Chimay and a cracked cylinder head which at first seemed to be a major disaster. Fortunately Leslie Brooke had good connections at Alfa Romeo and through Guidotti obtained the factory's only spare monobloc casting for the sum of £70, so that we were able to rebuild the engine.

As soon as we bought the Alfa, we sent it to Monaco Motors for a checkover and I explained to John Wyer that I could not afford to spend a great deal on the car. John Wyer was very good to me and that was the start of a long friendship. This was really the extent of preparation that Monoposto received while I was racing it.

My first outing with the Monoposto was in the Formule Libre Grand Prix des Frontières at Chimay in Belgium, enabling me to combine my first Continental race meeting with a holiday. Of this race John Eason Gibson wrote in his review of the year, *Motor Racing 1947*: 'One lap measured 6.75 miles and had to be covered 12 times. The circuit was of roughly triangular shape and the surface was incredibly loose and bumpy, one corner having a horrible bump right on the apex. ... The organisation was not of the highest, spectators being permitted to wander about at will both in the training and in the actual race. ...'

In practice I had trouble with the Monoposto's gearbox and I drove in the race using top gear only. The torque of the straight-eight engine was good enough for me to be able to get away with this, though the acceleration was of course badly affected. My main problem was overtaking. With the Monoposto weaving all over the road, it seemed a very hit-or-miss affair whether I went round the car in front or over the top! If I took my hands off the wheel on the straight, the car would steer itself, just weaving from side to side of the road as it did so. I finished fifth.

I ran the Alfa in a few other events in England during the year and my best drive was at Gransden Lodge in July. On this airfield circuit the road was so wide that I hardly noticed the weaving of the Alfa. In the main race of the day, the Grandsden Trophy, I drove a good race, despite locking brakes, to finish third behind Dennis Poore (3.8-litre Alfa Romeo 8C-35) and George Abecassis (Bugatti Type 59). Later in the year I ran the Alfa in the Southsea Speed Trials (third fastest) and at Shelsley Walsh (second fastest in class), but these events merely served to confirm my preference for circuit racing.

1948

For 1948 I looked for a suitable supercharged 1,500 cc car that would be eligible for Formula One races. My biggest problem was to find a buyer for the

Monoposto and I ran in the Luton Hoo Speed Trials and the Castletown Trophy on the Isle of Man before I eventually arranged a deal with the father of Ronnie Moore, the world champion speedway rider. All I could get for the Alfa was £1,000, so Mansfield and I took a substantial loss and the car was shipped to New Zealand where it enjoyed a very successful racing career in the hands of its new owners. They cured the weaving by modifications to the Dubonnet front suspension and by running the car on much lower tyre pressures than I had been using on the advice of Dunlop.

I bought an old, 1934, 4-cylinder Maserati 4C-1500 ex-Rayson from Charles Mortimer. I paid around £1,250 for the car and concluded a deal with Mortimer, who was a partner in a garage at Byfleet known as Rowland Motors, that his firm would prepare the car and transport it to meetings for me. Their charges were very reasonable, the sort of level that even I could afford. The Maserati was a good car and very enjoyable to drive; it handled very well, it had excellent brakes and it was almost as fast at the later 6-cylinder model. The engine peaked at fairly low revs and if I exceeded 6,000 rpm then I was quite likely to do some damage to the engine.

My first outing with the 4C was in the Jersey Road Race on the St Helier road circuit. I drove a very steady race, not pushing my luck too much, and finished seventh, some way behind Bod Gerard's winning ERA. A month later I competed on the very difficult Douglas road circuit. I ran the Alfa Romeo in the Castletown Trophy, but it gave trouble and I was forced to retire. In the main race, the Formula One British Empire Trophy, I over-revved the engine of the Maserati and retired with valve trouble.

There was only a limited number of events that I could enter, partly because motor racing was still re-establishing itself after the war and there were not many race meetings, and partly because the age of my car and my limited racing experience prevented me from entering the major International races. On June 1

With the Alfa Romeo Monoposto in the 1948 Castletown Trophy on the Douglas circuit in the Isle of Man. This photograph vividly illustrates road racing as it used to be (Louis Klemantaski).

I ran at the Stanmer Park hill climb, but was unclassified, and I did not compete again until August 7 when the BRDC organised the inaugural meeting at the new Zandvoort circuit near Haarlem. The race was a Formule Libre event with two 65-mile qualifying heats and a 108-mile final. I ran in the second heat and was classified eighth and last, although I was not running at the finish because of gearbox trouble; as a result I did not run in the final which was won by 'Bira's' Maserati.

On September 18 the first-ever Goodwood race was held and I drove the Maserati in the 5-lap Goodwood Trophy race for 1,500 cc supercharged racing cars. The opposition was very strong, Reg Parnell won with the latest 4CLT/48 Maserati on loan from the works and I was not at all displeased with my seventh place. My final outing of the year was in the RAC Grand Prix at Silverstone on October 2. There was a very strong entry of Maseratis (including the Scuderia Ambrosiana 4CLT/48 cars of Villoresi and Ascari which took the first two places) and of Lago-Talbots and I finished eighth after a pit stop. I might not have achieved much in the way of success, but my appetite for Grand Prix racing had been thoroughly whetted.

1949

For 1949 I agreed a deal with the great Siamese driver Prince Birabongse ('B. Bira') to drive a 4CL Maserati. This was not the latest Maserati model, but it was a post-war car with the usual 1,490 cc (78 × 78 mm) 16-valve single-stage supercharged engine. The basis of the deal – a common arrangement at the time – was that I paid £2,000 in return for which the car was prepared at the works at Modena for the coming season, entered by an Italian in Milan and prepared on a routine basis at Bira's White Mouse garage in England (it was almost next door to the Hammersmith Palais) by his mechanic Stan Holgate. It

My first car eligible for Formula One events, the Maserati 4C-1500, seen here at the Stanmer Park Hill Climb (Guy Griffiths).

At the wheel of the Maserati 4CL in the 1949 Daily Express *International Trophy race at Silverstone* (Louis Klemantaski).

was transported to meetings in the old White Mouse garage transporter. At the end of the year when the car was sold I would receive a percentage of the sale proceeds. Bira was under contract to a number of entrants, including Enrico Platé in Formula One, but he wanted to keep his own *équipe* going and so the arrangement suited us both very well.

During the negotiations I went with Bira to the Maserati factory and met the Orsi family whom I thought were charming, kind and very capable and whom I soon got to know well, something that helped me in later years. I also went with Bira to the Ferrari factory, was shown round and had lunch with Enzo Ferrari. The contrast between the Orsis and Ferrari could not be more marked. Enzo was formidable in stature and personality. I soon realised that it is Ferrari who does the talking, Ferrari who bangs the table and he gives you the feeling that you should sit quietly and agree or forever hold your peace.

My first outing with the 4CL was in the Paris Grand Prix at Montlhéry on April 24. I collected the 4CL myself from the Maserati factory and transported it to the circuit. I had continuous problems with an oil leak, as a result of which I had to make several pit stops. I finished eighth and last, a disappointing performance. I then drove on to England and put the 4CL in the care of the very quiet and very able Stan Holgate who had three weeks to prepare the car for the RAC Grand Prix. Although he made a good job of it, we had troubles both in practice and in the race. In practice I was only 20th fastest out of 24 starters. In the race I drove steadily, gradually working my way through the field until I held eighth place at half-distance (50 laps). I had already had a bad spin, stalling the engine, but I managed to bump-start the Maserati and jump in. I later retired with gearbox trouble after what I regarded as a good race in formidable company. The winner was de Graffenried with a 4CLT/48 Maserati.

I did not race again until the *Daily Express* International Trophy at Silverstone on August 20. The opposition included the works Ferraris of Villoresi and Ascari and the latest Maseratis driven by Farina, Bira, de Graffenried and Parnell. I went well in practice, lapping faster than the similar 4CLs of Murray

The 4CL burns furiously after the crash in the 1949 Wakefield Trophy on the Curragh circuit (Independent Newspapers).

and Shawe-Taylor. In my heat I finished fifth, a lap behind the winning Maserati of Farina. I was out of luck in the final and retired with engine trouble when I was in tenth place.

The following month we took the Maserati to Ireland to compete in the Wakefield Trophy on the Curragh road circuit. The main opposition came from Peter Walker with the E-type ERA and Dudley Folland with a 2-litre unblown Ferrari. It was indicative of my improving form and experience that whilst Walker was fastest in practice in 3 min 34 sec, I was alongside him on the grid and only two seconds slower. The race started in heavy rain. Walker took the lead at the start and I was close behind. As we came down the long straight and over the brow of the hill before the first corner, all I could see in front of me was a great cloud of spray – and this hid both Walker's ERA and the corner. Suddenly through the spray I caught sight of the ERA broadside across and I braked, thinking, 'Well, that's the end of the main opposition.' At that moment my Maserati was struck up the rear with tremendous force by Watson's Alta and I do not think that Watson had even begun to brake for the corner. My car was accelerated forwards by the impact, the ruptured fuel tank caught alight and I stood up in the seat, steering the car until it was clear of the crowd in the grandstand. I then jumped off the car, but my right foot struck the steering wheel and I fell between the nearside wheels with the result that the rear wheel ran over my foot. The car straddled a ditch, hit the bank and was completely burnt out because it was mainly constructed of magnesium – at one stage the flames were thirty feet high. We were left with only a box of spares to take home and we had some difficulty in satisfying the Customs about the disappearance of the car – until we showed them photographs that had appeared in the national press! The one consolation was that the Maserati was fully insured and I recovered some of the £2,000 that I had paid Bira earlier in the year.

1951

For financial reasons I was unable, with one exception, to afford to race in 1950.

Joe Kelly, purchaser of my Riley, was by this time racing an Alta Grand Prix car and he encouraged me to run in the 1950 Wakefield Trophy held as a handicap race. I drove a Riley-engined Healey Silverstone sports car (a car that I could easily sell through my business after the race) and I stayed with Joe while I was in Ireland. I finished fifth in the race.

When I returned to racing in 1951 I could not afford a Formula One car and I looked for a competitive sports/racing car that would be less expensive to run and could be driven to meetings on the road, thereby saving the cost of a transporter. The choice fell on the Frazer Nash Le Mans Replica, powered by a 120 bhp version of the Bristol engine, slim, light, at that time dominating the 2-litre class of British sports car racing and costing about £3,000 including purchase tax. I discussed the purchase of one of these cars with Tony Crook, who was a Bristol distributor and the most successful and experienced Frazer Nash driver. I arranged to buy a car from Tony and we also agreed that he would prepare and enter the car for a nominal sum and make available a mechanic at race meetings without charge. I knew that this arrangement would mean that I would get a good car, even if it would not be as carefully prepared and as painstakingly lightened as Tony's own Frazer Nash.

My first outing with the Nash was at the *Daily Express* Silverstone meeting where I drove in the 2-litre Production Car race. There were eight Frazer Nashes entered and I was fastest of all in practice. This was encouraging after my lay-off from racing, and I was hoping to do well in the race. I took an early lead, but we were all tightly bunched and fighting hard, and after only eight laps I had started to lap some of the slower cars. Of what happened next I remember nothing and know only what I have been told.

On the approach to Stowe I caught up with Hadley's Jowett leading the 1,500 cc class by a narrow margin from the MG of Jacobs and Lund. Rather than wait till we were clear of the corner – and possibly jeopardise my lead – I tried to pass this battling trio on the outside of Stowe. I slid wide, the Frazer Nash hit the marker drums filled with concrete and rolled over and over several times. I was half thrown out of the car and as it rolled, it rolled over me and I suffered the most terrible head and other injuries. I was rushed to hospital, but I had suffered three fractures of the skull and brain haemorrhaging. My chances of survival were very slim and as it was thought that I would not even last an hour, I was given the Last Rites. My parents were contacted by telephone and were warned that I was unlikely to be alive when they arrived at the hospital.

In fact something close to a miracle happened and I made a gradual recovery, regaining consciousness after some days. When I was able to take stock of my injuries, I felt very sore, my face was rather a mess including a broken nose and I had a dreadful and persistent ringing sound in my right ear, amongst other injuries. I thought this would ease in a matter of days but it continued and after some weeks I went to see a Harley Street specialist. He told me that I was completely deaf in my right ear and so ever since I have had to live with this. In fact I am so used to it that I only hear the ringing if I get depressed, which,

A sequence of shots of the crash with the Le Mans Replica Frazer Nash at Silverstone in 1951 taken by a Pathé cameraman (Pathé News).

fortunately, is hardly ever, or if I talk about it or I get very tired. My main concern was to start racing again, but the Frazer Nash was being rebuilt by Tony Crook and would not be ready for some while. It was ironic that the only two racing cars that I ever insured were the Maserati which got burnt out at Curragh and the Nash, as good reasons as any for not wanting to insure a racing car again.

I decided to buy a standard production Jaguar XK120 because of the delay in rebuilding the Frazer Nash. At Boreham on August 9 I ran the Jaguar in two races in pouring rain, taking third place in the XK120 race behind the modified cars of Hamilton and Swift after a spin, and third place again to Hamilton and Tom Allard (Allard) in an Unlimited Sports Car race. I had driven really hard, thoroughly enjoyed myself and was looking forward more than ever to my Nash being ready to race again. The car was repaired by September and I ran it at Shelsley Walsh and Castle Combe (finishing third in the Unlimited Sports Car race behind Sydney Allard, with a Cadillac-Allard, and Tony Crook).

1952

This year was to prove the turning point in my career as a racing driver. My driving was faster, I was learning from experience and very soon I was being asked to drive cars for private owners. I continued to race my Frazer Nash but with the difference that I maintained it myself with the help of friends and made my own arrangements at race meetings. The Nash was a superb car to race, even though I had nearly killed myself with it.

My first race of the year with the Frazer Nash was again at Castle Combe on Easter Saturday and Tony Crook was entered with his maroon car. Tony's car was the fastest and best-prepared Nash in the country and he was a very quick driver – to me he acted as a yardstick and if I could stay with him I knew that I was doing well. Our first race was for 1,500–2,500 cc sports cars and I was narrowly beaten by Tony. There was no real opposition to us and we were able to play around. The Unlimited Sports Car race was much more serious and we had a clash with Ian Stewart at the wheel of one of the Ecurie Ecosse XK120 Jaguars – the finishing order was Crook – Stewart – Salvadori. Our last race of the day was a competition relay event in which Tony Crook, Stirling Moss and I all shared my Nash, but we were disqualified because Tony completed one lap too many!

I ran at Ibsley the following weekend, finishing second to Dennis Poore's Aston Martin DB3 in the 3,000 cc Sports Car race, but I was eliminated in the Formula Two race when I was unable to avoid a spinning Cooper-JAP. On May 10 I raced in the Production Car event at Silverstone, the race in which I had crashed the previous year, but this did not seem to inhibit my driving. In 1952 the 2-litre and Unlimited classes were run together and I drove perhaps my best race to then to finish sixth overall, win the 2-litre class – finishing ahead of Walker with a Jaguar C-type and ahead of Crook. I then took the XK120, which I was still using as a road car, to the Maidstone and Mid-Kent MC meeting on the Club circuit at Silverstone and finished second to Phil Scragg's Jaguar-engined, ex-Grand Prix Alta in a scratch race.

At this time my Frazer Nash was being prepared for the British Empire Trophy, held as a Handicap Sports Car race on the very difficult Douglas road circuit in the Isle of Man. As helpers I had John Young and Fred Hart (father of engine-builder Brian Hart). In practice I found that the Nash was overgeared and on the night before the race Fred and John changed the axle ratio for me while I got some sleep. The race was run over a distance of 200 miles (52 laps), but cars of up to 1,500 cc received four credit laps and cars of up to 3,000 cc two credit laps. The Unlimited class included the new C-type Jaguar of Duncan Hamilton and the Ecurie Ecosse XK120s of Ian Stewart, Sir James Scott-Douglas and David Murray, but on this circuit the very powerful cars were unlikely to beat their handicap. In my class there was a works Aston Martin DB3 driven by Geoff Duke and four Frazer Nashes, including Stirling Moss with Sid Greene's car and Mike Hawthorn; Hawthorn was at the wheel of Len Potter's streamlined Mille Miglia Frazer Nash, generally reckoned to be slower than the Le Mans Replica, but lapping very fast in Hawthorn's hands. Hamilton, Duke and Moss all had problems and the race devolved into a chase of the 1,500 cc cars by Hawthorn, myself and Mitchell with another Le Mans Replica. That was the order in which we finished behind the Lester-MGs of Griffith and Ruddock. I finished well in the money and combined the race with a good holiday.

On June 21 I ran the XK120 at Boreham where I had two magnificent dices with Hugh Howorth's much modified but very well driven XK120. It was great stuff, very close, and we were constantly swapping places, occasionally making contact, with me being pushed back to second place in the XK120 race and beating Howorth to finish second to Oscar Moore's HWM-Jaguar in the Unlimited Sports Car race. The following weekend I ran the Frazer Nash in three races at Snetterton, winning the 2,500 cc Sports Car race (run together with the Unlimited category in which I finished second overall to Moore's HWM-Jaguar) and finishing second in a handicap and fourth in a Formule Libre race. It was another very satisfying day.

Next on the calendar was the Jersey Road race, run in two qualifying heats and a final, and in this race Tony Crook asked me to drive his Frazer Nash. The opposition included Ian Stewart with the new Ecurie Ecosse C-type Jaguar, works DB3 Aston Martins driven by Abecassis and Parnell, and Ken Wharton with the lastest works lightweight Mk II Frazer Nash Le Mans Replica. My chances of success in my heat were ruined when a wasp was sucked into the air

At the wheel of Tony Crook's Mk II Le Mans Replica in the 1952 Jersey International Road Race (Roy Salvadori collection).

intake and blocked a carburettor jet. After a long pit stop I finished at the tail of the field. The final was dominated by Ian Stewart who won by over a minute from Wharton, followed across the line by Abecassis and Parnell. I finished seventh, partly because I had to make up a lot of places after starting from well back on the grid.

For the British Grand Prix at Silverstone I was given a marvellous opportunity when Ulster driver Bobbie Baird asked me to drive his Tipo 500 Formula Two Ferrari. Baird preferred road circuits and was none too keen on racing on the vast expanses of airfield circuits like Silverstone. The Ferrari did not seem particularly quick on the straight, it did not handle that well and was difficult to drift, there was absolutely no 'feel' and it seemed to need a very precise driver; on the credit side it was beautifully built, it had excellent brakes and it was very reliable. I started from the sixth row of the grid, diced for much of the race with Parnell's Cooper-Bristol (which seemed just as fast on the straights despite its much lower power output), gave myself a bit of a fright when I tapped one of the marker tubs at Stowe (I would never cease to have trouble with Stowe Corner) and carried on steadily to finish eighth, three laps behind the winning Ferrari of Ascari.

Not long after the Grand Prix Bobbie Baird asked me to attend a test session at Snetterton. We drove both the Tipo 500 and Baird's 2.7-litre Ferrari sports car. I was consistently quicker than Bobbie and as a result he asked me to drive for him in several of the remaining races in 1952. The first of these was the Boreham meeting on August Bank Holiday Saturday and here I drove my own Le Mans Replica in the One-hour race for sports cars up to 2,000 cc and Bobbie's 2.7-litre Ferrari in the One-hour Unlimited Sports Car race.

In the first race there was a very strong Frazer Nash entry and the main opposition consisted of Warton with the works Mk II, Tony Crook and Hawthorn with Potter's Mille Miglia. I was away very quickly at the Le Mans start, settling into second place behind Wharton and immediately ahead of Crook, while Hawthorn was left trying to start his engine. When Mike did get going, he came through the field like a rocket to pass Crook on lap six, me on the next lap and Wharton on lap 12. Wharton repassed Hawthorn, Mike retired because of clutch trouble on lap 27 and the finishing order was Wharton – Salvadori – Crook.

The Unlimited race was even more exciting. The opposition included three C-type Jaguars, two works Aston Martin DB3s and another 2.7 Ferrari driven by an American Tom Cole. I made a dreadful start, but charged through the field, spinning the wheels furiously through the corners (sometimes this helps as it keeps the engine on its power curve) and getting Tom Cole, second in the class, in my sights. *Autosport* commented: 'Now Roy Salvardori, who is revealing remarkable versatility by his able handling of many different kinds of car, had his 2.7-litre Ferrari within sight of Tom Cole's sister car and forthwith set out to catch it. On the 24th lap there were a good 20 secs. between the white and blue and the red car; by the 27th lap Salvadori had reduced this to five secs., and on the following round he drew level with Cole at Orchard, to pass in the rush down to Railway corner. Cole had a wild slide at Hangar Bend, following Salvadori through. . . .' I finished fourth overall behind the C-types of Moss and Hamilton and not far behind Reg Parnell who won the 3,000 cc class with his works DB3.

Apart from the brakes and the rear wheel lift, I thought that the 2.7-litre Ferrari was an excellent sports car with an almost unbreakable engine, excellent gearbox and reasonably good roadholding.

Two days later, on the Bank Holiday Monday, I was in action at Thruxton. It was here that I first met John Coombs, who won the 500 cc race with his Cooper-Norton, and he was to become a close friend and my entrant over many years. I won three races, closely beating Wharton in the 2,500 cc race, just managing to pull one over on Oscar Moore (HWM-Jaguar) in the Unlimited race (and also beat Wharton again) and rounding off the day by winning an Invitation race (again beating Moore and Wharton).

For the last race I offered to swap cars with Ken Wharton. The reason for this was that Ken had been telling John Young and myself that he preferred the handling of the Mk I Replica to his Mk II, and I was very keen to try the Mk II – but Ken declined on the grounds that he did not think that the works would approve. I never really got on with Ken, there was always a slight 'edge' between us and it may have all started at Thruxton!

For the first Goodwood Nine Hours race – run between 3:00 pm and midnight – I received invitations to drive several cars, but I opted for Baird's Ferrari 2.7 which was a serious contender for outright victory. The race attracted works entries from Aston Martin and Jaguar and Tom Cole entered his 2.7 Ferrari with Graham Whitehead as co-driver. Isobel, Bobbie's wife, who was running the pit, told me during Bobbie's first stint at the wheel, 'If we're going to get anywhere in this race, you will have to do most of the driving', and that is what happened.

Bobbie started the race and held fifth place during the first hour; I quote from the report in *Road & Track* by Alan Clark '[Baird] began tiring and spun out three times at different points on the circuit. He was called in at 4:50 pm and co-driver Salvadori took over. The advent of Salvadori altered the whole character of the race. From being a playboy motor dealer he has now become one of the most accomplished drivers in England and proceeded to show just how quickly a Ferrari can be made to go. In half an hour he rose from seventh to third place, passing Cole's Ferrari and the Collins' and Abecassis' DB3s. . . .'

Just before 6:00 pm the third-place DB3 of Parnell/Thompson came into the pits, pouring out smoke from the rear axle and leaking oil on the undertray. While the Aston mechanics were refuelling the DB3, petrol was spilt on to the undertray and the car went up in flames, badly burning John Wyer and two of the Aston Martin mechanics. I was now in third place behind the two surviving works Jaguars and a lap ahead of both Cole/Whitehead and Collins/Griffith with the sole remaining DB3.

At just after 6:30 pm I had to hand the car over to Baird because no driver could spend more than two hours at the wheel without a break. It was only now that our troubles started. The intensity of the heat from the Aston Martin pit, which adjoined ours, had melted the tarmac; when the mechanics tried to change the Ferrari's wheels, the jacks sunk into the tarmac and so we had to try again with wooden blocks placed under the jacks. By the time Bobbie handed the car back to me at about 7:30 pm, having spent the bare minimum at the wheel, we were five laps behind the leading Jaguar and had dropped to fifth place. I quote again from *Road & Track*, 'At 7.28 Salvadori took over the red Ferrari and once more his progress was meteoric. In twelve minutes he had passed Tom Cole, after an hour he was on the same lap as the DB3 and by 8.15 he had passed Collins again to lead the 3-litre class. . .' . I lapped Collins and as I closed up on the leading Jaguars, Lofty hung out 'faster' signals to Hamilton and Walker. I handed over to Baird again at 9:20 pm, he covered just one lap to comply with the regulations and then I took the wheel again. This all cost time and once more I had to chase and catch the Aston Martin, but in the meanwhile Hamilton's Jaguar shed a wheel and when Moss retired his Jaguar with rear axle trouble I was leading the race.

At 10:23 pm I stopped to refuel and hand over to Baird, who was to cover only one lap before I resumed at the wheel to finish the race. To quote *Autosport*, 'The Belfast man pressed the starter, there was a click – and silence! His two mechanics worked desperately to coax some life from the battery, but to no avail. Eventually another battery was produced, leads fed to the dead component and the engine burst into life. Baird took off like a scalded cat, with the Ferrari's one-lap lead altered to three in arrears . . .'.

Back at the wheel again I started a frantic chase after the leaders, but everything was now against us. At the instigation of Reg Parnell, who was deputising in the Aston Martin pit for John Wyer, I was black-flagged because one of our lights was out; this stop further delayed us, and afterwards I was trying much too hard, had an enormous spin at Madgwick, stalled and was push-started, for which we were penalised one lap. When the race finished we were still in third place (278 laps) behind the Aston of Collins/Griffith (283 laps) and Cole/Whitehead (281 laps). I had driven throughout as though the race was a ten-lap sprint and it was the best performance of my career to date.

It was about this time that I sold my Frazer Nash, to which we had done nothing all year except change the plugs, oil and tyres. They were popular cars and I obtained a good price. From this point on I always drove for entrants on a professional basis and during the remainder of 1952 all my drives were for Baird. With the Formula Two car I could manage no better than fifth and sixth places in two races at the September Goodwood meeting, but I scored the car's one and only win in the Formula Two race at Castle Combe the following weekend, setting a new lap record of 85.38 mph (bettered later in the day by Gerard with his 2-litre blown ERA who lapped at 86.25 mph), and I finished fourth in the Formule Libre race. I rounded off the year by driving Baird's sports Ferrari into third place behind the C-types of Ian Stewart and Moss at Charterhall the following weekend. It had been a very good season for me and had started me off on my professional motor racing career.

Chapter 2

Connaught works driver

Introduction by 'Wilkie' Wilkinson of Ecurie Ecosse

'During my 50 years of preparing racing cars and driving them myself I soon learned to assess the skill of various drivers. I watched Roy Salvadori over the years driving many different makes of cars and always performing well with great skill and courage. My motto through life has been, 'Fortune favours those who take a chance' – and Roy did this on many occasions. He won many races and was a force to be reckoned with if you were competing in the same race.

'David Murray and I used to chat about drivers and their abilities. Roy was high on the list. We therefore negotiated with him to drive for us on special occasions. I believe that I am right in saying that he was our first paid driver. His first drive for us was at the Nürburgring in the 1953 1,000 Kilometres Sports Car race. The Nürburgring is a very difficult circuit, with a wide range of corners to negotiate and with some long, fast straights. It is very hard on the cars.

'We had entered three C-type Jaguars and one of these was to be driven by Ian Stewart and Roy Salvadori. With two such fine drivers at the wheel, we had great hopes of success. However, Ian was a bit temperamental and he had just got married. He was to drive the first half of the race, but on race day he insisted on Roy driving first. Roy went well and when he came into the pits at the end of his stint he was high up the field. The circuit was very tough on the suspension and Roy told me as he got out of the car that the suspension was rather soft, but manageable.

'During the pit stop we checked the oil and water, filled up with petrol and gave the car a quick check, including the shock absorbers. Ian Stewart did not seem very happy when he took over and as I had a funny feeling about Ian's attitude, I asked Roy to stay in the pits. After only one or two laps Ian came back in, complaining that the car was not handling very well and saying that he did not want to carry on. Without any hesitation Roy got back into the cockpit and he drove for the rest of the race, winning the Production Sports Car class and finishing second overall. We were delighted. After the race Roy mentioned that the car's handling had deteriorated and that it had been quite a handful. In fact after the prize-giving I drove the car down the tunnel to the pits and the suspension collapsed completely. We were very lucky to finish the race and Roy had been very plucky to drive a car in this condition.

'Roy drove for the team several times in 1954 and later in two races with our Cooper Monaco in the United States. He always finished in the money when he drove for Ecurie Ecosse and in the States shared a substantial part of his winnings with me.'

★ ★ ★

My original plan for the year was that I would continue to drive for Bobbie Baird who was proposing to have his Formula Two Ferrari completely updated at the factory, to acquire a new sports/racing 4.1-litre V-12 Ferrari to supplement the successful 2.7 which we had raced in 1952 and to buy a Cooper-Bristol Formula Two car. Bobbie's father controlled the *Belfast Telegraph* and I understand that he had made over his shares in the company to Bobbie on condition that he gave up motor racing. Accordingly Bobbie proposed to sign me up for the year as his driver and not to race at all himself.

Shortly before the Easter Goodwood meeting Bobbie changed his mind and said that he would like to drive in just a few races himself, starting with Goodwood. This rather upset my plans and when John Coombs heard about this, he arranged with Rodney Clarke for me to drive a works Connaught at Goodwood on a purely one-off basis. At Snetterton a fortnight later Bobbie and I shared the driving of his Formula Two Ferrari and shortly after this I received an invitation to drive for Connaught on a regular basis. Because Bobbie's change of mind had much reduced my season, it was agreed that we should go our separate ways and so I was free to sign up for the Connaught team.

Connaught, based on the Portsmouth Road at Send in Surrey, was financed by Kenneth McAlpine and since 1948, under the direction of that excellent engineer Rodney Clarke, had built first a small number of Lea-Francis-powered sports cars and from 1950 the A-series Formula Two single-seaters. Although the team's Formula Two car was powered by an engine based on the Lea-Francis, with push-rod operated overhead valves from two camshafts mounted high on the cylinder block in Riley fashion, it had in its developed state few components in common with the original production unit. There was an aluminium-alloy cylinder block, capacity was increased to 1,960 cc (79 × 100 mm), there were four Amal carburettors mounted in a so-called 'balance-box' in the airstream on the right-hand side of the nose and power output was around 135/140 bhp.

Clarke had designed an up-to-date tubular ladder-type chassis, converging in plan to the rear with front suspension by double wishbones and torsion bars and a de Dion axle located by a central torque rod and single radius arms and suspended on torsion bars at the rear. The transmission incorporated an Armstrong Siddeley pre-selector gearbox without clutch, and gear selection was made by operating a lever on the steering column and depressing what would normally be the clutch pedal to engage the gear. The A-series was beautifully engineered and most carefully planned. The big problem, however, was the lack of power – the A-series was some 40 bhp less powerful than the Ferrari Formula Two cars that were dominating racing – and throughout my year with the team Clarke was constantly battling to make the cars powerful enough and reliable enough to be competitive at an International level. It was, however, a battle doomed to failure.

I had known McAlpine, Clarke and development engineer Mike Oliver for some years. McAlpine was a great enthusiast, very anxious to make a success of the company. He drove the cars himself – and very well – but was always willing to hand his car over to Stirling Moss or me when we were in the team. The engineering side of the company had a superb reputation, for not only was Clarke a sound designer and a real go-getter, but Mike Oliver was a fine development engineer. He was also a first-class driver, only occasionally running in races, but as fast as the works drivers. The team manager was Basil Putt, and Connaught on the whole were well organised – probably better than some of the Italian teams who dominated racing at the time. Altogether it was a very friendly, first-class team to drive for.

After a testing session at Snetterton we agreed terms which were on the basis of the usual 50 per cent of the starting, bonus and prize money (less, in the last case, 10 per cent for the mechanics). I received no retainer from Connaught and paid my own expenses, but there were other advantages. The team had a contract with Esso for fuel which proved a good arrangement as I was soon to sign up with Esso as a result of my contract with Aston Martin and I was paid a very substantial retainer by Esso.

Connaught had planned a very full racing season but we only did a limited amount of testing, partly because in those days the cars would not stand it! The A-series came in two types, the original 7 ft 1 in wheelbase cars and the later 1953 AL version with the longer 7 ft 6 in wheelbase which I preferred. Both versions displayed strong understeer but had excellent roadholding. Another development for 1953 had been the introduction of American Hillborn-Travers fuel injection on the works cars and this boosted power by some 15 bhp, but at the expense of a marked time-lag before the power came in. The A-series had a strict 6,000 rpm limited and if you exceeded the limit only briefly a valve could jam in the guide, hit a piston and the engine could break most expensively.

Later in the year the team tried the very volatile oxygen-bearing nitromethane fuel additive. 'Nitro' was very expensive (around £10 a gallon) and very fashionable in 1953, and whilst this most definitely boosted the power output, it made the cars more difficult to start and it caused them to run roughly at low revs. The pre-selector gearbox was difficult and the ratios were badly spaced – I would have been much happier if the cars had had a normal 'crash' box which would not only have been easier to use, but would also have been lighter.

For my one-off outing for the team at Goodwood on Easter Monday I was entered in a total of three races with a short wheelbase, fuel injection car. In the Formula Two category the most serious contender was a 2-litre Maserati, an interim 1952–1953 car driven by the very experienced Swiss driver Baron Emmanuel de Graffenried. There was also a strong entry of other Connaughts and Coopers.

Above *With the fuel injection, short-wheelbase Connaught in the paddock at the Easter Goodwood meeting, 1953* (Guy Griffiths).

Above right *The Connaught being pushed to the starting line at Goodwood by the opposition – the works Maserati mechanics who had been loaned to de Graffenried for this meeting* (Guy Griffiths).

Right *On the starting grid with Sid Greene's Frazer Nash at Snetterton, May 1953* (Charles Dunn).

I was fastest in practice for the Formula Two Lavant Cup, took the lead at the start and drew away from de Graffenried's Maserati; I was going very quickly and I remember the tremendous understeer of the A-series in this race that made it necessary for me to throw the car around to get the rear end moving – it was only just acceptable at Goodwood, but the understeer was a major problem at some circuits and was never cured. On the last lap, as I approached the chicane just before the start/finish line, a connecting rod on the accelerator pedal came adrift and as I crawled to the line on tickover, de Graffenried swept past me to win the race. I did at least have the consolation of setting the fastest lap of 89.44 mph. I spun off at Woodcote in my next race, the Formule Libre Chichester Cup.

Connaught were having throttle problems with the new fuel injection car and Clarke thought that he had it sorted out by the start of the main race of the day, the Richmond Trophy for Formule Libre cars. We got my A-series on to the grid, but the throttle trouble was still there. Ken McAlpine offered me his car running on Amal carburettors and I gladly accepted. This meant that I had to start from the third row of the grid and I came through to finish fourth behind Wharton (BRM V-16), Taruffi (Ferrari 'Thin Wall' Special) and de Graffenried.

By the *Daily Express* Trophy meeting at Silverstone in May I was a regular member of the Connaught team. Also entered by the works were McAlpine and John Coombs. The race was run in two qualifying heats and a final and in my heat the principal opposition came from Mike Hawthorn, who was having one

of his first drives as a member of Scuderia Ferrari (Modena had sent only the one car), and Ken Wharton who, with his Cooper-Bristol, had been one second faster than Hawthorn in practice. These two dominated the heat and I came through to finish third ahead of Peter Whitehead (Cooper-Alta) and Louis Chiron (Osca).

The Connaught went beautifully, if rather down on power compared with some of the opposition, but it was to prove a lucky race for me. Moss dropped back in the final with an engine misfire, Trintignant's Gordini shed a wheel (a common occurrence with these very fragile French cars), de Graffenried retired in a huff because of the penalty that he had incurred for jumping the start and Wharton's Cooper developed a misfire so that I was able to slip by into second place. I was able to keep Hawthorn in my sights, but every time I closed up, he turned on the power and the Ferrari pulled away. At the flag I was twelve seconds in arrears, ahead of Tony Rolt with Rob Walker's private Connaught and Bira's Maserati. It was a very satisfying performance and gave us cause to hope that we should get some good finishes later in the year.

Connaught entered a full team of cars in the Ulster Trophy race at Dundrod, a circuit that I was soon to learn to hate for its narrowness, bumpiness, adverse cambers, banks and stone walls. At least on this circuit the understeer of the Connaught was almost desirable, but it was very unhappy on the bumps. In addition to myself and McAlpine, the team also entered Stirling Moss, available because of problems with his Cooper-Alta, and we all drove fuel injection cars. The opposition included Hawthorn with the Ferrari that he had driven at Silverstone, de Graffenried, Wharton, a team of HWMs and a number of private Connaughts and Cooper-Bristols.

In the first of the two qualifying heats Stirling finished second behind Duncan Hamilton (HWM) despite a pit stop and losing top gear, whilst, perhaps showing rather too clearly my feelings about the circuit, I finished sixth in the second heat. Between the heats and the final the mechanics worked feverishly to transfer the gearbox from McAlpine's car to Stirling's, only to find when they had finished the job that McAlpine's gearbox had broken and he had forgotten to tell Rodney Clarke! Stirling was obviously going to be a non-starter, so I immediately offered him my car. Apart from the fact that he would obviously go better with it than I would it was now starting to rain and so far as I was concerned any of the spectators could have had my car on this circuit! The official to whom Clarke spoke refused permission for a change of driver and it was only after the race started that the team learned that they had been misinformed and a change of driver should have been allowed. In the final my car developed a bad misfire and I was forced to retire when a rear radius arm broke. Hawthorn won the race from Wharton and Baird.

Connaught had entered for the Coronation Trophy at the newly reopened Crystal Palace circuit on Whit Monday, but the cars could not be repaired in time following the Ulster Trophy so I was without a drive. Rob Walker asked me to try his ERA-Delage in practice. It was agreed that I should drive the car in the ten-lap race for supercharged cars in place of Tony Rolt. The car was the old 1927 Delage Grand Prix chassis as rebuilt by Giulio Ramponi for Dick Seaman to drive in 1936 Voiturette races but fitted in post-war days with an ERA engine because of the spares problems with the original unit.

I had insufficient practice to get used to the car which felt very peculiar, with a chassis that seemed to be flexing the whole time and almost non-existent brakes, but this was compensated for by a lot of power. I was not able in one short race to judge the poetential of the car and I was happy to drive a steady race to finish second to Graham Whitehead's ERA.

I next drove for Connaught in the Dutch Grand Prix at Zandvoort, where there was a three-car team for Stirling, myself and McAlpine. The general characteristics of Zandvoort are not so dissimilar from Goodwood and so we were expecting the cars to go well. Apart from the fact that the cars were slower than we expected we were plagued by sand getting into the engines. Ascari (Ferrari) was fastest in practice in 1 min 51.1 sec, Stirling was the fastest Connaught driver in 2 min 00.0 sec and I was half-a-second slower; I was holding twelfth place in the race when the engine started to run rough on lap 14. I pulled into the pits where a sticking tappet was diagnosed and the car withdrawn. McAlpine also retired, but Stirling worked his car up to seventh place, made a pit stop and rejoined the race to finish ninth and last, seven laps behind Ascari's Ferrari. It was a disappointing outcome, for if the cars had held together we would have finished in the first six.

I had driven Sid Greene's Frazer Nash at Snetterton at the end of May and I was back at this circuit with the Frazer Nash at the end of June, competing also with a Connaught and a Jaguar XK120. At Snetterton the Connaughts – the same cars as had run at Zandvoort – dominated practice for the Formula Two race. I made a poor start, Ken McAlpine took the lead and I was third behind Rodney Nuckey's well driven Cooper-Bristol, but I soon moved up into the lead and then Coombs went ahead of Nuckey to make it a Connaught 1–2–3. This was the order until the last lap when my engine packed up, leaving me only with the consolation of fastest lap. After I had finished fifth with Sid's Frazer Nash in the Unlimited Sports Car race, John Coombs offered me his Connaught for the final race of the day, the ten-lap Formule Libre event, and I was pleased to accept John's offer. I soon took the lead, set a new lap record of 88.04 mph and won by a little over eight seconds from McAlpine. I had driven three different cars in five races – for me a typical and satisfying day's racing.

The following weekend I was competing at Reims, both in the 12 Hours Sports Car race and in the French Grand Prix. It was a hopelessly unsuccessful weekend. In the Sports Car race Tony Crook had arranged for me to co-drive the Le Mans fixed head coupé Frazer Nash which in the hands of Wharton and Mitchell had won its class at Le Mans. On paper at least we had a good chance of success in the 2-litre class, provided that the new and very aerodynamic works Bristol 450 coupés failed just as they had at Le Mans. Tony had the first turn at the wheel and after a quarter of an hour the car was out of the race with clutch trouble – and the Bristol 450 of Wilson/Fairman went on to win the 2-litre class.

Two cars were entered in the French Grand Prix, for Bira and myself, but we were outpaced on this very fast circuit. I was plagued by mechanical trouble in practice and I never managed a decent, fast lap. I was out of the race with engine trouble at the end of lap two and poor Bira did not survive very much longer before his Connaught succumbed to differential failure. Out in front Mike Hawthorn (Ferrari) was battling with Fangio (Maserati) and went on to score perhaps the finest victory in his career.

It was back to more familiar territory the following weekend when I drove a works Connaught in the 15-lap Crystal Palace Formula Two race. The main opposition came from Tony Rolt who was fastest in practice with Rob Walker's dark blue carburettor Connaught. I reckoned that I should be able to beat Rolt in the race, but I made a terrible start and had to settle for second place and a new lap record of 73.59 mph.

It is a good illustration of the lack of competitiveness of British Formula Two cars at this time that Connaught should dominate minor British National races such as that at the Crystal Palace and the following weekend be outclassed in the British Grand Prix at Silverstone where they faced full Ferrari and Maserati works teams. I was once again plagued by mechanical trouble in practice, and as a result I started from the back of the grid. I worked my way up to ninth place, my shirt tail flapping rather uncomfortably in the wind, but a rear radius arm broke, the car was all over the road and I was forced to retire. Almost inevitably Ascari (Ferrari) was the winner and the sole Connaught to finish was Bira in seventh place. At the German Grand Prix I was completely out of luck and retired at the end of the first lap.

It was during practice at Snetterton at the end of July that poor Bobbie Baird crashed fatally. We were both practising for the Sports Car race, me with the Frazer Nash and he with the 4.1-litre Ferrari. The 4.1 Ferrari was very much of a handful and already a couple of drivers had been killed at the wheel of this model, including Tom Cole at Le Mans a fortnight previously. Bobbie was scratching hard to turn in a good time and as he went through Sears corner just after the pits, he got on to the ploughed field edging the road, the car flipped and he was thrown out. When I saw the shunted Ferrari, I stopped and went over to Bobbie who tried to get up – the worst thing he could have done – and as he did so, I believe he must have punctured a lung. He lay down again and by the time he was taken away in an ambulance, I think he was dying. The next news was that he was dead. He had been taken only as far as a wooden shed on the circuit and I later went there with his wife Isobel. His body was completely unmarked,

With the long-wheelbase, carburettor Connaught before practice at Charterhall in August, 1953 (Newcastle Chronicle and Journal).

for all his injuries were internal. If he had to die, it was the way that Bobbie would have wanted it, for he had no other interest in life outside cars and motor racing. I feel that I can say this about him, for I knew him and his wife well.

Connaught entered a full team of three cars in the Formula Two race at Charterhall on August 15. I drove the long-wheelbase car on carburettors that had originally belonged to private owner John Lyons, John Coombs drove a new long-wheelbase fuel injection car and Ron Flockhart drove my usual shorter-wheelbase fuel injection car. My car was not ready when we were called to the start of the Formula Two race, and I was still wearing my raincoat when the flag dropped. I had to put on my crash helmet and chase after the field. It took me some while to sort myself out, but I managed to get everything together and worked my way through to second place behind Wharton's Cooper-Bristol. The belt of my raincoat was getting caught in the steering wheel and I reconciled myself to finishing second, but found that Flockhart, who had settled down well with his car, had closed right up on me. Flockhart was slowed by the Connaught pit, I eased off and we finished in second and third places. Wharton had been going very well with the Cooper and I doubt whether we could have caught him. Later in the day I went off the road in the Formule Libre race and damaged my Connaught's steering. When I reached the pits on foot, Fairman was called in for me to take over – a pointless exercise as I could not make up time lost in the change – and I rejoined the race to finish third.

For the Charterhall meeting we stayed at the Kelso hotel and on the evening before the race there was the usual party. I had planned an early night, but as I passed through the lounge with John Coombs and Alan Brown we saw the first round of what was to prove a hectic night. A group of drivers that included Peter Walker, Ian Stewart and Ninian Sanderson, sitting round the glowing embers of a fire. Twelve-bore cartridges formed a circle round the fire and we realised that the drivers were playing their own form of Russian roulette. Later in the evening some of the drivers stuffed Peter Walker into a folding bed/settee and pushed it at a high rate of knots towards a plate glass window. Peter managed to abandon the settee just before it crashed through the glass and on to the street. The police were called and interviewed all the drivers. I was dealing with a policeman who did not seem to know much about motor racing, so I told him that I was Mike Hawthorn who was not in fact competing at this meeting. I thought that if this was motor racing, then it was just great – that was until we received our bills in the morning. Each bill had an enormous addition without explanation – the manager had simply apportioned the cost of the damage between the drivers.

At the end of August I was invited by Ecurie Ecosse to co-drive with Ian Stewart one of their C-type Jaguars in the first Nürburgring 1,000 Km race. It was the first of many drives with this team which was so well organised by David Murray and Wilkie Wilkinson. I was delighted to be asked to drive for the team, especially as I was being paid for it – a departure from their usual policy. The strongest contender in the race, but very much of a handful on this circuit, was a works-entered 4.5-litre V-12 Ferrari driven by Ascari and Farina, and this

scored a convincing and easy victory after teams of Lancias and 2-litre Maseratis had fallen by the wayside. In practice I made the fastest Production Sports Car time. I took the first stint at the wheel and made a good start, but on the first lap, trying much too hard, I lost the Jaguar and rejoined the race at the tail of the field. I gradually clawed my way back through the field but as the race progressed the Jaguar, shaken up as all cars are at the Nürburgring, began to lose its brakes, the steering began to kick, the shock absorbers started to go and the car was creaking and groaning generally. The driver gets used to this, as the car deteriorates progressively, but it is a shock to take over a car in this state.

When I stopped to hand over to Ian Stewart, Wilkie said, 'Roy, just wait in the pits will you?' I had anticipated going off for a snack and a rest, but obviously stayed when I was asked to. Ian had not driven for very long before he came back into the pits to say that he thought the car was in very bad shape and should be withdrawn. Immediately Wilkie grabbed me, hustled me into the car, I was off again and drove to the end of the race. As the race progressed, the car got worse and worse and each lap I would say to myself, 'Well, nothing fell off on that lap', and I would carry on for another lap, talking myself through the race on a lap-by-lap basis. Towards the end the car was in a desperate condition, but the moment I finished the last lap I was convinced that it would have lasted another 1,000 km – so much of success and failure in motor racing is governed by mental attitudes. Although I had crossed the finishing line in second place overall, the major awards of prize money in this race were for the first Production Sports Car to cross the finishing line, and the Ecurie Ecosse team were delighted.

When the mechanics examined the car after the race it was found that the fuel tank was only held in place by the bodywork of the tail. The front suspension mountings had broken and very much more was wrong with it besides, but that is how some cars finished the Nürburgring 1,000 Km. The other Ecurie Ecosse C-type of Lawrence and Jimmy Stewart finished sixth overall and was in rather better shape. The Scott-Douglas/Sanderson standard XK120 finished tenth overall (fourth in the over 2-litre Production Sports Car class) to clinch the team prize for Jaguar.

Left *One of my best drives for Ecurie Ecosse was with a C-type Jaguar in the 1953 Nürburgring 1,000 Km race. In this picture I have just taken over from Ian Stewart (left of the car) and I drove throughout the remainder of the race to finish second and win the Production Sports Car class. Wilkie Wilkinson, standing by the left-hand rear wing, is supervising operations* (Roy Salvadori collection).

Right *Garlanded with the enormous wreath awarded to us at the Nürburgring, both Ian Stewart and I look very pleased with our performance* (Foto-Hilburg).

It was on to Italy to drive a Connaught in the Italian Grand Prix on the road circuit at Monza. The race was marked by Fangio's only win of the year for Maserati (after Marimon's Maserati had collided with Ascari's leading Ferrari at the last corner) and by the speed of Stirling Moss' Cooper-Alta; Stirling's car, running on SU fuel injection and nitromethane, was so fast that it had more power than its roadholding could cope with and a voracious appetite for tyres that put it right out of contention. I went surprisingly quickly in practice with the long-chassis carburettor car and lapped in 2 mins 8.0 sec (110.10 mph), compared with pole position man Ascari's 2 min 02.7 sec (116 mph). My time put me on the fifth row of the grid and was very good by British standards of the time. In the race I worked my way up to ninth place ahead of de Graffenried when a throttle cable broke. I rejoined the race, right out of the picture, and retired when a shaft in the final drive reduction gears broke.

We stayed in Italy to compete in the Modena Grand Prix the following weekend. There was a strong Maserati entry in this race, but no works Ferraris. It was an easy aerodrome circuit, the sort of circuit with which I was so familiar, and I went very well in practice. I was entered with the same car as at Monza, but found that I was a little faster with the car entered for John Coombs, the original prototype Connaught also running on carburettors, and was offered this car for the race. We had hoped to do well at Modena, but it was to be the usual dismal outcome. On lap 11 my car broke a piston and I took over Coombs' car. He is rather shorter than me so the seating position was thoroughly uncomfortable, but the discomfort did not last long as this car also broke a piston!

At the September Goodwood meeting I drove the latest Connaught, a long-chassis car running on carburettors. I was incredibly quick in practice, joint second fastest in 1 min 35 sec with Hawthorn (Ferrari 'Thin Wall' Special), while Fangio (V-16 BRM) was fastest in 1 min 34 sec. I ran away from the opposition in my first race of the day, the Formula Two Madgwick Cup, defeating strong opposition that included Moss (Cooper-Alta), Wharton (Cooper-Bristol) and Rolt (Connaught), scored an easy win and set a new Formula Two lap record of 90.95 mph. In fact until the Formule Libre

Woodcote Cup later in the day, when Hawthorn turned in a lap of 93.91 mph, my speed in the Formula Two race stood, albeit briefly, as an outright circuit record. (I should add that Hawthorn made a further improvement on the lap record in the Goodwood Trophy when he lapped at 94.53 mph.) I was holding second place in the Formule Libre Woodcote Cup behind Hawthorn (Ferrari 'Thin Wall') and ahead of Fangio's BRM when I was forced to retire because of a leaking oil pipe, and I finished fifth in the main race of the day, the Formule Libre Richmond Trophy, after spinning off, getting a push-start and fighting my way back through the field. Of my driving at this meeting *Autocourse* commented, '. . . the Connaught, handled by Salvadori, was taken through every corner at the limit for both driver and car – generally in a four-wheel drift – which resulted in the bends being negotiated at a far greater speed than was achieved by its more complicated competitors . . .'.

The performance of the Connaught in 1953, especially at Goodwood, earned the team a lot of good publicity, but neither this success nor later fine performances, particularly Tony Brooks' win at Siracusa in 1955, brought the team the financial support needed to sustain a full Grand Prix programme with properly developed cars. Eventually Kenneth McAlpine decided that he could no longer afford the financial burden of Connaught and the team withdrew from racing altogether in May 1957.

For me this was the end of my career with Connaught, a season in which I had first competed regularly in International single-seater racing, in which I had established myself as a regular Grand Prix driver and in which I had tasted the immense promise and potential of the Connaught marred only too often by its mechanical shortcomings. I owed a great deal to Connaught who had given me the opportunity of regularly driving in Grands Prix.

Chapter 3

Aston Martin, 1953–56: the DB3S era

Introduction by John Wyer

'It gives me great pleasure to write this introduction because Roy Salvadori was the longest-serving member of the Aston Martin team.

'The first time Roy drove for me was at Le Mans in 1953 and the last time at Monza in 1963. Today, when the end of each season is the signal for something between an auction and a game of musical chairs, such fidelity may seem a dubious distinction. In the climate of the period, and to me in particular, it had great significance.

'I had, of course, known Roy before 1953. Indeed, in the 1940s, when I was with Monaco Motors at Watford, we had prepared his Alfa Romeo P3. My chief recollection is that he contested the very modest bill and I made a small reduction. He told me much later that he made a mental note that this chap Wyer was a soft touch.

'By the end of 1952 we had a fairly well established front line, with Reg Parnell, George Abecassis and Peter Collins. For most of our races, however, we needed two drivers for each car and I was less happy about our second line. We were entering the transition period between the talented amateurs such as Eric Thompson and Pat Griffith, and the professionals, or at least those drivers who were prepared and able to make motor racing a first consideration. In the Goodwood Nine Hours race, towards the end of 1952, we had scored a somewhat lucky win but Salvadori, driving Bobbie Baird's Ferrari, had given us a very hard time and was considered by many to be the moral victor. He was therefore a natural selection.

'Co-opting a new member into the team was not a matter to be treated lightly. We regarded ourselves, somewhat arrogantly, more as an exclusive club than a racing team. Compatibility was second only to driving ability. I therefore discussed the matter with Reg Parnell, the acknowledged senior member, and with George Abecassis. Both gave Roy their support and George said he would be happy to have Roy as co-driver.

'It happened that a few days later we were testing the DB3S prototype at Snetterton and Roy was there testing a Connaught. During a lull I asked him if he would like to drive for us. I will always remember his reply. He said simply, "John, of course you know I would." Neither of us mentioned terms.

'That was the beginning of an association which was to bring us both considerable success. It was also the beginning of a warm and lasting friendship which gets better with the years.

'It would not be appropriate, in this introduction, to list all the races in which Roy drove for me and the many in which he was successful. They have been recounted before and Roy can tell his own story. The best publicised was, of course, his victory at Le Mans in 1959. I will have more to say about this. The best, in my opinion, was the last, at Monza in 1963. This was motor racing at its best. For three hours he fought, *mano e mano*, against Mike Parkes in a Ferrari 250GTO, two great drivers in two cars which were incredibly evenly matched. Roy won by less than 100 yd because, about four laps from the end, passing a back-marker, he was able to outfumble Mike, who went too wide coming out of the second Lesmo. The only way he could win was by coming into the straight, on the last lap, with sufficient lead to prevent Mike from taking advantage of his five speed gearbox on the sprint to the finish. He knew it and did just that. His comment to me after the race was, "John, I nearly thought myself out of that one."

'But perhaps some personal opinions may be permitted. When Roy joined us, I do not think that, by temperament or inclination, he was a great long-distance driver. He enjoyed the cut and thrust of motor racing, being in the lead or fighting for the lead. If he was second he wanted to be first and equally if he was tenth he wanted to be ninth. He never gave up trying. This is a desirable, indeed essential, quality in any racing driver. But I do not intend to convey by this that he was hard on the car because in my experience he was not. It was rather that he used to the full, but within the prescribed limits, the potential of the car. The engine, the transmission and the brakes were there to be used for the purpose for which they were intended, which was to win races. It was the business of the engineers to design and build the cars for that purpose; it was his business to drive them and to get the best out of them.

'Over the years, however, because he was a highly intelligent driver and because endurance racing was our chosen field, he made himself, by sheer application, into one of the best long-distance drivers in the world. This was proved at Le Mans in 1959 when he won with Carroll Shelby as his co-driver. He drove a completely text-book race, and even after an unfortunate incident with a tyre, when he lost a lap to the sole remaining Ferrari, he never asked the car for more than it could deliver and still last for 24 hours. The temptation must have been great because he was certainly capable of driving faster. He continued to pace himself and when, with almost six hours still to go, he regained the lead to hold it to the end, it was a form of poetic justice. On that circuit, on that particular day, he proved himself to be the best driver around. No team manager could have asked for a greater performance.

'As our association progressed and our confidence in each other developed, Roy played an increasing part in our test programmes. He was always available and gave generously of his time. In the sense that he could tell the engineers what was wrong with the cars and how to put it right, Roy was perhaps not one of the great development drivers, but he had an asset which was far more valuable. Given any car, he could set a lap time which could be regarded as par for the course. If it was not a good time, it was simply because the car was not good enough and not because the driver was making less than the best use of the potential. Roy could, of course, tell you – and frequently did – where he thought the time could be improved but analysis in greater depth was the realm of the engineers; he simply did not consider it was his business. There have, of course, been some great designer-drivers and I do not underrate the contribution which they make, but they can also be dangerous. If the driver knows, or believes that he knows, the solution to a problem, it may affect his thinking to the point where he is insufficiently critical. To Roy only facts were important and the lap times told their own story. He rarely confused us with his theories.

'One final point: Roy has at times been accused of being a tough driver. It is interesting that such criticism came only from those who considered themselves his equals or superiors and who felt that they should have won. I never heard complaints from drivers whom Roy would have regarded as his inferiors in skill or ability. Racing against his peers Roy neither gave nor expected any quarter. Motor racing is not a softball game. If you can't stand the heat, stay out of the kitchen.

'Both as a driver and on a personal level, Roy did everything possible to justify his selection. He was popular both with the other drivers – not always easy – and with mechanics. I have already spoken of his loyalty. During all the years of his association with Aston Martin we never had a difference of opinion about terms, nor did he ever suggest the possibility of leaving us, although I am sure he had many attractive offers. In 1960, when we made a belated entry into Formula One with the underdeveloped DBR4, he remained faithful to us although he could have driven for Cooper with much greater prospects of success. It is difficult to imagine such quixotic behaviour in motor racing today and, indeed, it would be regarded as slightly insane.

'The only cause for disappointment I ever experienced with Roy was that I could never persuade him to drive in the Mille Miglia. As I continually pointed out to him, he had only to drive as he did normally on the public highway and he could hardly avoid winning. He remained adamant, although when, during the making of the movie *Checkpoint*, for which Aston Martin provided some of the cars, he was allowed to join in the race with a cameraman as passenger, he greatly enjoyed himself.

'I am very pleased to have the opportunity of paying this small tribute to a great driver and a very valued friend.'

★ ★ ★

1953

John Wyer has confirmed my belief that my drive with Bobbie Baird's Ferrari in the 1952 Goodwood Nine Hours race had much to do with my invitation to join the Aston Martin team. I filled the seat in the team vacated by Geoff Duke, the motor cycle World Champion, who had enjoyed rather mixed fortunes with Aston Martin and had decided to stick to two wheels.

Aston Martin always treated their drivers very fairly, but were unable to match the sort of money paid by Jaguar because their resources were so much more limited. On signing the contract with Aston Martin I received a retainer for the year of £250 and I also received retainers from the oil companies that supported Aston Martin: Castrol for lubricants and Esso for petrol. I met and negotiated terms with George Williams of Castrol and Reg Tanner of Esso. My meeting with Reg Tanner proved to be the start of a long and very successful relationship between Esso and myself.

Together these payments amounted to a fairly substantial package. In addition, as was usual, I received 50 per cent of the starting money and 50 per cent of the prize money (less 10 per cent to the mechanics), but what was unusual was that in the Aston Martin team prize money was shared between all drivers and not just those who won it. All expenses were paid by Aston Martin who always provided very comfortable hotel accommodation. A final and very important point was that belonging to the Aston Martin team enhanced my prestige and as a result I was never short of a drive with private owners.

Aston Martin was superbly organised by John Wyer and the cars were immaculately prepared by an outstanding team of mechanics. I think that the standards of dedication and enthusiasm set by the Aston Martin mechanics was way above the high average in motor racing and the result was that the drivers (and here I really mean me) could race without worrying about bits falling off the cars. When something did break, it usually happened during testing. I remember three occasions in particular. At Goodwood in 1953 I was testing a DB3S and something in the front suspension broke at Fordwater when I was travelling at around 130 mph. A wheel tucked under, I went off the course and into the long grass, luckily avoiding lumps of concrete that were lying around, but the car took a great deal of stopping. The following year we were testing at Chalgrove airfield in Oxfordshire and on this occasion I was driving the Lagonda (this was unusual because the Lagonda was Reg Parnell's pet and he did most of the testing with the car). The de Dion axle broke at around 160 mph, I went off the road and it took a very hairy half-mile to bring the car to rest. On another occasion a stub axle broke during testing at Castle Combe. The team learned by these testing failures and they were rarely repeated under racing conditions.

My first race for Aston Martin was Le Mans in 1953 and the story of this race sums up how well Aston Martin looked after their drivers and the sheer pleasure of racing for the team. Much of this pleasure was derived from travelling to the races and for me an overseas race with Aston Martin was a holiday in itself. At this time motor racing was my relaxation and I did not take holidays. I know that Peter Collins felt the same way and even went to the extent of taking along his bucket and spade!

The arrangement was that the drivers would either meet at the Racing Department at Feltham or be picked up, and they would drive in pairs to the race in the latest production Aston Martins. For the Le Mans race we motored to Southampton, stayed there overnight and took an early ferry to Le Havre.

We would than motor gently across northern France in convoy, stopping at a good restaurant for a leisurely lunch that had been booked in advance.

In 1953 Aston Martin stayed for the first time at the Hotel de France at La Chartre on the Loir, some 25 km to the south of Le Mans itself, and John Wyer still used this hotel in his Ford, Gulf-Porsche and Mirage days. It was a small, family hotel with exceptional cuisine and a large garage in which the team could work on the cars. As Aston Martin used the hotel year after year, so it gradually expanded, adding bedrooms, bathrooms and enlarging the dining room. Not only was the Hotel de France patronised by the motor racing world during Le Mans week, but it became well known to motor racing enthusiasts who visited it throughout the year. Close by was the river with safe bathing and plenty of chance for relaxation in the sun. After night practice when we arrived late back at the hotel, there was always an excellent meal ready. It proved the perfect headquarters for a motor racing team.

When I joined Aston Martin I had a reputation as a very fast but rather wild driver who was frequently going off the road. I was rather worried whether I would be accepted by the other members of the team who, Peter Collins apart, were very experienced and senior drivers. In fact all the drivers made me very welcome. I soon blended into the Aston Martin atmosphere at La Chartre.

John Wyer always went out of his way to take a close interest in new team members, breaking them in gently, talking to them at length about the car after practice and the way it had gone and making detailed notes of their comments. I would have loved to know what John made of these comments – especially mine – and to a certain extent he humoured new drivers by taking their comments very seriously. With the old hands John could be very cutting, almost savage, and he quickly cut down anyone who got out of hand. Then there were John's black moods – when he was in such a mood everyone took great care to keep well out of his way. For me John was the one team manager for whom I always wanted to do well. I consistently kept faith with Aston Martin and that is probably the reason why they kept me as a member of the team for so long and why John brought me in later when he was involved with the Ford GT40 programme.

When I first competed at Le Mans, I found it difficult to believe that cars could last 24 hours at racing speeds and thought that tremendous luck was needed to finish. I had of course driven in one long-distance race previously, the Goodwood Nine Hours, where I had driven flat out the whole time. At Le Mans a different approach was required. So much depended on tactics and pacing the cars to last the distance, but it took me a long time to adjust to this attitude. I was not alone in feeling this way, for Reg Parnell (who was co-driving with Peter Collins at Le Mans in 1953) was always a goer who wanted to be out in front and George Abecassis, with whom I was co-driving, treated Le Mans as though it was a ten-lap race. George, who had been a bomber pilot during the war, was an incredibly quick press-on driver and I often thought that the only thing that could have been worse than co-driving with him would have been to be a member of his crew in the RAF!

It was during a conversation with John Wyer after one of George's many shunts that George is reputed to have said to John, 'During the war after I shunted a bomber, they gave me the DFC, but all I get when I shunt one of your bloody cars is a rollicking! The third Aston at Le Mans was driven by Dennis Poore and Eric Thompson, two excellent drivers who had a very much more responsible approach to Le Mans than the rest of us and who were far more likely to be successful.

Aston Martin were racing the new DB3S which was making its International debut. It was a lighter, more shapely and more aerodynamic version of the DB3 sports/racing car that had first appeared in the 1951 Tourist Trophy. The six-cylinder, 2,922 cc twin overhead camshaft engine, originally the work of W.O. Bentley and designed to power the post-war Lagonda, had been developed to produce 182 bhp at 5,500 rpm. Transmission was through a David Brown four-speed gearbox and single-plate clutch. The chassis was a tubular structure, with front suspension by trailing links and transverse torsion bars and rear suspension by a de Dion axle, trailing links and transverse torsion bars. Girling drum brakes were fitted, originally inboard at the rear, but by 1954 the rear brakes were also mounted at the hubs. The DB3S was a thoroughly competitive sports/racing car with good roadholding, good aerodynamics and low weight, but with one serious handicap: it was much less powerful than contemporary rivals such as the 4.1-litre V-12 Ferrari and the C-type Jaguar, simply because it had a smaller capacity engine.

At Le Mans John Wyer's instructions were that the drivers who started the race should hold their positions as at the end of the first lap. Both George and Reg were determined to be in front at the end of lap one and it seemed that several drivers were treating their own team-mates as their most serious rivals, rather than the very strong Jaguar team that was destined to win the race. John Wyer held a long briefing before the race, setting target times and making provision for every possible contingency. Reg/Peter and George/myself were set the same target lap speeds, but Dennis/Eric were to lap a little slower to conserve their car. John made it very clear that he did not want to see any dicing between members of the team.

George was as good as his word at the start of the race and was the leading Aston driver at the end of the first lap. It was obvious that George and Reg were dicing round the circuit well out of sight of the pits, but this did not last long because on lap 16 Reg lost concentration at Tertre Rouge and crashed. When George handed over to me, the car felt decidedly second-hand, very different from the car that I had driven in practice, very loose, with spongy brakes and a slipping clutch. It was not long before clutch slip caused my retirement. This had nothing to do with George, but was a problem with the single-plate clutch used by Aston Martin at the time. The remaining team car of Poore/Thompson survived until the 17th hour of the race when it succumbed to overheating.

For me the 1953 Le Mans race had been a completely new experience. I had never been involved in such a spectacle, with scrutineering that seemed to last for days, enormous publicity and showmanship of the American style. However I thought then and still do that there was far greater driver satisfaction to be derived from winning the Nürburgring 1000 Km race than Le Mans.

I was pleased to be asked to drive for Aston Martin in the Sports Car race at the British Grand Prix meeting at Silverstone in July, but I was also a little surprised. I was very much the new boy in the team, regarding myself as sixth string, and I was already being promoted to the team of three entered in short-distance events. I made the point to John and his answer was short, 'I am asking you to drive. If you want to drive, drive, but leave me to organise my own team.'

Reg was fastest in practice at Silverstone in 1 min 54 sec (92.43 mph) and I was alongside him at the Le Mans start with a time of 1 min 56 sec which was matched by Phil Walters with one of the big American Chrysler-powered Cunninghams. Other entries included Tony Rolt with the only works Jaguar C-type entered (seventh fastest), Peter Collins with the third of the DB3S entries (eighth fastest), Ecurie Ecosse C-type Jaguars and George Abecassis now racing his new HWM-Jaguar.

I was very hopeful of doing well in this race, but I made an atrocious start. I always had difficulties with Le Mans starts because since I had lost my hearing in one ear and was worried about damaging the hearing of my sound ear, I always made sure that my ears were well plugged; the result was that because I could not be certain when the engine had fired, I was always at risk of pushing the starter again before the engine had come to rest. In addition, because of my leg injury I was not a good sprinter. On the first lap at Silverstone I was in twelfth place and with such a fast and competitive field it took me until lap 14 to make up into fourth place behind Reg, Tony Rolt and Peter Collins. I passed Peter going into Stowe and Rolt retired the Jaguar with a broken piston, so I finished second in an Aston Martin 1–2–3 with Spear's 4.1-litre Ferrari fourth. There were no team orders in this race, so I was free to pass Collins and we were still chasing after Rolt. Nevertheless I did notice a slight atmosphere in the Aston pits after the race!

Next on Aston Martin's programme was the Goodwood Nine Hours race in which three DB3S cars were driven by Parnell/Thompson, myself/Poore and Collins/Pat Griffith. The really strong opposition in this race came from Jaguar who fielded their full team of Le Mans-winning disc-braked C-types. I went well in practice and well in the race until an hour and a half after the start when I called into the pits to report that the engine was misfiring. A mechanic lifted the bonnet, had a quick look and slammed it shut – there was a rod through the side! I, of course, was wearing ear plugs and could not hear what was going on. Even so, if you have the misfortune to throw a rod, then the engine will misfire! It was an unusual breakage on an Aston and not attributable to over-revving by me. The permitted maximum on the DB3S was 6,000 rpm, but it was difficult to attain more than 5,800 rpm on the straight and I would not exceed 5,600/5,700 rpm in the gears. Dennis Poore, with whom I co-drove at Goodwood, did not even get a drive, but the other members of the Aston team were rather luckier. The works Jaguars ran into trouble caused by overheating oil

Goodwood Nine Hours race, 1953: I am mixing it with Stirling Moss (works C-type Jaguar). I was co-driving the DB3S with Dennis Poore, but we retired because of a broken con-rod (Charles Dunn).

and Parnell/Thompson and Collins/Griffith took the first two places ahead of the surviving, but very sick works C-type of Whitehead/Stewart.

My final outing with Aston in 1953 was in the Tourist Trophy on the Dundrod road circuit in Northern Ireland. Here I was again paired with Dennis Poore. The race was likely to prove another needle match between Feltham and Coventry, for three works Jaguars were entered. The odds were in Aston's favour for the race was run on a handicap basis with the cars of over three litres such as the Jaguars having to cover 107 laps, the 3-litre cars 106 laps and the 2-litre cars 102 laps. On the Dundrod circuit the Jaguars and the Astons were very closely matched – in the race the best Jaguar time was 5 min 1 sec by Moss/Walker and the best Aston time was 5 min 2 sec by Collins/Griffith – so it was most unlikely that the Jaguars were going to make up a lap on the Astons.

I thoroughly disliked the Dundrod circuit and thought that it was dangerous. It was very narrow, very bumpy, all the cambers were wrong, many of the corners were blind, banks lined the road in many places and it was usually raining. Although the press often described Dundrod as a driver's circuit, in my opinion any driver that liked Dundrod needed psychiatric threatment. An additional problem in 1953 was that the road had recently been resurfaced with loose chippings. This caused a very high rate of tyre wear and frequent pit stops for wheel changes. After only a few laps the cars took on a very second-hand appearance with chip-scarred noses, and the drivers stood a very real risk of facial cuts from chips thrown up by cars in front.

Despite my feelings about Dundrod I went well in practice and in the race. The start of the race was delayed 90 min because of fog, but once we had started the order soon settled down to Moss/Walker (Jaguar) leading on the road, but the Aston Martins leading on handicap. After only five laps the Rolt/Hamilton Jaguar was eliminated by gearbox trouble and this problem also caused the retirement of the Whitehead/Stewart Jaguar later in the race. I handed over to Dennis Poore after 21 laps when we were in third position, and he went well for another 18 laps until he tried to lap Wharton's Frazer Nash at Tornagrough, a left-hander three-quarters of the way round the circuit. Wharton was very much in with a chance of winning the race on handicap and was not willing simply to wave Dennis through; the DB3S got on to the rough stuff at the edge of the road, Dennis lost control and shunted the DB3S into the ditch. The car was badly damaged and Dennis suffered a deep cut over the eye; he was lucky enough to get the attention of a superb surgeon who was acting as the course doctor.

Collins/Griffith and Parnell/Thompson went on to take the first two places on the road and on handicap ahead of the Wharton/Robb Frazer Nash. The Moss/Walker C-type also suffered gearbox trouble and Stirling, who had been waiting at the finish, juddered the surviving works car across the line into fourth place.

I did make one more appearance at the wheel of an Aston Martin in 1953, albeit in a private entry. The team had agreed to support Frenchman Mike Sparken who was running his DB3 in the Casablanca 12 Hours Sports Car race on December 20. Sparken's ex-works DB3 had been updated by fitting the latest DB3S engine and very aerodynamic coupé bodywork by Vignale. Orignally Peter Collins was going to co-drive with Sparken, but he had to drop out at the last moment and I took his place. The Whitehead brothers, Peter and Graham, also received full works support for the standard DB3 which they ran in this race. David Brown, John Wyer, the Aston mechanics, the Whiteheads and myself all flew to the race via Madrid in Brown's de Havilland Dove company aircraft.

The opposition in the race included Ferraris, Gordinis and Talbots. Sparken was a very capable, fast and reliable driver. We ran strongly in the race and in the closing hours we were holding third place when one of rear lights started to flicker on and off. Immediately behind us was the Talbot of Etancelin/Rosier, and the Talbot pit lodged on objection about the lights on the DB3. The light was repaired in the pits, which took some time, and we rejoined the race to finish fourth behind the Talbot with the Whiteheads in fifth place. The race was a splendid mid-winter break.

1954

Every year the Aston Martin contract was re-negotiated. I was not, however, expecting any problems, because I was very happy with the team and it seemed that they were happy with me. During the winter of 1953 we had the first of what was to be a regular annual meeting. Every year I would go to see John either at the Feltham works or at his home at Fulmer in Buckinghamshire and over a meal we would discuss the prospects for the coming year, the planned programme, what he expected from the drivers and what he proposed as a retainer. I never bargained with John about money, as I was happy to accept the terms he offered, but I am quite sure that John was firm as to what he intended to pay and that there was no real scope for negotiation! He would then arrange meetings with all the team's sponsors and this resulted in very good deals for the drivers with Esso, Castrol and Avon. For 1954 Aston Martin were planning to contest every round in the Sports Car Championship.

We were no sooner back from Casablanca than the team was preparing to travel to the Argentine to compete in the first round of the Championship, the Buenos Aires 1,000 Km race on January 24. For this race the only changes to the cars were the fitting of stronger, triple-plate clutches, (which of course became standard) and, because 100/130-octane Avgas fuel was to be used, the raising of the compression ratio to 9.4:1 and the boosting of the power output to 194 bhp at 5,500 rpm. Although three DB3S cars were taken to the race, the only British pairings were Reg Parnell/myself and Collins/Griffith, as the third car was to be driven by local drivers Mieres/Tomasi. In addition Aston took over an older DB3 car which was to be driven in the race by its buyer, Eric Forrest-Greene, an Englishman living in Buenos Aires.

The flight to Buenos Aires was by Aerolineas Argentinas Douglas DC-4 that was routed via Lisbon where the aircraft stopped overnight so that a radio operator could be found. There was no announcement as to the reasons for the delay and this led to a furious argument between John Wyer and the captain and glacial relations between them on the long flight as the aircraft made stop after stop on the South American mainland before eventually arriving at Buenos Aires. On the flight I palled up with a very scruffy individual whom I thought was an Italian mechanic, but he surprisingly spoke several languages and I later learned that he was the Marquis de Portago, a very well known international horseman and playboy and, later, a member of the works Ferrari team. At Buenos Aires he was co-driving a private Ferrari with Harry Schell.

Because the DB3S cars had been plagued by distributor drive shafts breaking, it was decided to do some endurance testing at Buenos Aires and I was selected to do the driving. The test, carried out prior to official practice, was run in torrential rain and there were no other cars on the circuit except the Ecurie Ecosse C-types which David Murray quickly brought in because he was worried that they might aquaplane off the road. So I was left lapping in solitary misery on the Autodrome part of the circuit with instructions from Wyer to keep going for several hours, while everyone else except a couple of mechanics returned to the hotel. I mildly objected to this – and said so – but John was firm and I was left to carry on until either the distributor shaft broke or the car skated off the road. Unfortunately, the test was satisfactory (which was to have repercussions in the race) and I returned late to the hotel for my dinner, soaked to the skin, thoroughly miserable and very bad-tempered – but did not receive the sympathy I thought that I deserved from either John or my team-mates. In fact when I mentioned that the whole exercise was dangerous, John Wyer replied, 'But Salvadori, didn't you know that you are the expendable member of the Aston Martin team?'

The circuit used for the 1,000 Km race combined the outer section of the Buenos Aires Autodrome with public roads (including a fast section using one side of a dual carriageway, round a roundabout and back down the other side) to give a lap distance of 5.89 miles and lap speeds approaching 100 mph. Both the Astons and the Ecurie Ecosse Jaguars went well in practice and stood a good chance against a mixed bag of Ferraris.

Farina took the lead with the works 4.5-litre Ferrari early in the race and he and Maglioli went on to score a convincing win. Reg and I were driving really well with the DB3S and I moved up into second place. Even so, I nearly had one of my biggest shunts ever at the long, quick, right-hander just after the pits. I was getting the DB3S into some beautiful four-wheel drifts through this bend, nearly flat out, but on one lap it almost got away from me. Our race came to an end when the distributor shaft broke on lap 66. As is sometimes the case, testing had failed to reveal a weakness that showed itself under the greater stress of racing conditions. After our retirement Schell/de Portago moved up into second place and Collins/Griffith finished third ahead of the Ecurie Ecosse Jaguar of Scott-Douglas/Sanderson. Mieres/Tomasi retired their DB3S with final drive trouble. Poor Forrest-Greene overturned the DB3 which caught fire; he suffered terrible burns from which he died the following day.

The cars were then shipped to Sebring for the 12 Hours race on March 7. There was simply no time to return the cars to England for rebuilds and this was to contribute to their downfall in Florida. For this race the compression ratio was reduced to 8.5:1 (power fell to 182 bhp) and the cars were fitted with new Girling brakes having automatic adjustors to compensate for drum expansion. Opposition came from a strong team of four works Lancia D.24 Spyders, a brace of private 4.5-litre Ferraris and a single 5.4-litre Cunningham. Sebring was notoriously hard on brakes and this was to cause problems for most of the teams competing.

Although the Astons lacked the speed to challenge for the lead, they ran swiftly and smoothly in the opening laps of the race and by the end of the first hour were seventh (Collins/Griffith), eighth (Reg, with whom I was co-driving) and ninth (Shelby/Wallace). I never got a drive because a bare 30 minutes later Reg stopped out on the circuit because of a broken con-rod and then pushed the car all the way back to the pits where it was realised at once that nothing could be done. For this achievement Reg was awarded a magnificent trophy as 'Man of the Race', but I thought that Reg, who had more mechanical knowledge than any other Aston driver, could have saved himself a lot of effort by simply looking under the bonnet! The funny thing is that when I threw a rod at Goodwood, I got no trophy but just harsh words. Both Collins/Griffith and Shelby/Wallace were eliminated by brake trouble caused by the new brakes stripping the linings from the brake shoes and overheating the hub assembly. The race was won by Cunningham's 1,500 cc Osca driven by Stirling Moss/Bill Lloyd from the surviving Lancia of Rubirosa/Valenzano and the Austin-Healey of Macklin/Huntoon.

For Sebring we had been joined by Rob Walker, a close friend of David Brown and John Wyer. I had know Rob for several years, regarded him as the perfect English gentleman, very reserved, and with of course a fine reputation for the high standard of preparation of his cars – but I knew nothing of the lighter side of his character. After the race the team returned via New York where we stayed at the Gothen hotel. We went out on the town as the guests of Esso, took in the Gay Nineties Club and had a thoroughly good time. Rob had been getting increasingly lively and as we left the club, he grabbed a policeman's cap. As we scuffled with the policeman, I realised that this could lead to terrible problems and although I was not so fast off the mark at Le Mans starts, I was first away from this incident and we ran down Fifth Avenue to the accompaniment of police whistles.

We managed to get clear of trouble and as we strolled on down Fifth Avenue, Rob decided to jump into one of the trash cans in the street. He made a good jump, jamming his bottom into the top of the can and we rolled him down the street back to the hotel. The party started in the hotel foyer with a wrestling match between Rob and Reg Parnell. The management seemed to take rather a dim view of this, so we retired to the team's suite of rooms. After Rob had insisted on demonstrating how easy it was to tear telephone directories, Reg and Rob started to wrestle again. It was all getting rather out of hand with Reg constantly on top, so John Wyer brought the match to an end by pouring a jug of iced water over the struggling pair. Later, at about three in the morning, I saw Rob with a long glass of foaming liquid – gin and Eno's, which Rob claimed was the perfect tonic for that time of day.

Next on Aston Martin's schedule was the Mille Miglia, but John Wyer has mentioned in his introduction that he could never understand why I would not compete in the Italian road race, saying that all I had to do was to drive as I normally did on the road and I couldn't help but win! I believed that the British teams competing in the race were on a hiding to nothing and that the Italian drivers who knew the course intimately would always win, but more importantly it was far more lucrative for me to stay and compete in England. While Stirling Moss and other top drivers were in Italy for at least a fortnight practising for the race and competing, I had a good chance of cleaning up most

of the British races in which I was entered! This was good for my principal sponsors, Esso, good for the private owners for whom I drove and good for my pocket. I never dared admit my reasons to John Wyer and I should add that it took Stirling to prove me wrong when he won in 1955 at the wheel of a Mercedes-Benz.

By the time the *Daily Express* Silverstone meeting arrived in May the Aston team had several new developments ready. All three DB3S entries were powered by new engines with twin-plug cylinder heads, larger Weber 45 DCO carburettors and a much improved power output of 225 bhp at 6,000 rpm. Peter Collins drove an open car, while Graham Whitehead and I were entered with very stylish fixed-head coupés. The coupés were Aston's great hope for Le Mans and the Silverstone race was very much of a test run. The cockpit of the coupé was adequately roomy, but headroom was decidedly limited and I was thoroughly uncomfortable – that, however, was nothing unusual because my height made me uncomfortable in most cars I drove. The team also entered Reg Parnell with the new V-12 Lagonda. The opposition included a works 4.9-litre Ferrari driven by Gonzalez, Abecassis with the HWM-Jaguar and a strong team of Ecurie Ecosse C-type Jaguars.

In practice the new coupés proved slow and difficult to handle – although at Silverstone there was nothing inherently vicious about their handling – and practice was dominated by Ian Stewart (Jaguar) and Gonzalez who lapped in 1 min 54 sec.

The race was run in the wet, the coupé's cockpit misted up badly and it was a miserable drive, enlivened only by a dice between Peter Collins and me. This was, however, one of those rare occasions when I went really well in the wet, and I closed up on Peter, uncertain whether I should have a go at taking him. I decided to press him fairly hard, he was getting slightly out of line under pressure and I was not surprised when he lost the DB3S at Becketts and spun in front of me. I kept clear of the spinning DB3S and moved up into seventh place, while Peter kept his engine running and rejoined the race some distance behind

Left *A party after Sebring, 1954, at the 'Latin Quarter' in New York with, left to right, Reg Parnell, Peter Collins, myself, the Esso representative and John Wyer* (Roy Salvadori collection).

Right *With the Duke Richmond and Gordon at the May 1954 Silverstone meeting. In the background is one of the ill-fated DB3S coupés, but I drove this one into first place in the 3,000 cc class of the Sports Car race* (Roy Salvadori collection).

me. The race was easily won by Gonzalez from Abecassis who had gone very well with the HWM, Walker and Stewart finished third and fourth for Ecurie Ecosse and Reg brought the misfiring Lagonda across the line in fifth place ahead of Hamilton (private Jaguar). My seventh place was good enough to win the 3-litre class, which was to prove the coupé's only success in its career.

On the basis of my experience at Silverstone I did not want to drive the coupé at Le Mans. Happily, as co-driver to Reg Parnell the situation was out of my control and Reg, who was in a position to choose which car he drove, opted for a Lagonda; when it became obvious that only one Lagonda could be ready in time for Le Mans, Reg with his love of unusual cars switched to an open DB3S fitted experimentally with a Wade supercharger, which with single Weber carburettor, single-plug head and 7.0:1 compression ratio developed 240 bhp at 6,000 rpm. At Le Mans the Lagonda was driven by Thompson/Poore, and the two coupés were handled by Collins/'Bira' and Graham Whitehead/Jimmy Stewart. In addition a single-plug open DB3S in American white and blue colours was entered for Carroll Shelby/Paul Frère.

For Aston Martin the 1954 Le Mans race proved a most terrible *débâcle*. In the opening laps of the race, whilst the 4.9-litre Ferraris and the new D-type Jaguars battled for the lead, Reg was ninth with our blown DB3S (which was not expected to last because of a gasket weakness), Collins 13th and Shelby 14th. The Lagonda was eliminated after only 25 laps when Thompson spun at the Esses, badly damaging the rear of the car.

The new coupés proved disappointingly and inexplicably slow and, although it was not fully appreciated at the time, suffered from a serious aerodynamic defect that caused the rear end to lift at high speed. In torrential rain both coupés became airborne over the hump on the approach to White House and crashed heavily. After five and a half hours' racing Jimmy Stewart lost control of the coupé which shot down the right-hand side of the course, hit a marker stone, bounced on to its roof and cannoned across to the other side of the track. Stewart was thrown out and was incredibly lucky to escape with only a badly fractured elbow and bruises. In the early hours of the Sunday morning 'Bira' crashed very close to the same spot, the car was again completely wrecked and he escaped with minor injuries. Already the Shelby/Frère DB3S was out of the race because of a broken stub axle, perhaps the result of an earlier off-course excursion when Shelby put the car into the sand rather hard.

This left only the blown DB3S driven by Reg and myself and now in fourth place. I was close to joining the coupés when I nearly lost the DB3S over the hump on the approach to White House after hitting a puddle, and I gave myself a terrible fright as I skated down the road sideways. Earlier, not long before dark on the Saturday evening, I came into the Dunlop bend just after the pits, normally flat out but somewhat slower on a wet road, to find a 'creeper' right in the middle of the track instead of hugging the bank. I was completely committed to my line so I either hit the 'creeper' or changed my line and most probably hit the bank; I braked as hard as I dared on the wet road, but could not avoid nudging the 'creeper' up the chuff. The extra horsepower his car suddenly acquired was just too much for the driver and he lost control and hit the bank. For several laps afterwards the driver stood on the bank and shook his fist at me at I went past. I looked the other way and although I thought that he was going to throw his crash helmet at me, he eventually lost interest. When I stopped at the pits to hand the car over to Reg, he asked me how the car was running and I told him that it was perfect, quite forgetting my little shunt – and anyway, I am not really the type to stir up trouble! About an hour later Reg was back in the pits complaining that the headlamps were useless – instead of shining on the road they were lighting up the birds in the trees! It was then discovered that I had tweaked the front of the bodywork when I nudged the 'creeper' and Reg rejoined the race after telling everyone very clearly just what he thought of his co-driver! Reg and I soldiered on until a little after midday on the Sunday when our blown DB3S succumbed to gasket failure.

As the result of a prodigious effort the Aston team managed to recover from the Le Mans disaster to field four cars at the Grand Prix meeting at Silverstone on July 17. Reg drove the Lagonda, both Peter and I had twin-plug cars and Carroll Shelby drove his nominally private single-plug car. Tony Rolt with an Ecurie Ecosse C-type Jaguar was fastest in practice, I was second fastest and the race had all the makings of another good Aston-Jaguar battle.

Inevitably I was slow off the mark at the Le Mans start and on the first lap was in sixth place. It had rained just before the race and as this was the last race of the day the track was not only damp, but had a good coating of rubber and oil. I began to pick up places, but then I lost the DB3S at Copse, nearly hitting the bank. I kept going and was driving really well, pulling right through the field to finish second behind Peter Collins. I was pushing Peter really hard and getting frantic 'easy' signals from the pit, but there was no way that I would have tried to pass him. At the flag I was a mere second behind Peter and set the fastest lap, and Shelby and Reg finished behind me to make it a very satisfying David Brown 1–2–3–4.

The Aston team did not race again until the Tourist Trophy at Dundrod on September 11 and there was a strong DB3S team consisting of Reg/myself, Collins/Griffith and Graham Whitehead/Poore. The opposition included a full team of D-type Jaguars (two of which were fitted with 2.5-litre engines to take advantage of the complicated handicap system on which the race results were decided), four works Lancias and a single works 3-litre Ferrari Monza shared by Hawthorn/Trintignant. Both Reg and I had similar thoughts with regard to the circuit – and it showed in our practice times – so the team's hopes were really pinned on Peter Collins who was superb at Dundrod.

It proved a miserable, wet race and a poor race for Aston: Peter completed only 23 laps before retiring with final drive failure, and I was near the end of my spell at the wheel when I received a pit signal calling me in rather earlier than I expected. I was so relieved at the thought of getting out of the car and drying out that I pressed on rather too hard, realised that I was going into the bend over the railway bridge at Leathemstown too quickly, was unable to break off my drift early enough and touched the wall on the inside of the circuit. I felt a heavy thump and I was thrust against the door, cutting my elbow. The car's handling, not surprisingly, deteriorated, and when I stopped at the pits it was obvious that the DB3S was too badly damaged to continue. It was only then that I learned that Collins was going to take over the car and of course there was every prospect that he would have been able to get the car up with the leaders. This was just about the only shunt that I had in a race with an Aston. I felt very distressed about this, as it was entirely unnecessary. I am sure that John Wyer realised how I felt for he never criticised me for the accident. John, who could be so very cutting at times, was very forgiving and understanding when the chips were down. The surviving DB3S of Poore/Graham Whitehead was plagued by problems and finished thirteenth. The winner on handicap was the 750 cc DB of Armagnac/Loreau, while Hawthorn/Trintignant were the winners on scratch. It was small consolation for Aston that the Jaguars had been plagued by mechanical trouble and their highest placed finisher was the 2.5-litre car of Peter Whitehead/Wharton in fifth place.

1955

Aston Martin adopted Girling disc brakes for 1955 and the main advantage of these was their consistency and their durability in long races. Once I had driven a DB3S with disc brakes, I never wanted to go back to drums (although there were of course drum brakes on the car I owned personally in 1955). Peter Collins was on record as saying that he preferred the DB3S with drum brakes and he opted for drum brakes at Rouen in 1956. I think that the real point is that Rouen is a circuit on which the brakes are not too heavily used. From my point of view, whilst drum brakes were quite adequate for short races, the discs were infinitely preferable for long-distance racing. There were also a number of other, minor changes made for 1955.

Over the winter I did quite a lot of testing for Aston, mainly because Reg Parnell and Peter Collins were otherwise engaged. My first DB3S drive of the year was at the British Empire Trophy at Oulton Park in April, racing my own car entered in Gilby's name, and I also drove this at Goodwood and Ibsley, winning at both circuits. I did not race with a works car until the *Daily Express* meeting at Silverstone in May and here the team fielded a four-car entry for Reg Parnell, Peter Collins, newcomer to the team Peter Walker and myself. Both Reg and I were driving new open cars rebuilt from the wrecked coupés and fitted with disc brakes. Peter Collins was at the wheel of his own car loaned back to the works and my car had been loaned back for Peter Walker to drive. The race was over 117 miles and the opposition included a strong team of works Jaguar D-types driven by Hawthorn, Rolt and Hamilton, together with Titterington driving an Ecurie Ecosse-entered car – a typical Aston versus Jaguar thrash.

The two disc-braked cars arrived late at the circuit so Reg and I missed the first practice session, practised only in the second session in the wet and were well down the line of cars for the Le Mans start headed by Hawthorn's D-type. Both Reg and I had a lot of work to do if we were to get anywhere in the race and

On my way to second place with the DB3S in the Sports Car race at the May Silverstone meeting, 1955. The DB3S is displaying tremendous understeer and the angle of the front wheels to the road indicates that I am trying to induce a rear-end breakaway to set up the drift for the corner (Roy Salvadori collection).

we battled through the field so that the race order by the end of lap five was Hawthorn leading Rolt with Reg and myself in third and fourth positions respectively. Reg passed Rolt, but as he closed up on the leading Jaguar, Mike set a new lap record of 95.79 mph on lap 15 to maintain his lead. Two laps later I passed Rolt and equalled Mike's new record. The prospects of catching the D-type were remote, but only four laps from the end the Jaguar blew its top radiator hose and Mike fell back to finish fourth behind Reg, myself and Rolt. Of the other two team cars, both drum-braked, Collins finished sixth and Walker eighth.

For Silverstone races the Aston Martin team always stayed about five miles from the circuit at the Wicken Rectory, which was run by the Rev Paul Hoskins. His regular clientele were elderly residents who moved into other accommodation in the village during the Silverstone races. At these times the hotel was run in the usual Aston party atmosphere and the champagne flowed the moment we arrived. Each night when we returned to the hotel and went up to the bedrooms, something would have happened – maybe your bed had been hidden or thrown out of the window by other members of the team, or there was a snake in the bed or a dead rat. We behaved just like a pack of kids, but sometimes the humour wore just a little thin – there is nothing like being on the receiving end of a jet of cold water from the garden hose just after getting into bed for destroying one's sense of humour!

Next on the calendar was Le Mans in June. Heading the entry list was a team of three of the new Mercedes-Benz 300SLR cars, Jaguar fielded three of their

Above *Le Mans, 1955. It's raining and you know how I feel about wet weather driving!* (Roy Salvadori collection).

Above right *Le Mans, 1955: I am leading Peter Collins during our long dice. My DB3S retired with crankshaft problems, but Peter and Paul Frère went on to take a well deserved second place* (Roy Salvadori collection).

new 'long-nose' D-types and from Ferrari came a trio of new 4.4-litre six-cylinder cars. The Astons had braking and roadholding that were more than a match for any of these cars, but were substantially less powerful. Aston Martin tactics were to try to last the distance and hope that the opposition would break. There were DB3S entries for Collins/Frère, myself/Walker and Tony Brooks/John Riseley-Prichard (both of whom were having their first drive for the team), while the revised Lagonda was driven by Parnell/Poore.

In the opening couple of hours of the race there was a titanic battle for the lead between the Ferraris, Jaguars and Mercedes, while Peter Collins and myself were running steadily close together in about eleventh and twelfth places. As in 1953 the race order had been determined as at the end of the first lap, which meant that I led Peter, and we had a comfortable lap target of about 4 min 35 sec of which we were well in advance. After two-and-a-half hours there occurred the terrible accident when Levegh's Mercedes collided with Macklin's Austin-Healey and was launched into the spectator area opposite the pits.

We knew that there had been a bad accident, but we had no idea how bad and as far as we were aware no spectators were involved, for the accident seemed to have happened in the pits area. Every time we came past the pits we were slowed down by the marshalls to around 50 mph, but round the back of the circuit we were having the most immense dice, constantly swapping positions and then sorting ourselves out so that we re-appeared at the pits in the right order. On one lap I spun at Arnage – one of the very few occasions on which I spun a DB3S

– and Peter waited while I restarted and caught up with him. He laughed and waved me by so that we could keep the order right as we passed the pits. Peter was really as nice as they come.

In the early hours of Sunday morning the Mercedes team was withdrawn from the race and the D-type Jaguar of Hawthorn/Bueb went on to win by some 60 miles from the DB3S of Peter and Paul Frère. Walker and I held tenth place at one stage, but we had difficulty in starting the car after a pit stop because of a solenoid problem caused by me pressing the starter button before the engine had stopped. We fell back a couple of places and retired after 138 laps because of a broken crankshaft. The Brooks/Riseley-Prichard DB3S was eliminated after 83 laps because of dynamo failure and the Lagonda survived 93 laps before succumbing to fuel problems.

At La Chartre we were well known to the villagers, we used to talk to many of them who followed the fortunes of the team and we used to sit out on the front of the Hotel de France playing gin rummy watched by the locals. Villagers from La Chartre would come to the race and try to get a position in the stand opposite the Aston Martin pit; it was here that Levegh's Mercedes crashed and I am told that some of them were amongst the casualties.

Although many races were cancelled following the Le Mans disaster, it in fact made little difference to Aston's programme in Sports Car races. Four DB3S cars were entered at the British Grand Prix meeting at Aintree and took the first four places, just as the four works Mercedes-Benz W.196 cars took the first four places in the Grand Prix itself. The Astons were driven by Parnell, Collins, myself and Walker and again the real opposition came from Jaguar, a works D-type for Hawthorn and an Ecurie Ecosse car for Ninian Sanderson. Aston were particularly anxious to win the Sports Car race because the whole meeting had attracted substantial publicity as a result of the Mercedes entry in the Grand Prix.

I was fastest in practice the first day and joint fastest with Peter Walker the second day, and although Hawthorn was going exceptionally well with the D-type, I thought that we would beat him in the race. As far as my team-mates were concerned I thought that my toughest opponent would be Reg Parnell and I doubted if Peter Walker would repeat his practice form in the race. John Wyer's instructions were, 'If you get in front of Mike (Hawthorn), I don't want any inter-team fighting. Whoever is leading should hold the lead and the rest of you should hold your positions.' If I was to win, I had to be the leading Aston driver at the start, and I was helped in this because it was a normal grid start with engines running.

The result was that the start was an absolute shambles as the Aston drivers jockeyed for position, trying to edge each other into the outside wall or the pit lane, and while we were taking care of each other Mike accelerated away into a lead of several cars' lengths. I would have hated to have been anywhere near John Wyer while this was happening. I managed to hold off my team-mates to snatch second position, trying to get past Mike; the problem was that if I tried to pass Mike and messed it up, it was quite likely that I would be passed by one of my team-mates and my rear view mirror was full of Astons. I made two unsuccessful attempts to pass and behind me the other Aston drivers were queueing up to have a go at me. On lap two I scrambled through at the corner before the long straight, edging Mike on to the rough stuff at the edge so that he had to lift off, and by Melling Crossing I had pulled out a slender lead; Peter Collins was the next to pass, but it took him a couple more laps, and both Reg and Peter Walker passed Mike who had now lost much of the will to fight back.

When I passed the pits at the end of lap four I was greatly relieved to see the 'Hold' signal and thought that I was going to have an easy run home. However, Peter Walker was not content to sit in fourth place but passed Reg and started to pressure Peter Collins who pressured me – the whole Aston Martin team was lapping flat out, while the pits held out frantic 'Hold' signals. Once Reg had re-passed Peter Walker, the pressure eased again and I was able to relax a little. After the race there was a somewhat strained atmosphere between Reg Parnell and Peter Walker whom, I suspect, had received an earful from John Wyer for disobeying team tactics. Rudi Uhlenhaut, the Mercedes chief engineer, commented that it was a good thing that Mercedes had not entered one of their 300SLR sports/racing cars in this event, for he doubted whether it would have been a match for the Astons on this circuit.

At the end of July Aston entered a single DB3S for me at the Crystal Palace, but on this difficult circuit there was a very real risk that I would be beaten by Archie Scott-Brown with the Lister-Bristol. Scott-Brown led for the first lap, but I passed him at Ramp corner on the second lap – a very difficult place to pass with a very real risk of colliding, but I was not going to let the chance go by and

Peter and myself after the Sports Car race at the Grand Prix meeting at Aintree in July 1955. At least two members of the Aston team were pleased with the race results! (Roy Salvadori collection).

Archie was so good that there might not be another chance – and once I was in front I pulled steadily away to win by a margin of eight seconds.

Prince Bertil of Sweden, a very good friend of Aston Martin and David Brown, was involved in the organisation of the first Swedish Grand Prix held on August 7 and persuaded the team to send two DB3S cars. If he had been a *real* friend of the team he would have kept the Mercedes team away, for on the very fast but rather narrow and bumpy Kristianstâd circuit the 300SLRs were untouchable and took the first two places by a substantial margin. Both Peter Collins and I, driving our own cars prepared at the works, were hopelessly outpaced in practice, and Peter became a non-starter when his car broke a con-rod. I struggled through the race, not expecting to achieve anything, and finished a poor seventh. What I do remember about Sweden was the social life – a pale shadow of what we had been led to expect. Several cocktail parties and dinners had been arranged but, unfortunately, they all finished early in the evening and the drivers were in bed and on their own much sooner than expected!

A great disappointment for me followed at the Goodwood Nine Hours race where Aston had entered three cars and I was co-driving with Reg Parnell a DB3S fitted with the latest, more powerful engine developing 236 bhp at 6,000 rpm. There were no works Jaguars in this race, so the opposition came from private Ferrari Monzas and Jaguars. During the first day's practice Mike Hawthorn (Ferrari Monza) was fastest in 1 min 37.6 sec, I was second fastest in 1 min 38.0 sec, but on the second day Mike improved to 1 min 36.2 sec. Reg and I reckoned that we had a very good chance of winning, but at the Le Mans start Reg let in the clutch too fiercely, overstrained a rear hub and retired at the end of the third lap. The Ferraris proved very quick but very unreliable and Peter Walker and Dennis Poore scored Aston's third successive win in this race from the Ecurie Ecosse D-type of Titterington/Sanderson. Peter Collins and Tony Brooks led for much of the race with their DB3S, but were delayed by an electrical fault and finished third.

More disappointment for me followed in the *Daily Herald* Trophy at Oulton Park the following weekend. After his mishap at Goodwood, Reg persuaded John Wyer to enter a works car at Oulton Park for him, and Peter and I, who had entered our own cars privately, unexpectedly had full works support. The works and Ecurie Ecosse D-type Jaguars were not entered, but once more there was a strong entry of private Ferrari Monzas. Mike Hawthorn was fastest in practice in 1 min 58.6 sec, I was second fastest with my drum-braked DB3S in 2 min 0.4 sec and Reg with the works disc-braked car was third fastest in 2 min 0.8 sec.

I was well up in the fight for the lead on the first lap, but I lost the use of third gear (the one gear needed more than any other at Oulton) and while I was struggling with the gearbox, Archie with his Lister-Bristol ran up the back of me. I eventually finished eighth, four laps in arrears. Reg won the race with a brilliant, smooth drive, Mike finished second with the Monza (which was a real handful on Englebert tyres) and Peter took third place with his drum-braked

DB3S. The best social life of all was when we were racing at Oulton Park and Aintree and the Aston team usually stayed at Rowton Hall Country Club where the proprietor, Denis Uren, laid on the most fabulous parties.

Aston's final race of 1955 was the ill-fated Tourist Trophy at Dundrod, another tragic race which cost the lives of three drivers (including the young and talented W.T. Smith at the wheel of the works Connaught) and led to the abandonment of the circuit – certainly not before time. Mercedes-Benz dominated the results with first three places with their 300SLR cars, but only after a long battle with a single works D-type Jaguar driven brilliantly by Mike Hawthorn and Desmond Titterington which ended when the Jaguar broke its engine and spun off on its own oil. Apart from the Collins/Brooks car which was right up with the Mercedes, the Aston Martin team was competing in what amounted to a secondary race with the works 3-litre Maseratis and Ferrari Monzas.

Much as I disliked the circuit and thought it dangerous, I was reconciled to driving there, as was Reg Parnell with whom I was co-driving, and we both put up quite a good show. Neither Reg nor I was happy with the handling of the car in practice, but our dislike of the circuit was such that our complaints were not taken seriously. In the race I found the throttle sticking wide open at times and I made several pit stops; the mechanics would open the bonnet, flip the throttle and say, 'Look, it's all right.' This was all I needed when I was struggling with a circuit that I disliked so much and I had some terrible moments because of the sticking throttle. It got to the stage where I would lift my foot, the throttle would close and operate normally but when I put my foot down again and then braked for the next corner, it would stick wide open.

Eventually I convinced the mechanics there was a problem – they knew me well enough to appreciate that I did not invent problems – and they took a closer look. What was happening was that when the bonnet was closed, the bonnet stay cleared the throttle linkage by only a small margin and on this occasion it was fouling the linkage over bad bumps. The mechanics bent the stay and that was the end of our problem. There were more delays when the exhaust pipe dropped off – I had to stop out on the circuit to pick it up (it was damned hot) and put it in the passenger side so that it could be refitted in the pits. We lost a tremendous amount of time through all these stops and did well to finish seventh. The best Aston Martin placing was fourth by Walker/Poore behind the Mercedes, whilst the third team car driven by Collins/Brooks – the team's real hope on this circuit – were eliminated by a broken con-rod bolt.

1956

Aston Martin soldiered on with the DB3S in 1956, although it was now near the end of its competitive life. The DBR1, on which I did some of the testing, was under development, but it was not raced on a regular basis until 1957. Perhaps the most significant event was that Stirling Moss joined the team. I thought that this was simply marvellous because he was the greatest British driver and unquestionably the best in the world after Fangio retired. Aston Martin had pushed out the boat to secure Stirling's services and this meant that they would have to protect their investment by putting even greater effort, if that were possible, into the preparation and development of the cars – and that was good for the team as a whole. When Stirling made up his mind to set a really fast lap in an Aston, we knew that his lap time was the ultimate for the car on that course and the time at which we should be aiming. Stirling's driving always stimulated me to greater effort, but it tended to demoralise other members of the Aston Martin team. Tony Brooks never seemed to go quite so well when Stirling was in the team (and this was also true of Tony's driving for the Vanwall team – he seemed to go faster after Stirling had retired from the race). Dennis Poore had now retired from racing for business reasons, but Peter Collins stayed with Aston Martin even though he was driving for Ferrari in Formula One.

Our first race of 1956 was the Sebring 12 Hours in which three cars were entered for Moss/Collins, Parnell/Brooks and myself/Carroll Shelby. Carroll was an excellent driver, very experienced, and as he was about the same height as myself it made life as easy as it could be with regard to the pedal and seating arrangements. The cockpit of the DB3S was particularly uncomfortable for a tall driver and we always thought that the Aston design team had built the car with Stirling's measurements very much in mind. At Sebring there was strong opposition from teams of V-12 3.5-litre Ferraris and from D-type Jaguars entered by Briggs Cunningham, but we thought that our chances of success were fairly good.

Moss/Collins set the pace for the Aston team, but were eliminated by oil pump drive failure that caused the engine to seize when they were in second place. As the race drew on Aston hopes were still high for Parnell/Brooks were fourth and we were fifth, but with the major problem that we had lost second and third gears and were worried in case the gearbox packed up altogether. The Parnell/Brooks car also succumbed to oil pump drive failure at three-quarters race distance, but we struggled on to finish fourth overall behind two works Ferraris and a Cunningham-entered Jaguar and to win the 3-litre class.

After the race Carroll and I borrowed the chef's car at the Pinecrest Lakes Club at Avon Park where we were staying and drove into Sebring for the evening. After a rather wild party and in the early hours of the morning Carroll drove back to the hotel, but managed to get lost. I was complaining rather sleepily that he really ought to know the way when I saw the hotel and pointed to it. 'Do we turn here?' Carroll asked and although I could see no turning I agreed. Carroll turned sharp right and drove down a steep bank, there was a thud, a lot of wallowing and the car bogged itself in soft earth. We returned to the hotel on foot, intending to make our apologies to the chef in the morning. When we came down to breakfast, there was the car smack in the middle of a cabbage field and in full view of the dining room window. I left Shelby to explain to the chef exactly what had happened – he was always so good at explanations.

For the Sports Car race at the *Daily Express* Silverstone meeting I was asked by Aston Martin to lend my car, DB3S/5, back to the works as they were short

An Aston Martin Grand Slam: Silverstone, 1956, with, left to right, one of the mechanics, David Brown, Reg Parnell, Charles Mortimer, myself and Peter Collins (Louis Klemantaski).

of cars. I had been allowed to buy the prototype car DB3S/1 for 1955 and enjoyed a good season with it so naturally I wanted another car the following year. Initially John said that there were no cars to spare, but when I pressured him he offered me DB3S/5, pointing out that it was the 'lemon' which no one wanted to drive and I remembered that I had not enjoyed driving it myself in 1955.

I was entered with my own car at Silverstone and the other Aston drivers were Stirling, Collins and Parnell. As you will see, however, Stirling became convinced that there was something special about my DB3S. The opposition at Silverstone included a full team of works Jaguar D-types driven by Hawthorn, Titterington and Fairman and Ecurie Ecosse D-types driven by Flockhart, Sanderson and Brown. I always seemed to drive well at Silverstone and I made fastest practice time jointly with Titterington.

Stirling was obviously unhappy with his car and I later learned that he had asked John Wyer whether he could try my car. John explained to Stirling that I was driving my own car and if Stirling wanted to try it, he should ask me. In fact, although Stirling was convinced that my car was superior, he merely asked me if I would like to try his car. I lapped very quickly with Stirling's car and could find nothing wrong with it, but I would not have chosen the same width of tyres and said so. Stirling opted for 6.00 tyres on the back (the other Aston drivers ran on 6.50 rear tyres) and I think that these made the back end of the car too lively. Another point was that Stirling changed down to third for Stowe, while I stayed in top (thereby, I believe, saving time). I think that these two factors contributed to my faster lap times in practice and the race.

If I had known that Stirling wanted to try my car I would gladly have let him.

On my way to a controversial win with my own, but works-entered DB3S in the Sports Car race at Silverstone in May 1956 (Richmond Pike, Roy Salvadori collection).

In fact I would willingly have given it to him for the race, just as I had done at Goodwood a few weeks previously (see Chapter 5). The result of all this was that Stirling started the race in a less than happy frame of mind.

To beat the Jaguars at Silverstone it was necessary to build up a lead on the first lap. This had been highlighted in practice when I was lapping very quickly and caught up with Mike Hawthorn's D-type. Although I could lap faster than Mike thanks to the superior road holding and brakes of the DB3S, the D-type was so much faster than the DB3S along the straights that I was stuck behind him unless I could overtake him in a corner and this was difficult and could be dangerous. The result was that my lap times were slowed down to the speed of Mike's.

At the start of the race Stirling led away in an enormous power-slide; I was right behind him and behind me was a Jaguar driven, I thought, by Hawthorn. On the approach to Stowe, Stirling waved me past, but I did not have enough speed; I waited until we were almost into Stowe corner and passed him as he moved over to line up for the corner. Unfortunately the works Jaguars were right behind me and I pulled them through with me. It was vital that I held my lead through Club Corner, for if the Jaguars passed me now they would have the straight leading up through Abbey curve to extend their lead.

Going up to Club Corner I had a Jaguar which I thought was Hawthorn's right up my chuff. Now the last thing I wanted was a Jaguar inside me going into Club, so I started moving over to the right of the circuit, clearly inviting the Jaguar to pass me on the left if it could. If it had passed me, I was confident that I could then dive in on the inside of the Jaguar and out-brake it before the corner, after which I would be more able to hold my own and build up enough lead over the Jaguars before we got to Stowe straight which was the most likely place for the Jaguars to overtake if they were close enough.

I was quite convinced that the Jaguar driver was Mike, as hard as they come and not willing to give an inch. If I had realised that it was Desmond Titterington, very able but far less experienced than Mike, I might have reacted differently.

As we went deeper into the corner the Jaguar was still trying to pass on the inside. I knew that we were far too deep into the braking area for him to make it and then all I could see in my mirror was a puff of smoke. I accelerated away, presuming that the Jaguar had overbraked, locked everything up and spun, but I did not know until I came round on the next lap the carnage that the incident had caused. Mike and Stirling slipped round the spinning Jaguar but Collins struck it amidships, Reg went off into the ditch and Sanderson's D-type mounted the bank. Hawthorn chased me hard for some time but I went on to win what I consider to be a thoroughly well-deserved victory, and Stirling moved up to second place after Hawthorn stopped at the pits. Mike finally retired with steering problems and third place went to Bob Berry at the wheel of Johnny Broadhead's private 1954 ex-works D-type.

I really do not think that this incident would have occurred if it had been Mike – he would have known my thinking and would have made his attempt to pass on my left. It certainly caused plenty of dissension within the Aston team. Stirling thought that I was very much at fault, but I was supported by both John Wyer and Peter Collins. I dropped out of the inquest when my 250F Maserati crashed in the International Trophy race later in the day and once again I was taken unconscious to Northampton hospital. Later the BRDC held an enquiry into the accident, but drew no firm conclusions, merely urging that drivers took greater care on the first lap.

Because of the damage to two cars at Silverstone the team borrowed my DB3S for the Spa race the following weekend. It was driven by Reg Parnell who lapped little faster than Paul Frère had the previous year at the wheel of a DB3S in production form with cast-iron block, single-plug ignition and 40 less bhp. This proved that there was nothing special about my DB3S.

The injuries I had suffered in the crash with the 250F at Silverstone made it most unlikely that I would be fit enough to drive in the Nürburgring 1,000 Km race at the end of May – I was in very considerable pain and the bad burn on my left arm, caused by the hot exhaust of the Maserati, was painful and healing slowly. John Wyer was very kind and suggested that I came to the race as the guest of the team, made a holiday of the race and stayed at the hotel or came to the circuit as I wished.

Aston had entered only two cars in the 1,000 Km race, but as time passed it became clear that they would be desperately short of drivers. Under the terms of his contract with Aston Martin, Stirling was released to drive a Maserati in this race and poor Reg had a very bad shunt with Rob Walker's Connaught at the Crystal Palace on Whit Monday which put him out of racing for much of the season and ultimately caused him to retire at the end of the year. John telephoned more and more frequently to see how I was. I was very keen to drive if at all possible; John had his doubts as to whether I should drive, but when it came to the crunch there was no alternative.

When we got to the Nürburgring and started practice, I found that I was in serious trouble. I was in great pain when I lowered myself into the car and when I pushed myself up to get out again, but while I was seated it was not too bad, although the bumps at the Ring gave me a fair pounding. My arm was very painful, but John looked after me with great care, changing the burn dressing and my bandages after practice, and somehow I managed. Peter Walker, with whom I was co-driving, was also far from well and together we made a terrible pair of invalids. Mike Hawthorn, outwardly a tough character, was in fact a 'softie', and was most concerned that I should be racing in my condition. He tried hard to talk me out of driving, even to the point of threatening to take up the issue with John Wyer.

I usually started the race, but there was no way that I was going to be able to manage a Le Mans start so the first session was down to Peter. In a strong field of works V-12 Ferraris and 3-litre Maseratis, plus the works D-type Jaguars (which were a complete handful on this circuit) we did very well, rising to fourth place. Unfortunately our run came to an end on the last lap when the de Dion tube broke and I went off the road into a shallow ditch. Thankfully I escaped further injury, but I was very badly shaken. From this race right through to August I was in terrible pain and it was only after I crashed on the Bank Holiday Monday that it was discovered that I had broken two ribs, which I think dated back to the Silverstone accident.

An interesting addition to the racing calendar in 1956 was the Sports Car Rouen Grand Prix limited to 3-litre cars and run over a distance of 203 miles. Works entries came from Ferrari with three cars, there were two 300S Maseratis, Aston Martin entered a full team of cars for Moss, Collins, Brooks and myself and Ecurie Ecosse fielded a single D-type with the engine linered down to three litres. Peter Collins was very keen to drive a car with drum brakes because he thought that the roadholding was better and so a car in this trim was prepared for him. Tony Brooks was entered with a standard disc-braked DB3S and both Stirling and I were to drive new cars, destined for Le Mans, with smoother nose featuring faired-in headlamps and streamlined headrest.

We all went well in practice and Peter was especially happy with the drum-braked car; however, Stirling decided that he would like to try it. John Wyer's attitude was that the car had been specially prepared for Peter at Peter's request and, if Stirling came to his own arrangement with Peter, all well and good, but he was not going to insist that Peter should allow Stirling to drive it. Stirling persuaded Peter to swap cars and then set a time that was fastest of the Aston drivers – 2 min 32 sec compared with Peter's 2 min 35 sec.

In the opening laps Peter, possibly irked at giving up his originl car, drove really hard, holding second place behind Perdisa's Maserati, taking the lead briefly, dropping back to third and finally retiring with run bearings on lap 16. It was only too obvious that the car had been over-driven, for not only was the tachometer 'tell-tale', pointing to 7,300 rpm (which could have been a flash reading or caused by a missed gear), but John Wyer noticed that the oil temperature gauge was off the clock indicating that high revs had been consistently used. Stirling then took up the gauntlet and on this fast road circuit drove a brilliant race to finish less than four seconds behind Castellotti's winning Ferrari. Behra (Maserati) took third place, Tony Brooks was fourth and I finished fifth. I had a problem with my car: the brakes jammed on at the hairpin and would not release. I had to get out of the car and bend part of the scuttle panel which was jamming the pedal. I lost a lost of time and had to fight my way back through the field from thirteenth place. It was another race that illustrated just how badly the team needed the extra power of the DBR1 that was under development and with a few more bhp under the bonnet Stirling would certainly have won.

Only a single car for Reg Parnell was entered in the Sports Car race at the British Grand Prix meeting in July and I was to drive my own car. My car threw a rod in practice and as Parnell was still not fit to drive as the result of a crash at the Crystal Palace, it was decided that Tony Brooks should take his place. Tony crashed badly with a BRM in the Grand Prix and at the last moment John asked me to drive. Practice had been dominated by Stirling with a works 300S Maserati in 1 min 47 sec; Titterington with an Ecurie Ecosse D-type was second fastest in 1 min 51 sec and I matched this with my DB3S. The race was summed up neatly in *Autosport*: 'Moss in the Maserati, at the head of the line, was first away, first into Copse corner, and first thereafter to the end, drawing remorselessly away, and coming within a few seconds of lapping the second place car, Salvadori's DB3S, at the finish.

'Roy Salvadori, equally, had the rest of the opposition well in hand, so that, so far as the two leaders were concerned, there was little excitement.'

In 1956 the Le Mans race was postponed to the end of July because of alterations made to the circuit following the 1955 disaster. In an effort to keep the speed of the cars down, prototypes were limited to 2.5-litres and anything above that capacity was supposed to be a production car. In addition there were fuel consumption regulations which affected the performance of the cars. Both the Jaguar D-type and the Aston Martin DB3S were listed as production cars and both were accepted as such by the organisers, although the D-types with long-nose bodywork and fuel injection were very different animals from the production car, as were the works DB3S entries with disc brakes, twin-plug ignition and restyled bodywork. The DB3S entries were driven by Moss/Collins and myself/Walker, whilst the brand-new DBR1 ran in 2.5-litre prototype form with Parnell/Brooks at the wheel.

The favourites to win were the works D-types but Paul Frère spun his car on the second lap and Jack Fairman rammed the bank whilst trying to avoid his team-mate. The remaining works D-type driven by Hawthorn/Bueb lost 21 laps in the pits while the mechanics sorted out the fuel injection system. This put the Ecurie Ecosse D-type of Flockhart/Sanderson and the DB3S of Moss/Collins in contention for the lead and that was where they finished after 24 hours' racing with the Aston unable to push the Jaguar too hard because of gearbox problems. Peter Walker and I drove steadily and consistently, holding fifth place by midnight after we had lost time in the pits when the engine backfired and bent the starter shaft. All went well until 7:30 am on the Sunday morning when Peter lost the DB3S in the biggest possible way in the wet at the Dunlop bridge, smashed the car against the bank and was thrown into the road. Poor Peter, who had been due to hand over to me at the end of the lap, suffered serious injuries that brought his racing career to an end. The DBR1 survived until the Sunday lunchtime when it ran its bearings.

Three weeks later a full team of four Astons ran in the *Daily Herald* International Trophy at Oulton Park. Moss (1 min 58.2 sec) and Brooks (1 min 59.2 sec) dominated practice and I was fourth fastest, fractionally slower than Flockhart's D-type. Race day dawned to low stratus, heavy rain and strong winds and long before the race the circuit was flooded. The start was delayed while the marshalls and the local fire brigade tried to clear the water off the course. There was talk of the race being cancelled and eventually David Murray withdrew the Ecurie Ecosse cars on the grounds of safety; there was much criticism of Murray, but my own view was that on this rare occasion the race should have been cancelled.

Moss was all in favour of racing, but I thought that the conditions were incredibly dangerous with great clouds of spray thrown up as the cars passed through small rivers running across the circuit. Moss was, of course, the absolute maestro in the wet and for him the conditions were easier to cope with. His mastery showed itself on the first lap when he pulled out a 6.2 seconds' lead over Brooks; some way back, Reg and I were lapping rather gingerly, taking our time in passing Archie Scott-Brown's Lister-Maserati. Towards the end I pushed Reg a little and he turned, shaking his head as if to say, 'You silly bugger', but I was not seriously attempting to take him – just trying to upset him! Astons took the first four places, completely unopposed, and I was very glad when it was all over.

My last race of the year with Aston was at Goodwood in September and cars were entered for Brooks and myself. As I had already won two races with Coopers that day, I was expecting to do well in the Sports Car race. I led on the first lap with one of the Le Mans cars, but then Tony went ahead to score his first win in an Aston. It was not one of my better races, but it was no disgrace to be beaten by Tony Brooks.

This was my last drive with a DB3S and after four immensely enjoyable and very satisfying seasons with this car, the Aston team was about to embark on a new phase in its racing history with a car that would have the roadholding to beat the opposition on most circuits and, ultimately, when sports car racing was limited to cars of three litres, win both Le Mans and the Sports Car Championship.

Chapter 4

The Gilby Maseratis, 1953–54

Introduction by Keith Greene

My involvement in motor racing started in 1950 at the tender age of fifteen years. The first event that I attended was the Brighton Speed Trials on September 1 that year and I have been involved in the sport ever since. I drove in International events between 1955 and 1964 and since 1967 I have been involved in test driving and team management. Currently I run the Richard Lloyd Racing Canon Porsche 956 team in World Endurance Championship events in both hemispheres.

Cutting back, however, to the good old days, my first recollections of Roy driving for Gilby Engineering were when he handled our Frazer Nash Le Mans Replica. Later the company bought a Maserati A6GCS and I remember Roy's tremendous battles with Archie Scott-Brown who raced the Lister-Bristol. At about the same time Gilby Engineering beat Stirling Moss to the draw by getting Board of Trade permission to import into the country a brand-new Maserati 250F Grand Prix Car — also, of course, for Roy to drive. By today's standards the team was pretty compact — three mechanics; my father as patron, team manager and time-keeper; myself as 'go-fer', polisher, race number putter-on-er and signaller; plus a few friends to run errands. Transport was also a slightly different scene from today — one converted BOAC observation coach to carry the Formula One car, no elaborate awning, but a primus stove for brewing the tea. Dad drove the A6GCS on the road and I usually went with him.

Something that I really miss today is the early morning start to get, to say, Aintree, about three and a half hours from our Essex home, and the customary stops for egg, bacon and coffee; there was hardly any traffic and no speed limits. Also, you could talk to the police, if you know what I mean! If Roy were racing regularly today, he would almost certainly have no licence. He always drove flat-out everywhere and used to use a small-capacity car as a means of limiting his terminal speed on the road!

Later Roy raced his Aston Martin DB3S as part of the Gilby team and I remember that we enjoyed immense success. Roy is one of the few (maybe the only?) driver to have won four different classes of racing on the same day — Formula One, Formule Libre, Sports Car and Saloon. It goes almost without saying that those days of motor racing were much more fun and much more social than today's more sophisticated and commercial motor racing scene.

* * *

In 1953 I achieved a breakthrough in my racing career – I successfully completed the transition from an enthusiastic and fairly successful amateur driver to a professional appearing regularly in International events. I was a member of the works Aston Martin team, I drove a works Connaught Formula Two car, and lengthy discussions with Sid Greene early in that year led to one of the happiest and most successful periods in my racing career.

I always enjoyed driving for Sid when the chance arose; he was direct in his dealings, he had a superb sense of humour and he got along very well with everybody from the mechanics to the sponsors. For him motor racing was purely a sport, but he believed that his sport should pay its way and bring publicity to his company, Gilby Engineering Limited, based at Woodford in Essex and mainly engaged in machine work for Ford. Because of his physical disability (he had lost his left arm in an accident) Sid was unable to compete himself except in sprints and he usually engaged an experienced professional to drive his cars.

Sid told me that he was thinking of importing one of the new Maserati A6GCS 2-litre sports cars, no example of which had been seen in the United Kingdom, but which had already done well in long-distance Continental road races. The A6GCS was very similar mechanically to the Maserati Formula Two cars that were challenging the supremacy of Ferrari in Grand Prix racing. With a claimed power output of 165 bhp at 6,750 rpm, the A6GCS had a top speed of over 130 mph and it had a reputation for being both rugged and reliable. Sid believed that if he could put together the right financial package, he would have a car with which we could perform strongly in the 2-litre class in British sports car racing and he would more than cover his costs.

Esso were already one of my sponsors and so I arranged a meeting between Sid and Esso Competitions Manager Reg Tanner. An agreement was hammered out whereby Esso would put up the money for the purchase of the Maserati (just under £3,000) and contribute a substantial sum towards its racing costs. For 1954, when Gilby were racing two cars, I believe their Esso sponsorship was around £10,000 for the year. I received a similar sum for using only Esso products exclusively in all my drives. As a concession, and provided that it did not clash with Esso's interests, Reg Tanner would consent to me having the occasional drive for an entrant not using Esso products. Sid paid me the usual split of starting and prize money. With the 250F Grand Prix car the starting money ranged from £250 or so for small meetings at Snetterton up to about £650 for Grands Prix.

In May 1953 Sid and I went to Modena to order the Maserati. I was already well known at the factory by Signor Adolfo Orsi and Bertocchi, as I had been introduced there by Prince Bira back in 1950, and Sid soon became a firm friend of the Orsi family who controlled Maserati – mainly because Gilby always settled their accounts promptly. We ordered the A6GCS off the shelf and we believed that the claimed 165 bhp would cope with the 135–140 bhp Bristol-powered Frazer Nash Le Mans Replicas, Coopers and Cliff Davis' Tojeiro that were dominating British 2-litre sports car racing at the time. The only stipulations were that the A6GCS should be painted British Racing Green and the Maserati factory should supply a mechanic to maintain the car whilst it was in England.

The six-cylinder twin-cam sports car, chassis number 2052, arrived in England in time for Sid to secure an entry at Goodwood on September 26. As soon as the car arrived, Sid telephoned the local motor taxation office to obtain a registration and make the Maserati road legal, as he always drove his sports cars to race meetings. He *thought* he was given the number XMC 601 and this was hastily painted on the nose and tail of the car. When the paperwork came through, it became clear that he had not heard the number properly over the telephone and the correct number was XEV 601. This explains why the car appeared with different registration numbers in 1953!

There was no time for testing before the Goodwood race and the Maserati's qualities – and shortcomings – soon revealed themselves to me in it first race. On the credit side the A6GCS was very well balanced and it had excellent brakes. However the left-hand steering was a major handicap: as most British circuits are clock-wise, the majority of corners are right-handers and at right-hand corners not only was the driver's weight in the wrong place, but it was not possible to 'sight' the car properly for the corner; it was fine on left-handers. I also found that the cockpit was very cramped, but there was not much that we could do about this, except move the seat back a limited amount.

With plenty of power at the top end of the rev range and its rugged construction, the A6GCS was the perfect car for Continental road circuits with long straights and long-distance endurance races – the sort of event for which it was designed. However, with this type of power band and with an engine that we were convinced developed rather less power than its makers claimed, it was a handful in British events. Even so it achieved a substantial measure of success.

The interest and publicity attracted by the A6GCS on its début at Goodwood convinced Sid Greene that his investment was justified. Starting from the back of the grid because I had missed practice, I could manage no better than sixth in a five-lap Sports Car race at the Sussex circuit. The following weekend the racing season ended at Castle Combe; I was now adapting myself to the power range and handling of the A6GCS and I drove a good race to finish second to Reg Parnell's works DB3S Aston Martin, well ahead of the 2-litre opposition.

It was now that Sid informed me of his latest plan, the acquisition of a Formula One Maserati. For two years Grand Prix racing had been run to 2,000 cc unsupercharged Formula Two rules, but a new Formula One of 2,500 cc unsupercharged came into force on January 1 1954. Connaught, for whom I had driven in 1953, were developing a completely new Formula One car, but it would not be ready for some time and I had doubts as to whether it would be competitive. For me Sid's decision gave me an opening into serious Grand Prix racing for the first time.

At the end of January we flew to Italy and I was able to drive Fangio's Argentine Grand Prix-winning 250F car at the Modena Autodrome. I was delighted with the 250F and as I familiarised myself with its power and handling, I motored faster and faster, unofficially breaking the lap record set in 1952. The 250F had a power output at this stage in its development of around 220 bhp, with a much wider power band than the Maserati sports car, a de Dion rear axle that significantly improved roadholding and, of course, a central driving position so that the driver's legs straddled the prop-shaft tunnel. It was a very well balanced car, with a slight understeer (which I preferred), powerful drum brakes that experience was to prove could withstand the rigours of a long race and a quick, positive right-hand gearchange in an open gate. Like most Italian competition cars of the time, it was fitted with a central throttle, something that I was already used to on the sports car. I never found this a handicap, even at race meetings where I was driving other cars and these were fitted with the usual right-hand throttle. Another good feature – and unusual with an Italian car – was the very roomy cockpit.

Sid ordered the 250F at a price of around £4,000, a figure doubled by import duty and purchase tax, and we soon found that we headed a queue of customers awaiting delivery. These included the Owen Organisation (who wanted a competitive car to race while the new Formula One BRM was developed) and Stirling Moss. Stirling was never happy with the central throttle and on his car and the Maseratis he later drove for the works it was moved to the right. right.

Compared with most of our rivals, the Gilby organisation was working on a very tight budget. We had very little opportunity for racing outside the United Kingdom and Sid tried to take in all the British races that our sponsors favoured. Many of these were very minor races. Apart from the question of cost, both Sid and I were running businesses on a full-time basis and we could not spare the time for travelling needed to compete regularly on the Continent. To conserve the life of the 250F engine and components we did very little testing and with the 250F I tried to observe a strict rev limit of 7,500 rpm. The works drivers frequently took their 250Fs up to 8,000 rpm, but this resulted in excessive bearing wear and more frequent overhauls than Gilby could afford. Work on the car between races was kept to a minimum and, because of the length of time it took, we only changed the axle ratio if absolutely necessary.

In the few International Grands Prix for which we would be competing with the 250F in 1954, our chances of success were slim. Apart from the works Ferrari and Maserati teams, the opposition would include new cars from Mercedes-Benz and a number of private owners who would be prepared to drive their cars without regard to the cost of mechanical repairs. Even in British events the opposition would be strong: apart from the private Maseratis of Stirling and the Owen Organisation (whose car was driven by Ken Wharton), my good friend Reg Parnell was racing the ex-Baird Ferrari which had been completely rebuilt and now had a 2.5-litre engine. In Formule Libre races I would face Tony Vandervell's Ferrari 'Thin Wall' Special and the BRM V-16s.

With the A6GCS in my heat of the 1954 British Empire Trophy at Oulton Park. The headlamp was damaged in a collision with Alan Brown's spinning Cooper-Bristol (Motor Sport).

We still raced the A6GCS sports car in 1954 and I drove this in a couple of races before the 250F arrived from Italy. At Castle Combe on April 3 I scored an easy win in the race for sports cars up to 2,500 cc and followed this up with another win in the race for unlimited-capacity sports cars. In the latter race the main opposition came from Jimmy Stewart with one of the Le Mans C-type Jaguars now owned by Ecurie Ecosse. The Jaguar had much superior acceleration and top speed, but the Maserati was nimbler and quicker through the corners. To get the best out of the Maserati I had to throw it into the corners and, to prevent the engine falling off the narrow power band, try to keep the inside wheel spinning to maintain revs. Throughout the race I stayed right on Stewart's tail, but left my braking desperately late at the last corner on the last lap; using the grass I shot through into the lead while Jimmy spun off, but he recovered to finish second.

A week later I drove the A6GCS in the British Empire Trophy at Oulton Park. In my heat I collided with Alan Brown's spinning Cooper-Bristol and spent the next ten laps making up lost ground and catching and passing Tony Crook's Cooper-Bristol to take the lead. In the final, trying rather too hard in my pursuit of Alan Brown, I went off the road at Knickerbrook, spinning through the sandbanks until the Maserati stopped with its rear wheels in the Upper Lake. I managed to get the car back on the road and finished second to Alan, but with the consolation of setting a new outright circuit record of 1 min 48 sec (74.33 mph).

By the Easter Goodwood meeting the 250F had arrived. From now on Gilby Engineering fielded two cars at most race meetings. Initially the Maseratis were looked after by Italian mechanics, but these soon became homesick and wanted to return to Italy. After three had spent only short spells with us before returning home, we decided that for 1955 the cars would be maintained at my garage on the Kingston bypass by Les Wilson, (whose experience dated back to 1926 and who had worked for Thomson & Taylor before the war) and Michael Norris. Both were brilliant mechanics. All the other helpers were enthusiastic unpaid friends of Sid Greene or his son Keith.

If you can't beat them, join them! Pushing Wharton's BRM on the debut of the 250F Maserati at the Easter Goodwood meeting, 1954. This duel in the Richmond Trophy race ended when we collided and spun at Lavant (Roy Salvadori collection).

The transporter carrying the 250F and Sid at the wheel of the A6GCS would start out early for a race meeting so as to arrive in good time for scrutineering. I would make a much more leisurely start and meet them at the circuit. The cars would usually be started and warmed up by 17-year-old Keith Greene (in later years a member of the Gordon Spice organisation and racing manager of the Rondeau team). Much of the pleasure of driving for the Gilby team came from the friendly and relaxed atmosphere – although the atmosphere sometimes became rather strained when Sid shot off with the A6GCS between races for a quick visit to the nearest pub. After the meeting was over, regardless of results, Sid always gave a dinner party for the team and some of the 'opposition', usually held at a hotel on the way home.

The 250F, inevitably, was far from trouble-free. Throughout 1954 we were plagued by clutch, drive-shaft and prop-shaft problems and – rather more seriously – by a sticking throttle mechanism. I also found the 250F very difficult to get off the line which usually meant that I lost a lot of time at the start of a race and could not always make it up. Only at the end of the year did we discover that for no good reason our 250F had been fitted with an unusually high and non-standard first gear.

At Goodwood I made a poor start in the seven-lap Lavant Cup and had to settle for second place behind Reg Parnell's Ferrari. Next came the Formule Libre Chichester Cup and I again finished second, this time behind Ken Wharton with the V-16 BRM, which for once was running really well, but ahead of Reg and the Ferrari. The big race of the day was the 50-mile Richmond Trophy in which I again faced Reg with the Ferrari plus the V-16 BRMs of Wharton and Flockhart. I was now getting the hang of the 250F and was optimistic of doing well.

In the race I sat close behind the leading BRM of Wharton; the V-16 was slowing through the corners and throwing out oil and fuel which soon spread over my windscreen, goggles and face. The BRM was a big car and I had difficulty in seeing my line through corners; I had no chance to get alongside it and I was almost running into the back of it as it slowed for the corners. The race was getting progressively slower, but if I could have got ahead of the BRM my lap times would have been very much faster. The situation was just the same as in Formula One in 1981–82 when the turbocharged Renaults and Ferraris were holding up the Ford-powered cars through the corners, while the drivers of the unblown cars cooked their tyres and their brakes as they tried to get by on the twisty sections only to have the turbocharged cars sail away on the straights. In 1954–55 the drivers of unblown Formula One cars suffered exactly the same frustration as they strived to pass the BRMs in Formule Libre races.

As the Richmond Trophy progressed, so I became more and more bad tempered, waving my arms furiously. On lap 19 I tried to force my way through at Lavant corner, hoping that Wharton would let me through. Ken was one of the very hardest drivers, I should have known better than to expect him to give way and the two cars collided and spun. Both of us restarted, but on the next lap my clutch blew up. There was a lot of clutch trouble with 250Fs in the early days, because they were not strong enough to take the power, and it was particularly nasty because bits of clutch were exploded through the bell housing and, at Goodwood, even punctured holes through the bodywork like shrapnel. Very shortly afterwards Maserati introduced a stronger clutch and there were no more problems.

Sid Greene decided to enter a protest against the BRM, but this was rejected. However, even if Sid's protest had been upheld, it would not have benefited us as our car had retired. Nevertheless, the incident brought a lot of publicity which was probably very good for the Goodwood circuit and Gilby Engineering. Later I received from the Duke of Richmond and Gordon, the owner of Goodwood, a silver cigarette box inscribed, 'In acknowledgement of a splendid show at Goodwood on Easter Monday, 19 April 1954'. I was quite convinced that the Duke thought that I had been hard done by until I learned that Ken Wharton had also been presented with a similar cigarette box!

The 250F was now out of action for a few weeks while the new clutch was awaited from Italy. I drove the A6GCS at meetings at both Snetterton (finishing

Left *The 250F in the paddock for the* Daily Express *Trophy at Silverstone in May 1954. My anxious expression and the bonnet off the car are both evidence of the mechanical trouble that we suffered at this meeting* (T. C. March).

Right *A fine view of the 250F with its original, heavily louvred bodywork at the opening meeting at Aintree in May 1954* (Louis Klemantaski).

second in two races) and Ibsley (winning my class), and at the Hampshire circuit I also won a short race for closed cars at the wheel of Rob Walker's very special and very quick Aston Martin DB2.

By the *Daily Express* International Trophy race at Silverstone on May 15, the 250F was ready to race again. After finishing fourth in my heat on a damp track, I lost a lot of time in the final when the throttles jammed open and finished tenth after a two-minute pit stop. A fortnight later I drove the 250F in the Aintree '200' run in torrential rain. I finished second in my heat and set fastest lap, but in the final I threw away my chances of success, as I often did in those days, by spinning and I finished a poor fifth.

Snetterton on June 5 was, statistically, the most successful day in my racing career, for of the six races in which I competed, I won four and finished second and third in the others. In addition to the two Maseratis I also drove an ex-works disc-braked C-type Jaguar for Ecurie Ecosse. The Edinburgh team asked me to drive for them only occasionally when, as David Murray put it, 'It was better to have me in the team than the opposition', and I was one of the very few drivers ever paid by Ecurie Ecosse. I enjoyed the sheer power of the C-type, its sure-footed roadholding and its slight understeering characteristics. I personally was not, however, very happy with the disc brakes of the C-type which were power-assisted, with the result that it was only too easy to overbrake in the dry or wet and lock the wheels. Much of the development testing of the C-type's Dunlop disc brakes had been carried out by Stirling Moss so the result was a brake pedal pressure that suited him, but not many other drivers. Stirling liked brakes that you just had to breathe on for them to work. When Stirling joined the Aston Martin team for 1956, he was most unhappy about the brakes of the DB3S which were not power-assisted and required far more pedal pressure than he was used to.

There was a certain amount of 'knock-off' with all disc brakes which meant that as the car twisted round the circuit, the discs themselves deflected and pushed the pads away from the discs. When you reached a corner, it needed

almost the full travel of the brake pedal to get the brakes to operate. 'Knock-off' was not a problem for Stirling, as he would pump up the pedal on the straight with his left foot so that when he needed the brakes at the next corner, the pedal was right up. Most drivers are much too busy to do this and when they needed the brakes of the C-type at the next corner, they would have to depress the pedal a long way before the brakes gripped. With the DB3S, as the driver depressed the brake pedal, he would get a very hard and progressive grip from the brakes, but with the C-type the driver would depress the pedal further and further until suddenly the brakes gripped with immense power.

Despite the brakes I always felt that I would have been just as happy at the wheel of a works Jaguar as an Aston Martin. What a luxury it would have been driving a Jaguar and having the power to pull away on the straight and let the opposition have the problem of trying to catch me!

At Snetterton I finished third in the William Lyons Trophy handicap for Jaguars, won scratch and handicap races, all with the C-type, as well as finishing second with the A6GCS to the Cooper-Bristol of Tony Crook in the 2,000 cc Sports Car race; in the absence of any serious opposition I won both the Formula One and Formule Libre races with the 250F. And I set fastest lap (jointly with Crook in the 2,000 cc event) in every race.

I competed with three different cars at Snetterton, but sometimes I raced as many as four or five different cars on one day. It was always an immense problem to change rapidly from one car to another, each with its different handling, engine and gearbox characteristics. For example, the 250F engine peaked at 7,600 rpm, while the A6GCS peaked at 6,700 rpm which made the gear-changing points different. Because of its narrow power band, with absolutely nothing below 5,000 rpm, I had to work very hard to keep the A6GCS engine in its restricted power band. In contrast, the C-type had a strict maximum of 6,000 rpm, suberb torque throughout the power range and a superb performance.

It was fatal to think of the last race with, say, the 250F when I was about to drive a C-type and just as bad to think about the next race, trying to remember gear-change points, speeds and braking points with the vastly different types of car. My technique was to hustle myself from one car to the next which would usually be waiting ready for me in the marshalling area or the pits, avoiding any discussion with my entrant about the last race, and letting my mind totally relax. On the first lap the subconscious mind did its work, everything slotted into place and everything was (hopefully) organised. Would I have done better if I had restricted the number of races in which I competed? Probably, but my racing would have been far less enjoyable and far less remunerative.

Gilby Engineering was not really equipped to run in Continental Grands Prix, because we carried very few spares for the 250F and the team wanted to avoid the cost of major engine overhauls – and a major overhaul was really necessary after a hard-driven Grand Prix of over 300 miles. Nevertheless we decided to run in the French Grand Prix at Reims on July 4 and in the non-Championship Grand Prix at Rouen the following weekend. To conserve the engine we knew that we would have to restrict practice and that I would have to observe a strict rev limit in the race.

I drove to the French races in my Morris Minor – I have always preferred small cars for road use. I thoroughly enjoyed the Continent because of the excellent food, the change of surroundings and the atmosphere, but the general standard of race organisation was well below British standards. There were seemingly endless difficulties over scrutineering and passes and the standard of marshalling was abysmal. Another problem was that drivers and entrants had always to queue up to collect their starting money and prize money after the race. I was always at the head of the queue in case they ran out of money! In reality I much preferred racing in Britain where, for example, I could sometimes drive to a meeting, practice, compete in five races and drive home again the same day.

I started from the third row of the grid at Reims and soon found myself dicing with Behra (Gordini), Mieres (Maserati), Manzon (Ferrari) and Villoresi (works Maserati); most of the time we were three abreast down the straights, slip-streaming each other and scrabbling for positions in and out of the corners. I was taking the 250F beyond my set maximum revs and holding tenth place when the rear axle stripped on lap 16.

Rouen was a particularly attractive race for us, as high prize money was paid to all finishers, although there was no starting money. Twice during the race I was called into the pits because the officials thought my car was dropping oil on the course; because of an oil breather problem on the 250F we had a pipe linking the breather to a one-gallon can in the tail of the car and it seemed likely that as the can filled, oil was spilled at some of the corners. However, when the car was stationary in the pits the stewards looked round the engine and no trace of a leak was found, so I was allowed to rejoin the race, although I had lost a great deal of time. I still managed to finish third, slowed in the closing laps of the race because the steering box had worked loose on its mountings. I was all of five laps behind Trintignant's winning Ferrari, but we were delighted to have competed in these two Continental Grands Prix and to have done so well financially.

At the British Grand Prix, held on July 17 at Silverstone, we were still running the same, now rather tired engine with which we had started the season and it must have been down on power compared with the latest engines fitted to the works 250Fs. In fact the works Maseratis missed practice and started from the back of the grid, thereby precluding any pre-race comparisons, but I was pleased with my practice time of 1 min 48 sec which put me on the second row of the grid alongside Karl Kling's Mercedes-Benz. In the race I held tenth place, harrying Kling until he went off the road at Copse, but any chance of a good finish was lost when my fuel tank worked loose and I lost five minutes in the pits while it was re-attached. I rejoined the race in 19th place and eventually retired when the gearbox seized. We next ran at the Crystal Palace on August Bank Holiday Monday, but I made a bad start in both my heat and the final with the 250F and finished second to Reg Parnell with the Ferrari. In the 2,000 cc Sports Car race I chased Tony Crook's Cooper-Bristol hard, doing everything possible to pass, until the last lap when the A6GCS put a con-rod through the block. This was an expensive blow for Gilby, but the engine had not been stripped since the car was delivered.

The following Saturday I was in action again with the 250F in the first Gold Cup race to be held on the Oulton Park circuit. We had problems in practice and the best I could manage was a place on the third row of the starting grid. However, Stirling, the most likely winner, was driving a works 250F which did not arrive until race morning and he started without practice from the back of the grid. I held fourth place during the first couple of laps, Stirling was carving through the field and took the lead on lap four and I moved up into second place on the next lap.

Although I had no hopes of catching Stirling, the Maserati was running really well and lapping faster and faster. On lap 15 as I went up Clay Hill, I lifted my foot for Druids, the engine note changed and the throttles jammed open. On our 250F Gilby had fitted two cut-out switches of the push-button type (so that they could test each magneto individually) and I quickly pushed these in. I did not throw out the clutch because this would have wrecked the engine. In fact I had pushed only one cut-out button, so the engine was still revving flat out; I approached Druids corner much too fast, the Maserati slid sideways, mounted the bank and crumpled itself against a tree. The 250F started to smoke and flare, but any impending blaze was extinguished when the top of the tree collapsed on to the engine!

In the impact I was thrown forward onto the steering wheel and the 250F's thick perspex windscreen. Although I was badly dazed by the impact with the windscreen, my face was saved by the visor I had been wearing in anticipation of wet weather. My other injuries were restricted to bad bruising and cuts around the knees and the chest. The 250F was less fortunate – it had to be returned to Italy for a complete rebuild, including the fitting of a new chassis frame (the original frame was later repaired and used on one of the works cars driven by

Leading Archie Scott-Brown and the Lister-Bristol at Snetterton in August 1954 – but Archie passed me to win the race by a margin of six seconds (Motor Sport).

Showing the controls of the 250F to Jimmy Stewart at Goodwood in September 1954 (Roy Salvadori collection).

Stirling Moss). What had caused the problem was that the engine had swallowed a valve and the valve head went straight through one of the carburettors and wedged the butterfly. The Maserati factory was very sympathetic and charged only a modest price for completely rebuilding the car.

For the time being I could only race the Maserati sports car and the following weekend I was back in action at Snetterton. I had a memorable dice with that magnificent driver Archie Scott-Brown at the wheel of the Lister-Bristol. Archie had been born with no right hand, but merely the stump of a forearm with partial palm and thumb. That he could drive so well and so fast, getting the Lister in and out of the most incredible attitudes, was almost miraculous and at the end of a race his stump would be red raw and bleeding. I led him for a while at Snetterton, but was scrubbing out of line through the corners and it was all very untidy. Eventually I spun the Maserati and rejoined the race to finish second. The following weekend at Castle Combe I made a superb start and led Archie by a matter of a few feet to win by two-fifths of a second. A week later I won the Sports Car race at Charterhall with an Ecurie Ecosse C-type Jaguar from Ninian Sanderson entered by the same team.

The 250F was back in action at the Crystal Palace meeting on September 18, but broke a drive-shaft while I was holding second place in the first part of the London Trophy Formule Libre race. I was entered at Goodwood the following weekend with both Maseratis and with an Ecurie Ecosse C-type Jaguar. In the 2,000 cc Sports Car race the Lister-Bristol was driven by Stirling Moss – I think that Brian Lister offered Stirling the drive so that he could make a direct comparison with Archie's performances and satisfy himself whether or not Archie was the right man to drive the works Lister. I believed that I had a good chance of beating Stirling. Archie had the Lister set up to suit his driving style –

he had the car breaking away at nearly every corner – and Stirling had very little time to have the car set up to suit his style. Once again I managed to make a good start and throughout the race I could see the green and yellow Lister in my mirror. Stirling tried hard all the way and made fastest lap, but I managed to finish three-fifths of a second ahead.

In the Formula One Goodwood Trophy the opposition included Stirling Moss with his private 250F and Peter Collins with the new 2.5-litre version of the Vanwall Special. Stirling won the race easily and set fastest lap, second place went to Collins with the Vanwall Special and I finished third. My second win of the day was in the unlimited capacity Sports Car race and I always seemed to go very well when I drove for Ecurie Ecosse. I made a very good start, as I usually did with a C-type, accelerating clear of the traffic jam at the start, hotly pursued by Masten Gregory with a 4.5-litre Ferrari. Not only was the Ferrari faster than my C-type, but the American was a very hard driver and I did well to hold on to a narrow lead to win by three-fifths of a second. I rounded off the day with fifth place in the Formule Libre race.

My 1954 season finished on October 23 when I drove a Jaguar C-type for Ecurie Ecosse in the Barcelona Cup, the Sports Car race held the day before the Spanish Formula One Grand Prix, over the Pedralbes road circuit that included cobbles, tram lines and a very fast and long straight. In practice I had engine trouble, but Sir James Scott-Douglas offered me his car and David Murray was insistent that I took this over. Obviously David was pinning his hopes on me!

Above *The Maserati A6GCS on its debut at Goodwood in September 1953 where it ran as* XMC 601. *A smiling Sid Greene stands to the left of the cockpit and standing by the right front wing is our Italian mechanic, Daniele* (Charles Dunn).

At Goodwood in September 1954 I had one of my best drives in an Ecurie Ecosse C-type and won the Sports Car race from Masten Gregory's 4.5-litre Ferrari (Roy Salvadori collection).

Jean Behra (Gordini) was easily fastest in practice and led the early laps of the race with me in second place, harrying the French car on braking. When the Gordini retired, I led for six laps and thought that I was going to win, but the C-type's brakes began to lock on and, also, I was worried because the crowds were pressing on to the road making the circuit look different from practice and spoiling my sight-line through corners. I was passed by Picard with one of the new Ferrari Monzas and although I tried to stay with the Ferrari, I gradually dropped back and had to settle for second place ahead of team-mate Ninian Sanderson. At the prize-giving I discussed the race with Behra through Harry Schell acting as interpreter. Commenting on my tactics of passing him on very late braking, which he considered dangerous, Behra said, 'When you know the Gordini better, you will have patience. The Gordini is fast, but never lasts. So do remember that!'

1954 was a demanding year during which I drove in a large number of races and at the wheel of a wide range of cars. I gained a lot of experience and I particularly enjoyed racing the Maseratis and the Ecurie Ecosse C-type. I received a number of offers for 1955, but I was happy to stay with Aston Martin and Gilby.

Chapter 5

Racing with the Gilby and Cooper teams, 1955–56

1955

Both Sid Greene and I were satisfied with the 1954 season and we continued into 1955 on the same terms, except that Sid insisted on paying me a retainer of £1,000. Over the winter the 250F was given a complete overhaul at Modena, but mechanically it remained in its original 1954 trim. It was very clear that the A6GCS sports car was no longer competitive and so, after discussions with Charles and John Cooper, Gilby ordered a Cooper chassis very similar to that of the Cooper-Bristol sports car with tubular frame and transverse leaf spring independent suspension front and rear. To this chassis we transferred the A6GCS engine and gearbox and it was fitted with an aluminium body designed and built by Maurice Gomm.

The Cooper-Maserati was a complete disaster and with the benefit of hindsight I realise that we should have abandoned it immediately. It had the most appalling understeer, it was not competitive and we had no opportunity to carry out any development work. The Gilby team also entered the DB3S which the Aston Martin company had sold me at a specially low price. This was the prototype car DB3S/1, and it was to prove very successful in British events, more than compensating for the shortcomings of the Cooper-Maserati. Part of my deal with Aston Martin was that they would maintain the car away from the circuit and could call it back into the team when necessary. In fact, I drove it as a works entry at several races during the year.

In a couple of races I drove the A-series Formula Two Connaught which my very good friend John Young had bought from Bill Whitehouse and had had prepared by John Coombs. This Connaught was the long, 7 ft 6 in-wheelbase car with fuel injection that I had raced for the works in 1953. It had been an excellent car in 1953 and the passage of two years had not diminished its qualities.

My 1955 season started with an easy victory in a Formule Libre race at Snetterton and an early retirement the following weekend in the British Empire Trophy in which the throttle linkage of my DB3S broke on the first lap.

Next came the International meeting at Goodwood on Easter Monday. Goodwood was a circuit on which I usually did well and meetings there, even so early in the year, had a delightful garden party atmosphere. I drove four different cars, ran in six races, won three and finished second in two. Competing in so many races and achieving such success was just what was needed to make our racing viable and I personally made a substantial sum. We had negotiated better starting money than any other British driver/entrant except Stirling Moss and at Goodwood we earned near to £1,000 in starting money alone. Prize and bonus money increased this to around £2,000 (bonuses from our sponsors for a win were high, but nothing for a place). All in all it proved an exceptionally successful day, but by the evening I was completely exhausted – it was too much even for me!

I won the Lavant Cup with John Young's Connaught and took second place in the Chichester Cup Formule Libre race with the 250F. Another win followed in the Unlimited Sports Car race, more by luck than anything else. Peter Collins, who was running his DB3S, and I discussed the race beforehand and we concluded that we had no real chance of beating either Mike Sparken (Ferrari Monza) or Duncan Hamilton (Jaguar D-type). Both Sparken and Hamilton jumped the start to the extent that they were almost into Madgwick before the flag fell and it was obvious that they were going to be penalised. They battled for the lead throughout the five laps, while I held on to third place on the road and, as expected, was promoted to first place by a margin of just over two seconds when Sparken and Hamilton were penalised 15 seconds.

Immediately after this race I jumped into the still unpainted Cooper-Maserati for the 2,000 cc Sports Car race and finished fourth. Next came the main race of the day, the Formula One Richmond Trophy, in which the only serious opposition was Moss with his 250F and, as I had beaten him in the Formule Libre event, I thought that I could beat him again. Stirling made a brilliant start and it took me a couple of laps to close up on him; instead of biding my time, as I could well have done in this 21-lap race, I tried to pass Stirling too early. Pressing him hard through the chicane, I spun at the exit; I managed to keep the engine running, reversed out of the way of the front runners and rejoined the race in sixth place. (I was always at my best when I had thrown the race away and had to start again from scratch!) I soon worked my way back to second place, making fastest lap in the process, caught and passed Stirling on lap 12 (he retired shortly afterwards with fuel injection problems and I presume that it was a problem throughout the meeting) and scored an easy win from Bob Gerard's Cooper-Bristol. The final race of the day was the Easter Handicap in which I finished second with the 250F.

The *Daily Express* Trophy at Silverstone on May 7 was one of the most important events in the British calendar and in 1955 attracted a strong entry, but none of the Continental works teams except Gordini. Tony Vandervell fielded two of his ever-improving Vanwalls for Mike Hawthorn and Ken Wharton; two of the new, streamlined Connaughts were driven by Jack Fairman and Ken McAlpine; and there were six Maserati 250Fs, all privately entered. It seemed unlikely that the British cars would last the distance (although they displayed good speed in practice). I was joint fastest in practice with Hawthorn in 1 min 48 sec, taking pole position, and rated my chances highly, although I expected Stirling with his 250F to be the most serious

On my way to second place behind Peter Collins (Owen Organisation 250F) in the 1955 Daily Express *Trophy at Silverstone* (T. C. March).

opposition. Stirling was two seconds slower in practice and seemed still to be having problems with his car, but I thought that these would be sorted out by the race. Rather foolishly I disregarded Peter Collins with the disc-braked Owen Organisation 250F who started from the second row of the grid with a time of 1 min 51 sec.

At the start Collins shot through from the second row into the lead, but I went in front at Copse. I expected to pull away from Peter, but he stayed with me – the quicker I went, the quicker Peter went. Stirling retired with engine trouble on lap ten and both Vanwalls were plagued by mechanical problems.

In an effort to pull away from Collins, I tried very hard for a few laps, setting a new lap record of 98.48 mph, and opened up the gap between us by a few yards. Peter soon closed the gap, matching my lap speed, and he passed me on lap 23; we swapped the lead a couple of times, but when Peter went ahead again on lap 31 he started to pull out a good lead.

In retrospect I realise that I should have allowed Peter to go ahead early in the race and played a waiting game. While he lapped fast enough to keep us clear of the rest of the field, I could probably have surprised him and slipped ahead near the finish. Instead I showed my full hand earlier and had nothing left for the finish. Resigned to finishing second I slowed a little and Peter Collins pulled further and further into the distance. I then noticed Wharton's Vanwall in my mirrors; he had lost a lot of time in the pits and was several laps behind, but was now lapping very fast, apparently trying to set a new lap record. We became involved in quite a dice, he tried to overtake me on braking for Copse, got on to the grass and in my mirrors I saw the Vanwall bounce off a corner marker, slew across the track and catch fire. I was fortunate not to have been involved. The Vanwall was almost completely destroyed, but luckily, Ken escaped with fairly minor burns.

Peter won the race at a speed of 90.94 mph for the 176 miles; at the finish I was still in second place, 39 seconds behind, and other Maserati drivers, 'Bira', Simon and Rosier took the next three places. Hawthorn's Vanwall and both the Connaughts retired. From my point of view it had been a very good race, even if I conceded the fight with Peter too easily.

At the Whitsun weekend I won two events with the 250F at Snetterton on the Saturday, but I retired because of an oil leak at Crystal Palace on the

Top *After a practice shunt we ran the 250F at the Crystal Palace on August Bank Holiday Monday without its tail. I finished third in the International Trophy behind Mike Hawthorn (Moss' Maserati) and Harry Schell (Vanwall)* (T. J. Duvall).

Above *This photograph of the Cooper-Maserati was taken at the same point on the circuit at the same meeting and shows off the distinctive Cooper lines and alloy wheels* (T. J. Duvall).

Monday. The following weekend I was due to drive the 250F in the Rouen Grand Prix but this was cancelled following the Le Mans disaster and so Gilby made a late entry with the DB3S in the Eastern Counties '100' race at Snetterton. The race was run as a scratch event, but it was also a class handicap which gave the 3-litre Aston a credit lap over the 3.4-litre Jaguar-engined cars. Positions on the grid were decided by drawing names out of a hat and I was on the third row. It took me until lap three to get into the lead, but I had to keep up the speed to beat the 1,500 cc cars which had to cover one lap less than the 3,000 cc cars. Not far behind me on the road was George Abecassis with the latest HMW-Jaguar, but he crashed badly ten laps from the finish. I won both the handicap and scratch races by a comfortable margin from Archie Scott-Brown's Lister-Bristol.

In practice for the British Grand Prix held at Aintree and dominated by the Mercedes-Benz team, the Gilby 250F was plagued by low oil pressure. My fastest practice lap was 2 min 11.6 sec (almost three seconds slower than my time with my works DB3S in practice for the Sports Car race!). My car was little more than a starting money special and I trailed round well down the field until the gearbox broke.

At the August Bank Holiday weekend we competed at both the Crystal

Palace and Brands Hatch. The opposition in the International Trophy at the Crystal Palace on the Saturday was strong and included Mike Hawthorn at the wheel of Stirling's Maserati, Horace Gould who had acquired a 250F, Harry Schell with a Vanwall and Jack Fairman at the wheel of Rob Walker's new, unstreamlined Connaught. During practice I went off the road, damaging the rear of the 250F, and throughout the weekend we were forced to race the car without its shapely tail. I finished second to Mike in my heat and third behind Mike and Harry Schell in the final. There was no doubt that my driving lacked sparkle, probably because I was rather jaded as a result of competing in too many races.

We made a very real mistake in running the 250F at Brands Hatch which was then just a very twisty and very bumpy 1.24-mile circuit. Not only did the circuit favour the old 2-litre Formula Two cars, but the 250F was bottoming badly and to try to avoid this I was choosing the smoother parts of the circuit at the expense of the proper line. We were very worried that the grounding of the car would tear off a fuel or oil line and so after practice we fitted distance pieces between the springs to raise the car so that it did not ground, but this of course affected the handling. I finished third on the aggregate of two heats which was satisfactory in all the circumstances.

Tommy Sopwith, son of aviation manufacturer and America's Cup yachtsman T.O.M. Sopwith, invited me to drive his 1,100 cc Climax-powered Cooper sports car at Snetterton on August 13. This rear-engined car was a complete revelation; it was incredibly easy to drive, its handling was superb, it was immensely sure-footed and it had excellent stability thanks to the 'Kamm' cut-off tail. Although the 1,500 cc Sports Car race was held in torrential rain, conditions in which I was usually far from happy, I simply sailed away from the opposition and won not only my class, but the race outright. I ran in three other races at Snetterton that day, finishing fifth in the Formula One race after a spin and second in the Formule Libre after a duel with Peter Walker with Rob Walker's dark blue Connaught. I was expecting to have the race much my own way, with what seemed to be the fastest cars out of contention, but I was in for an unpleasant surprise; Peter was really sticking his neck out, the Connaught seemed to have slightly better acceleration than the 250F, he passed me at the hairpin and I repassed at the Esses. We battled furiously, lap after lap, until Peter decided to have another go at passing me, misjudged his braking, locked his brakes and nudged the Maserati off the road. The Connaught accelerated away to win the race and I rejoined to finish second, over 50 seconds behind. I was far from pleased about this incident, but had to admit that his win gave Peter a much-needed boost.

Remarkably enough I managed to win the 2,750 cc class of the large capacity Sports Car race with the Cooper-Maserati – mainly because Archie Scott-Brown overturned the Lister when he missed a gear-change. I beat the Lotus-Bristols of Peter Scott-Russell and Cliff Davis, but whilst these cars were very aerodynamic and light, their handling was not much better than that of the Cooper-Maserati. In their report of the race *Autosport* commented that I was 'getting round corners by the simple expedient of turning the wheel about a hundred yards before entering them'.

I won the 1,100 cc class of the 1,500 cc Sports Car race with Sopwith's Cooper at Aintree on September 3, but the main race of the day at Aintree was the *Daily Telegraph* Trophy for Formula One cars. I was entered with the Gilby 250F and other 250Fs were driven by Stirling, Louis Rosier and Horace Gould (who had been loaned a works car). Works streamlined Connaughts were driven by Reg Parnell and Jack Fairman and Peter Collins should have been at the wheel of the new four-cylinder BRM, but this non-started after a practice mishap.

I made a dreadful start, but by lap three of this 17-lap race I had moved up into third place behind Parnell and Moss. I was driving really well that day, I turned in the fastest lap of 86.26 mph and passed Stirling as he slowed before pulling into the pits with mechanical trouble. With four laps to go to the finish Reg was probably too far ahead for me to catch him, but I pressed on at a fierce pace. On the last lap I caught up and was about to lap my old friend John Young on the approach to Tatts corner. Afterwards John said that he saw me in his mirror, but thought that there was no possibility of me passing him before the corner. As I rushed into the corner, John was right on my line and I could not avoid banging into the side of the Connaught. This rather upset me, because I do not like colliding with friends, especially when they loan me their cars!

Just before the finish I passed Reg who was motoring very slowly and I was quite convinced that he was on his lap of honour. In fact the Connaught's engine had broken and he eventually pushed the car across the line into sixth place. As I reached the finishing area I moved over to pull into the pits lane, but everyone waved me on and I carried on to take the flag and win the race. I was a lucky winner, but on the other hand it was one of those days when I was going really well, gaining on Moss and Parnell, and my win was by no means undeserved. I rounded off the day with a third with the DB3S in the Unlimited Sports Car race and finished second in the Formule Libre race to Peter Collins with the V-16 BRM, driving really well to make up ground lost after a spin. *The Motor*'s Grande Vitesse listing drivers who should be in a works Formula One team, wrote, 'Given works Grand Prix cars Collins, Parnell and Salvadori could match the best.' They also wrote, 'Salvadori . . . presses on with more zeal than any Fangio.'

The *Daily Dispatch* Gold Cup race at Oulton Park on September 24 attracted a very strong entry that included Ferrari-entered Lancia D.50s driven by Hawthorn and Castellotti, works Maseratis for Moss and Musso, Vanwalls driven by Schell and Titterington, three Connaughts and the new BRM driven by Peter Collins. I was experiencing handling problems with the Gilby 250F and in all the circumstances fifth place was an acceptable performance.

At Castle Combe on October 1 I drove a Lister-Bristol in the 2,000 cc Sports Car race finishing third. This was a 1955 streamlined model that had won its class in the Goodwood Nine Hours race and I had bought it for stock at Elmbridge Motors. I wanted to compare it with the Cooper-Maserati as Gilby were considering buying a Lister for 1956. I also drove the 250F in the Formula

One and Formule Libre races, but it was not running too well and I had to settle for fourth place in both races.

My last race of the year was the Syracuse Grand Prix on October 23, an event in which we competed because the starting money was good. This was the famous race in which Tony Brooks, then an almost completely unknown driver, at the wheel of a works Connaught, defeated a strong Maserati team to score an outstanding victory. I retired the Gilby 250F early in the race.

Winter Interlude

I am not very keen on rallies, which I think are an unnecessarily dangerous way of passing the time, but my friend John Young is an enthusiast for all forms of motor sport and he managed to persuade John Coombs and myself to join him on the 1956 Monte Carlo Rally. John took the rally very seriously, but as far as Coombs and I were concerned it was a joke and we planned to abandon at Paris, have a good time and return home again. The car chosen was a carefully prepared Ford Anglia, but somehow it managed to be involved in three shunts before it was despatched to the start at Glasgow and it followed this up by having a flat battery the day the rally started.

We had told everyone that John Young was doing all the driving (we were only going along to give him moral support) and the press had run stories on this. At the start of the rally we were on a ramp being flagged off by the Mayor of Glasgow. John Coombs, in the back, managed to ease the car out of gear and John Young let in the clutch, to find that there was no drive. He said to us, 'The gearbox had broken!' He soon realised what had happened, but I am not sure

On the 1956 Monte Carlo Rally with John Young, John Coombs and Ford Anglia (Roy Salvadori collection).

that he shared the joke. I had suggested a number of short cuts which avoided the centre of London so we arrived first at the Beckenham control to be received by the television cameras. This was just too much for John Coombs, who decided to take the wheel, and we left the control with Coombs hanging out of the driver's window, smiling for the cameras.

Once we were on the Continent, we split the driving sensibly. There was the inevitable row with John Young when we told him that we wanted to jack the rally in at Paris and he persuaded us to carry on. It was easy going until Grenoble where the weather conditions worsened and the difficult timed sections started. My road driving has always been pretty notorious and needless to say I pushed the Anglia hard, drifting through the corners and with my own technique for passing other competitors – flash the lights, sound the horn and if they do not move out of the way, lean on them. One of the other competitors whom we caught up was Chief Superintendent John Gott with a works Austin and he seemed reluctant to move over even though I recollected leaning on the Austin a time or two; eventually I managed to push through on the inside of a corner. The others took a pretty dim view of my driving; they were shouting at me – and each other – and at one stage of the rally Coombs, who could stand no more, wrenched the keys out of the ignition while we were straddling a level crossing. By the time we arrived at Monaco relations were very strained.

We had qualified for the Mountain Speed/Regularity Test, but neither of the Johns would agree to me driving, though I thought that our chances of success would be much better with me at the wheel. As we went to bed on the eve of the test, I said jokingly to John Young, 'See you at nine in the morning.' 'Don't be stupid,' he replied, 'you know perfectly well that the test starts at eight.' John Coombs and I just looked at each other, for we realised that he had really got the starting time wrong – it was 7:30 am. It seemed like the perfect answer to our problems for we were still arguing about who should drive. Coombs and I cheerfully slept on in the morning until John Young came thrashing back into the hotel at about 8:30 am, absolutely furious, to tell us that we had been disqualified for not being at the start on time. The joke had badly back-fired and it was very nearly the end of a good friendship. I never competed in a rally again.

1956

My decision to stay with the Gilby team for 1956 had been reached long before the previous year's racing had ended. The DB3S that I raced in 1955 was sold to Graham Whitehead and for 1956 Aston Martin sold me another works car, DB3S/5, which was again entered for me by Gilby Engineering.

I also agreed to drive for Cooper in 1956, but this involved only 1,500 cc sports cars and the new Formula Two single-seaters. Because my garage on the Kingston bypass was only about a mile from the Cooper works at Surbiton, I knew very well both Charles Cooper and his son John. I had a purely oral contract with the Coopers and they asked me to drive for them because I had beaten the works cars with Tommy Sopwith's privately owned car on a couple of occasions in 1955. Coopers did not offer to pay me a retainer that year, but later both Jack Brabham and I received written contracts that provided for a retainer of £5 per year. We never received this miserable sum and I think that the idea was that by paying a consideration the Coopers were making the contract legally binding. Charles Cooper was a mechanic of the old school (he had worked for Kaye Don in pre-war days) who did things properly. In contrast his son John was rather disorganised. Happily, John made up for this by his friendly, easy-going nature and good sense of humour. He could usually persuade mechancis to work late to get cars ready or persuade Coventry-Climax to speed up delivery of engines.

If John himself worked on a car, there was always a risk that in a last-minute rush a nut or bolt would be over-tightened (John Cooper was a strong man). While Jack Brabham was in the team, he would steer John well away from his car and so John used to practise on mine. My car was always looked after by Gordon Whitehead, a superb mechanic who usually managed to keep a close eye on the situation and ensured that no harm was done.

Jack Brabham spent much of his time at the Cooper works; he was a superb mechanic and engineer who contributed a great deal to Cooper's success and he always endeavoured to make sure that the cars were put together properly. In contrast to the Gilby team, who could not afford regular test sessions, Cooper were constantly testing and developing their cars. I was regarded by Cooper as their number one driver (a title which, as I have explained in the next chapter, I did not like) and so I did most of the testing and drove all the new cars. During 1956 Jack started to do some test driving and by 1958 was doing most of it. He was to prove himself an outstanding test driver who could clearly analyse faults in a car in way that I was just not able to. Jack and I had an arrangement that if I thought there was something special about his car, then, before we drove the cars in practice, we could toss a coin and the winner could have his choice of the cars. I knew Jack did his best to ensure that both cars were equally good, I trusted him and I never opted for tossing the coin! As Jack once said to me, 'Roy, even if you won the toss, you really wouldn't know which car to choose!'

As usual, my British season started with the Easter Goodwood meeting. In the Lavant Cup for 2,000 cc single-seaters the Cooper team entered me with one of the sports cars powered by the new 1,460 cc version of the single-cam Coventry-Climax engine, an interim design of which only very few were made before the appearance of a Climax twin-cam engine for 1957. I faced stiff opposition from Bob Gerard with his elderly, but still very quick Formula Two 2-litre Cooper-Bristol. I made an exceptionally good start, but was scratching to keep ahead of Gerard who made several attempts to get past; each time he tried to pass me on braking, I left my braking even later. I was close to losing the Cooper-Climax a couple of times, then Gerard nearly went off the road with his Cooper and at the finish I was a mere second ahead.

Gilby had entered my DB3S in the Unlimited Sports Car race, but I had agreed with Stirling Moss that he could drive the car if it looked as though I was going to have a good day. If my day was going badly, then I would drive. I

My first ever works Cooper drive was at Goodwood on Easter Monday, 1956. This is the car that I drove in the Lavant Cup. I am talking to, left to right, Bob Gerard, John Coombs and John Young (Charles Dunn).

thought that I could win the race myself, but with Stirling at the wheel the prospects of a win were even better. I had gone well in practice, and with one win under my belt I was happy to let Stirling drive; he scored a convincing win from George Abecassis (HWM-Jaguar) and Bob Berry (Jaguar D-type). As I had loaned my car to Stirling on this occasion, then it is only reasonable to assume that I would have let him have it at Silverstone the following month if he had made his wishes clear.

The next race for me was the up to 1,500 cc Sports Car event in which I drove a different Cooper-Climax, a new car fitted with Girling disc brakes. There was strong opposition that included my team-mate Jim Russell with a drum-braked Cooper-Climax, Reg Bicknell with a works Lotus Eleven and Ivor Bueb with his private Cooper. The disc-braked Cooper did not handle quite as well as the drum-braked car on this occasion, but I was not being pushed as hard as in the racing car event and won at a slower average from team-mate Russell.

The Richmond Trophy Formula One race attracted a very strong field that included Stirling with a works Maserati fitted with experimental fuel injection, the BRMs of Mike Hawthorn and Tony Brooks, three works Connaught 'Syracuse' cars driven by Archie Scott-Brown, Les Leston and Bob Gerard and two works Gordinis. My chances of finishing in the first three were slim indeed, but there were many retirements. I drove a steady race, using my head for a change, and finished a sound second behind Stirling.

For the British Empire Trophy at Oulton Park just under a fortnight later I lent my DB3S back to the works and it was raced by Reg Parnell, but with a reduced capacity 2.5-litre engine to take advantage of the handicapping. I drove a works 1,500 cc Cooper-Climax. The race was run in class heats and with what was supposed to be a handicap final. In fact the 1,500 cc cars were so fast in their heat that their advantage was reduced from one lap to 40 seconds and even if it had been a scratch final, a 1,500 cc car would probably still have won. The opposition in the 1,500 cc class was very strong, and I was well satisfied with second place in the heat behind Colin Chapman's Lotus but ahead of Stirling's Cooper and Hawthorn's Lotus, and third in the final behind Stirling and Chapman. 1956 was the year in which the British 1,500 cc cars, thanks to the new Climax engine, made a breakthrough and it was at Goodwood and Oulton Park that their tremendous speed and competitiveness was first seen.

A week later I was in action again at Aintree where I drove the 250F, my DB3S and a works Cooper-Climax sports car. Early in the day I finished second in the 2,000 cc Sports Car race, but was soundly trounced by Mike Hawthorn with Bueb's Lotus. For me the race was a disappointment, as I had been fastest in practice with my Cooper and believed that I could win!

In contrast the Unlimited Sports Car race provided me with a very good win at the wheel of my DB3S. Aintree, with its very long straight, favoured the Jaguars and so it was absolutely essential to make a good start with the Aston and lead into the first corner. Otherwise there was a very real risk of getting stuck behind one of the Ecurie Ecosse D-types (the team usually entered three) and by the time I had managed to get past if I could, I would then be too far back to get to grips with the leader. Ecurie Ecosse team tactics would be that one of the drivers would go all out to win the race, while the other two would do their best to stitch up Salvadori! With the Aston you lost a vast distance to the D-type on the straight – not just a couple of cars' lengths. I was away first when the flag fell and led into the first corner, but Titterington (Ecosse D-type) was breathing down my neck all the way and trying to pass me right at the end of the straight. As the race progressed I gradually extended my lead and at the finish I was nearly nine seconds ahead. I also set a new Sports Car lap record of 2 min 8 sec (84.38 mph).

The '200' Formula One race was marred by retirements and Hawthorn's crash with the new BRM. I retired because of low oil pressure. Stirling won the race and in third place was my Cooper team-mate Jack Brabham with the Maserati 250F which he had bought from the Owen Organisation. To my mind Jack never adapted to driving the 250F really quickly. Brabham's true skill was at the wheel of the much lighter rear-engined cars and he did not get on well with the heavier, front-engined designs. When he joined the Aston Martin team in 1958, he was again slow to adjust to the DBR1 and was never really as quick with this car as he should have been. I felt that Jack needed to be involved with the testing and construction of a car for him to achieve his Championship performances – just as it was to be at Cooper.

For me the Silverstone races in May provided a mixture of triumph and disaster. I was fastest in practice for the 1,500 cc Sports Car race, I led throughout (finishing 30 seconds ahead of Chapman) and I set a new class lap record of 96.67 mph, some six mph faster than the existing record and not much slower than the lap record of 98.48 mph set by Hawthorn with a works D-type Jaguar in the Unlimited race. Whilst I had plenty of reasons for disliking Silverstone, I usually went well there and I was able to throw the Cooper-Climax round with almost complete abandon, confident in its superb roadholding – it was far easier to drive than the much heavier DB3S. I also won the controversial Unlimited Sports Car race, the full story of which is told in Chapter 3, but it is interesting to note that my winning speed with the DB3S (94.79 mph) was slower than with the Cooper.

There was an immensely strong entry in the *Daily Express* International Trophy, including Lancia-Ferraris driven by Fangio and Collins, the new redesigned Vanwalls in the hands of Moss and Schell, a single BRM driven by Hawthorn and six Connaughts. I managed to get in very little practice, but I was pleased with my time of 1 min 44 sec which put me on the second row of the grid sandwiched between Collins (1 min 44 sec) and Scott-Brown (1 min 46 sec). Moss took pole position in 1 min 42 sec.

I made a mediocre start and was holding sixth place in the early laps, not driving particularly swiftly. As the race progressed I lapped faster and closed up on Archie. There had been a lot of retirements (one Lancia-Ferrari was already out of the race and the other was soon to follow) and the order was Stirling leading by a comfortable margin from Archie and myself. I squeezed past Archie's Connaught, but he fought back; we were both driving very hard, swapping places and lapping cars with me passing on one side and Archie on the other. I knew Archie's driving so well that I had complete confidence in him and it seemed that a problem could only arise when we were lapping a slower car.

Over the winter of 1955–56 the 250F was returned to the works for a major overhaul and came back with later-style bodywork. This photograph shows the tremendous dice with Archie Scott-Brown (Connaught) in the Daily Express *Trophy at Silverstone which ended when I crashed at Stowe* (T. C. March).

On the approach to Stowe on lap 49, when I was still holding second position, one of the drive-shafts of the Maserati seized up, the back end locked and there was nothing that I could do about it; I hit the bank, the car overturned and I was knocked unconscious. I suffered bad bruising, injured a knee and my left arm was badly burnt by the exhaust pipe. While Stirling carried on to score a fine win with the Vanwall, I was taken unconscious to Northampton General Hospital. Ironically, two of my worst crashes were at Stowe on Saturday May 5 (in 1951 and 1956) and yet so often during my career I overtook in or through Stowe corner. I was racing again by the end of May, but once again the 250F had to go back to the factory for a rebuild and was not ready to race again until the British Grand Prix in July.

On June 17 I drove a works Cooper-Climax in the City Cup race at Oporto. The race was held on the narrow, bumpy, fast and dicey 4.6-mile Boavista road circuit. There was a large entry although the only serious British opposition came from Reg Bicknell and Cliff Allison with works Lotus entries and there were several fast Porsche 550s entered. I was fastest in practice and I led away from the start – and throughout this 148-mile race. As the race progressed, so the shock absorbers overheated, the brakes were beginning to fade and the Cooper was dancing about the road. I was expecting the Porsche opposition, built to withstand the rigours of Le Mans and other long-distance events, to close the gap. Fortunately for me, none of the Porsche drivers turned out to be a budding 'Moss', and I won with a comfortable lead of over a minute from local driver Nogueira (Porsche) and Bicknell. In the early laps Jack Brabham was in second place, but he was forced out by steering problems.

The opening event of the British Grand Prix meeting at Silverstone was a race for the new category of 1,500 cc Formula Two cars which officially did not come into force until 1957. I was entered at the wheel of the new Cooper-Climax single-seater, the only monoposto in the race, for all the other entries were sports cars. The new Cooper, mechanically similar to the sports cars, had not been completed until the day before the race and was untested. I was fastest in practice, but in the race found that Chapman's Lotus was faster along the straights, but slightly inferior in terms of both cornering and braking. I made a very bad start because the Cooper slipped out of gear; I jammed it into third instead of first and it took me several laps to get to grips with Chapman. Because of the superior speed of the Lotus I had great difficulty in passing Colin, but eventually closed up on him at Woodcote and squeezed ahead under braking for Copse. I finished 30 seconds ahead of the Lotus at the end of this 30-lap race. For Cooper this was a magnificent victory with an untried car and it was followed by intensive development work so as to stay ahead of Lotus, who it was known would be bringing out their own Formula Two single-seater very shortly.

For me the British Grand Prix was a very good race. I was glad to be back at the wheel of the Gilby 250F and although it was now very outdated mechanically compared with the works Maserati, I lapped in practice in 1 min 44 sec (compared with the 1 min 41 sec recorded by Moss with a works 250F who took

One of my best drives with the 250F was in the 1956 British Grand Prix at Silverstone in which I held second place before having to make a pit stop (T. C. March).

pole position). The opposition in this race included four works Lancia-Ferraris, four works Maseratis, three Vanwalls, two BRMs and two Connaughts.

I made an excellent start and held fifth place in the opening laps; Stirling passed me and we were both going very well, moving up into third and fourth places behind the BRMs of Hawthorn and Brooks by the end of lap ten. Sometimes when I was at peak form I was completely relaxed and smooth and this was one of those rare days. By lap 30 the BRMs had shot their bolt, Moss was leading the race and I was in second place ahead of Fangio's Lancia-Ferrari and pulling away from the Maranello entry. I decided to conserve my engine as much as possible, still pulling full revs of 7,500 rpm along the straights (the car was geared so that it would not over-rev in top), but changing up at around 7,200 rpm.

Although I was driving to conserve the car, my lap times remained just as quick, and I held second place until lap 50 when I was black-flagged and called into the pits because the 250F was trailing a fuel tank retaining strap. I rejoined the race, having lost several places, and only a few laps later I was back in the pits because the engine had developed a misfire. We could not locate the problem (it was in fact dirt in the fuel – quite possibly muck got in the tank during the rebuild at Modena) and I restarted, but decided to retire on lap 55. If I had kept going, I would probably have finished fairly high up the field, in fourth or fifth position, but I was terrified in case the engine blew up. Gilby simply could not afford the cost of a major engine rebuild, apart from the fact that it would have cost us six to eight weeks' racing while the engine was sent to Modena. The race was won by Fangio (Lancia-Ferrari). Despite my retirement, it was one of my most satisfying and enjoyable races and I received a very good 'press' from both the motoring journals and the national newspapers.

The August Bank Holiday weekend was a very busy one for me indeed, as I was competing at the Nürburgring on the Sunday and Brands Hatch on the

Monday. Because Cooper had decided to compete in the Rheinland Cup race for 1,500 cc sports cars on the morning of the German Grand Prix, it was a suitable and convenient race in which to enter the 250F.

In the first practice session in the wet with the Cooper, I learned in the pits that so far I had lapped fastest which surprised me because I am not a wet-weather man. I went out again, determined to retain pole position, but overdid things by locking the brakes of the Cooper on a fast part of the course, slid off, straddled the hedge and slid along the top of it for some 200 yards which brought the car to a gentle halt and destroyed a good length of hedge. After practice John and I went to collect the car and it was badly battered. In these circumstances John came into his own; he persuaded the East German AWE team to let us use their garage at the circuit and he and Gordon Whitehead spent all night bashing my car back into raceworthy condition.

Because of the accident I missed the second practice session (held in improved conditions) and I was pushed back on to the third row of the grid. I made a superb start and led through the first few corners, but then fell back to third place and battled throughout the race with Stirling at the wheel of a much heavier Maserati. The Maserati seemed undergeared and slower than the Cooper on the straight (Stirling always preferred his cars undergeared). So whilst Stirling passed me on every lap through the twisty section of the circuit, I repassed him on every lap on the long straight before the start/finish line. We moved up into second and third places when Barth's AWE retired, but as the race progressed, so the shock absorbers of the Cooper deteriorated, the car was dancing all over the road through the corners and Stirling was finding it more and more difficult to pass me. By the last lap my car was handling so badly that it was on the grass almost as much as on the road; Stirling forced his way past and I had to settle for third place. If Stirling had had a clear run, he would probably have won the race.

Because of our efforts to conserve the 250F I had very little practice for the Grand Prix, but managed a quick lap in 10 min 32.4 sec which put me on the third row of the grid, sandwiched between Jean Behra (works Maserati) and de Portago (Lancia-Ferrari). In the opening laps I was well up with the works cars, dicing with Jean Behra and holding fifth place. I was feeling very happy and very confident, but my race came to a dismal end when the transverse leaf rear spring broke on lap four.

Herr Schmidt, the organiser of the Nürburgring races, was determined that his events should not be treated as second-rate and it was mandatory for all drivers to attend the reception after the race to collect their starting and prize money. Once dinner was over and the presentations had been completed at about 9:30 pm, all the drivers due to compete at Brands Hatch on the Sunday roared off and there was an even more intensely fought Grand Prix on the roads to Dunkirk. I think that this was a race that I won, but John Cooper, my passenger, was far from amused. We managed to snatch a couple of hours' sleep during the Channel crossing and arrived at Brands Hatch in time for early-morning practice. Then, with any luck, we had another couple of hours' sleep before racing started. Quite obviously no one was in any great shape to race, but the starting and prize money was a great incentive!

Brands Hatch was held in pouring rain and the circuit was flooded at certain points. In the second heat of the 1,500 cc Sports Car race, I was chasing Bueb's private Cooper down the hill from Druids when I hit a river of water running across the track, lost all steering and slid with considerable force into a well protected marshall's post. The Cooper was a complete write-off and I was feeling very groggy indeed.

Later in the day I finished third in the first part of the two-part Formule Libre race and won the Formula Two race, both with the single-seater Cooper. By this time I was feeling decidedly second-hand and John Cooper insisted that I should go to the medical tent; after a quick examination I was sent to hospital where it was discovered that I had two broken ribs. I had felt very tender round the rib cage ever since my Silverstone shunt and had been in considerable pain at several circuits. It seems very improbable that I had driven ever since May with broken ribs, but, quite possibly, Brands Hatch completed what the shunt at Silverstone had started. Once I had been strapped up at the hospital, I felt very much better and my driving at later race meetings was unaffected.

On August 18 I drove at Oulton Park, with a works DB3S in the *Daily Herald* Trophy and a works Cooper-Climax sports in the *Sporting Life* Trophy for 1,500 cc cars. It was another miserably wet day and whilst I felt distinctly unhappy with the Aston DB3S, which was a very 'skatey' car in the wet, I did not mind the Cooper so much and was reasonably happy with its handling on wet surfaces.

In the 1,500 cc race Moss took an early lead with his Cooper, but I was well in the hunt in second place and narrowly leading Mike Hawthorn at the wheel of Bueb's Lotus. As we approached Knicker Brook, Mike went ahead; I thought that he was motoring too fast on the approach to the corner, but he seemed to be holding a good line and it looked as though he was going to get away with it. Suddenly the back of the Lotus broke away, the car mounted the bank and turned a complete somersault. I tried to avoid the Lotus and instinctively ducked as parts of Mike's disintegrating car landed on top of my Cooper, hitting me on the head and breaking the windscreen. Completely dazed, I went off the road, just missing a small concrete building; the car spun and carried on backwards until I managed to get it pointing in the right direction and I cruised round to the pits. 'Lofty' England of Jaguar, a great friend of Mike's, was in the pits and asked what had happened to Mike. Still badly dazed, I said, 'He's dead.' This caused considerable, but rather needless, panic, for, although he had been thrown out of the car, he had only suffered bad bruising and a sprained wrist. For the first time in my career I opted out of a race for other than mechanical reasons and this indicates clearly just how stunned I was.

Gilby had decided to compete in both the Caen Grand Prix on August 26 and the Italian Grand Prix on September 2. In the non-Championship French race there was a strong entry of private Maseratis but the only works team was Gordini whose cars were notoriously fragile. Despite gearbox trouble I was fastest in practice, took an easy lead from Harry Schell (Maserati) and on lap two set a new circuit record. I had a comfortable lead of over a minute when the circuit was soaked by a violent rainstorm. I eased my pace, but by this time the circuit had a generous coating of oil and rubber and I completely lost the 250F on a stretch of road crossed by tramlines. I stalled the engine, it took me a long time to bump-start the car on my own and after a pit stop to check the Maserati, I finished third behind Schell and André Simon (Gordini). Gilby were very disappointed, as it had looked as though the race was in the bag.

The Italian Grand Prix was held on the combined road and banked track circuit at Monza and proved a complete fiasco for the Gilby team. The banked section of the circuit was so bumpy that every car in the race was so badly shaken that it needed a rebuild afterwards. I was trying to pick the best line on the banking to give the car the least hammering, the 250F was plagued by minor problems and after four pit stops I finished in 11th and last place, nine laps behind Stirling's winning 250F.

Both Jack Brabham and I were entered with sports Coopers in the Berlin Grand Prix held on September 16 on the banked Avus track. The opposition was formidable and included a full works Porsche team and the very quick, very aerodynamic East German AWEs. In practice I was attaining around 150 mph along the straights and was faster than all the Porsche entries – my time was bettered only by one of the AWE drivers. The German teams were astonished, as the Cooper was much lower-powered than their cars and power could be expected to be all-important on this high-speed track. After practice we stripped down the engine of my car because of a suspect cylinder head gasket. While we were working on the car, Porsche team manager Huschke von Hanstein and their leading driver Wolfgang von Trips appeared in our garage. We were convinced that they suspected us of using a 2-litre engine in practice and were hoping to catch us swapping engines before the race. We were delighted to show them that they were wrong! I believe that the high speeds which we were attaining at Avus were due to the superb aerodynamics of the Cooper.

I led the race initially, but dropped back to second place. The banking was so bumpy that it was blurring my vision and shaking the car badly. On the second lap I was alongside von Frankenberg's Porsche on the North Curve when suddenly I realised that his car had disappeared. It seemed almost incredible, but I could only conclude that this car had gone over the top of the banking. This is exactly what had happened and the Porsche had plunged into the paddock some 30 ft below, throwing out the driver whose injuries included a fractured skull. As the race progressed I was forced to ease off, because the pounding from the banking deranged the Cooper's suspension so badly that the wheels were slightly buckled under, fouling the bodywork. I finished sixth and Jack was one place ahead of me.

The Gold Cup at Oulton Park on September 22 was the Formula Two race of the year and attracted a strong entry that included Coopers driven by myself and Jack, Rob Walker's new Cooper driven by Tony Brooks and yet another new Cooper driven by Ken Wharton. The new Formula Two Lotus had yet to appear and so all the works team Lotus drivers were at the wheel of sports cars. A major attraction of the race was the very high prize money – £1,000 for first place. Apart from my team-mate Jack there was just one other driver that really worried me. Tony Brooks, who was an absolute natural on a road circuit – as we had seen in the Aston Martin team – and Oulton Park was just the sort of circuit on which he was at his best. In fact just to impress us he was fastest in practice and I was slightly slower.

I made a superb start and pulled away into the lead, while Jack diced with Tony. This was fine from my point of view, for the inevitable result was that Jack and Tony slowed each other down while I extended my lead. After the first five or six laps I began to feel really confident, lapping swiftly and smoothly, and unchallenged. Jack was forced to stop at the pits because of a fuel pump problem and I went on to win from Brooks by a margin of over 20 seconds and set a new lap record.

In his book *Racing Mechanic*, Alf Francis, Rob Walker's mechanic, wrote that he threw away Brooks' chances of winning the race by letting him start on new, unscrubbed tyres. This is not really correct. Although Tony would have been slowed during the opening laps, this was a long race and his tyres would scrub themselves in fairly early on so that he had the opportunity of making a late challenge or going for the fastest lap.

In practice for the Sports Car Shell Grand Prix at Imola near Bologna on September 30 both Jack and I went well with our Coopers in practice and in the

Receiving the Daily Herald *Trophy after winning the Formula Two Gold Cup race at Oulton Park in 1956.* (Roy Salvadori collection).

race I had a tremendous dice with the Oscas of Castellotti and Musso. I was able to stay with the Oscas which were much heavier, more powerful cars, but when I tried to pass on corners, they crowded me and tried to nudge me off the road. I had a go at getting between them, but it did not work and they were still edging me on to the grass. I started banging the Cooper against their cars, which was a rather stupid thing to do as my car was so light that it was likely that I would end up against a tree or a bank. Sometimes I did not think clearly when I was racing and this was one of those days! However, the tactics worked, the Oscas backed off and we were able to get on with the race. Soon afterwards I was forced to retire because of the distributor trouble that was plaguing the Coopers at this time. The state of my car led to reports that I had retired because of an accident, but in fact all that the car needed was a few hours' work by a panel-beater. Jack drove a particularly good race and came through to finish second, sandwiched between the Oscas.

On October 14 I drove my last race for the Gilby team with the 250F in a short Formula One race at Brands Hatch. Connaught entered four cars. I knew that I had slim prospects of beating Archie with our now very tired 250F, but I made a fantastic start and led for the first lap. We could never get the 250F set up for Brands Hatch and it was constantly bottoming and darting about. Whilst I was struggling to control the 250F, Archie passed me on lap two and Lewis-Evans went ahead just before the end of the race. I worked harder in that race than in many races that I actually won!

The Cooper team rounded off the season with an entry in the one-hour Sports Car Rome Grand Prix held on the Castelfusano circuit on October 21. On my way to the race I flew to Milan and drove to the Monza banked circuit to join in a record-breaking attempt by Bill Knight and Arthur Owen with a 1,100 cc Climax-powered Cooper. I set a new Class 'G' 200-mile record of 131.89 mph which reveals just how quick the small Cooper was. I was very surprised that Cooper could stand up to the treacherously bumpy Monza circuit, which certainly would not have been my choice of venue for record-breaking.

At Rome I was fastest in practice of the 1,500 cc runners and I led my class in the race until Cooper's usual distributor problem ended my run; Jack retired for the same reason, but before we retired we had the consolation of leading the much more powerful Oscas.

Sadly, my years with the Gilby team were at an end. The 250F was now obsolete, we were expanding at Elmbridge Motors so there was no longer room to prepare the cars and I was becoming more and more committed to Cooper. Gilby soldiered on with the 250F for another season and later developed and raced their own sports/racing and Formula One cars with Keith Greene at the wheel.

Chapter 6

Cooper, BRM and Vanwall, 1957

Introduction by John Cooper

'My motor racing associations with Roy go back a very long way. I first met Roy in 1947 at the West Court Speed Trials where he was driving the ex-Dobbs off-set single-seater Riley and I was driving one of the first of our Cooper 500s. As I raced Cooper 500s and 1000s and Roy drove various cars for private owners, so we saw each other regularly and became good friends. When Roy took over Elmbridge Motors on the Kingston bypass, just over a mile away from our workshops at Surbiton, we would see each other even more frequently and, of course, we always discussed motor racing.

'In late 1955 we asked Roy if he would drive one of our works central-seater sports cars during the 1956 season. Up until this time most of our works drivers had bought their own cars, but Roy was our first 'pukka' works driver. These sports cars, powered by the 1,100 cc Climax engine in their original form, handled well and the streamlining was very good because the body was based on the 500 cc car with body designed by Hawker at Kingston that we had used for record-breaking in 1953. It was thanks to Roy's driving that the sports car was so successful, but in addition Roy taught my father, Charles, and myself the business side of motor racing. Until Roy drove for us, we had not appreciated how best to raise sponsorship (Roy introduced us to Esso) and how to get the best starting money. Motor racing for us had been very much a hobby, but it soon became a serious business.

'By July 1956 we were racing single-seater Formula Two cars with enlarged 1,500 cc Climax engines and we fielded a two-car team for Roy and Jack Brabham. Later came the Climax twin-cam 1,500 cc engine, but at Roy's suggestion this was soon enlarged to 2 litres and for 1958 to 2.2 litres. Because we had only one 2.2-litre engine, Roy and Jack used this at alternative Formula One races. Roy and Jack were a superb combination because not only were they excellent drivers, but Roy was a very able business man while Jack had engineering ability, was able to set up the cars and helped us enormously in this way.

'Towards the end of 1958 it became obvious that our small Coopers, powered by the full 2,500 cc engine that everyone knew Climax were developing, would have an excellent chance of success in 1959 Grand Prix racing. There was, however, a real risk that we would lose both our drivers. BRM made an offer to

Jack, but I managed to persuade them not to poach him by making a direct approach to Alfred Owen. Then Reg Parnell made a very attractive financial offer to both Roy and Jack to drive the new Aston Martin Formula One car. Not only did Aston Martin want to keep them together as a team, but they themselves wanted to drive together. At this stage I was desperate because Roy and Jack drove so well together and I did not know how I could replace them. I discussed the problem with Reg Tanner at Esso and Esso came forward with sufficient sponsorship for both Roy and Jack to stay with Cooper. The new money was for Jack because Roy had his own arrangements with Esso. My father and I managed to persuade Jack to stay with Cooper, but Roy's commitment to Aston Martin, because of his long association with the team, was such that he could not go back on his word. The result is history.

'Roy and I remained good friends and, of course, Roy maintained close connections with Cooper through his drives with Cooper cars for private owners. Roy was instrumental in putting together the deal with BMC whereby the Mini-Cooper went into production and it was only through his assistance and support that the deal with Leonard Lord was finally concluded.

'Later Roy and I were to work together again. It was at Roy's instigation that Jonathan Sieff, who had already bought his business, should take over Cooper Cars. This was in 1965, not long after my father's death. The new 3-litre Grand Prix Formula was starting in 1966 and we believed that it would be immensely expensive with all the cars having four-wheel-drive and 24-cylinder engines! Sieff was the British Maserati concessionaire and we put together a deal whereby Maserati would supply V-12 engines developed from the design raced by them briefly in 1957. Roy became Racing Manager and a Director of Cooper and for two seasons we raced the Cooper-Maseratis with reasonable success. Coopers and Roy Salvadori were good for each other and it was an association based on friendship.'

* * *

Although I was driving for Cooper in Formula Two and Sports Car races, I was very keen to get a regular Formula One drive. During the winter of 1956–57 I met Raymond Mays in London on several occasions to discuss the possibility of me driving for BRM in 1957. I was wary of joining a team with such a long history of mechanical problems and I believed that most of the problems stemmed from the organisation of the team.

The new BRM had first appeared in 1955 when it was driven by Peter Collins, but it was too new to show anything other than immense potential. It was a very small, squat car with a markedly oversquare four-cylinder engine that produced as much power as any of its rivals, an unusual suspension layout with oleo-pneumatic struts at the front (as on the original V-16 BRM) and an even more unusual braking arrangement with normal disc brakes mounted at the wheels at the front and a single disc brake at the rear mounted on the transmission. Originally the brakes were made by Dunlop, but by 1957 BRM had switched to

Testing Rob Walker's Formula Two Cooper at Goodwood early in 1957 (Roy Salvadori collection).

Lockheed brakes. BRM drivers in 1956 had been Mike Hawthorn and Tony Brooks and they had had a really disastrous year plagued by brake, transmission and engine problems. The team had pulled out of racing for the rest of the year after Tony Brooks crashed badly in the British Grand Prix because of a jammed throttle.

BRM team manager Raymond Mays was dedicated to the cars which he had been nurturing through disaster after disaster since early post-war days and he was very charming and persuasive – if you listened to him long enough, he would make you World Champion! However much you tried to ignore all the flattery and optimism exuded by Ray, some of it stuck. Eventually, against my better judgement, I decided to throw in my lot with BRM. A major factor was the amount of money that BRM would pay me and the level of retainer from BRM's oil company, BP. I thought that even if I did not rate the car very highly, I would be driving in only a small number of Grands Prix (there were far fewer races then) and the money would compensate for the car's shortcomings.

For some while I had been thinking that if the Climax engine could be enlarged to two litres then it would be competitive in Formula One on British circuits and in some of the more tortuous Continental events. Already the Formula Two Coopers were lapping at speeds close to the times of the much heavier and more powerful Formula One cars and it needed only a little more power for us to be able to mix it with the Vanwalls and Ferraris. I mentioned the idea to John Cooper and we later discussed it at length with Wally Hassan of Coventry-Climax who was all in favour. One problem was that the small Cooper team was far too busy to do the work themselves.

In March I agreed to test Rob Walker's Formula One Connaught and Formula Two Cooper before they were despatched to run in the Syracuse

Grand Prix. I had known Rob for a long time, both liked and admired him and was very happy to do the testing for him. At Goodwood John Cooper and I talked to Rob and his mechanic Alf Francis about the idea of a 2-litre version of the Climax engine. Rob Walker was very excited and agreed to underwrite the development of a 2-litre car by Alf Francis, but it was also agreed that John Cooper would order the new crankshaft, cylinder liners and pistons from Coventry-Climax. The result was the 2-litre Cooper-Climax which Jack Brabham drove at Monaco. The original idea was that I should drive the 2-litre Cooper at Monaco but this was not possible because of my commitment to BRM.

We had regular test sessions with the BRMs at Silverstone and Snetterton. At BRM's insistence I was number one driver, as Ray said that I had more experience than Ron Flockhart. I have my own ideas about number one drivers – to me the number one driver is the guy who drives fastest and that can vary from circuit to circuit. My ideas were of course influenced by the Aston Martin team where there was no number one driver except, when he was in the team, Stirling Moss. I felt very sorry for my team-mate Ron Flockhart, who was a very able driver, had been with BRM since 1954 and deserved rather better treatment.

During testing neither Ron nor I went particularly quickly and our lap times were much the same. There were always mechanical problems and Ron, who was a far more able test driver than I was, seemed better able to cope with these. I soon found that I did not get on well with the BRM, but I admit that I had rather made up my mind in advance about it. I could not throw it round the circuit in the way I liked, it seemed little progress had been made since it was raced by Hawthorn and Brooks in 1956 and there were those constant mechanical problems.

Ray and I had specifically agreed that because of BRM's persistent brake trouble only Lockheed, who had made the brakes, should modify the system and that no other changes should be made to the brakes without the drivers being consulted. This agreement was completely ignored by Mays and was to lead to my break with BRM early in the year.

Early in 1957 I was contacted by Ken Gregory, Stirling's Racing Manager, offering me the chance to drive a works Maserati with Carroll Shelby in the Sebring 12 Hours race. Shelby had teamed up well with me previously and our driving styles blended. When we arrived at Sebring, no one in the Maserati team seemed to take much interest in us, there was a complete lack of organisation and no one told us when to practise or for how long; this chaotic state of affairs was to have repercussions in the race.

Carroll ran well in the opening laps, but because of a complete mess-up in the Maserati pits he was called in to refuel after 18 laps, whereas a minimum of 20 laps had to be covered between refuelling stops. I took over the car, knowing that we would be disqualified, and within a few laps the officials had hung out the black flag calling me back into the pits. We were very disappointed and Gregor Grant in his report of the race in *Autosport* wrote, 'It was a great pity, for the car was being exceptionally well driven. Both Shelby and Salvadori have similar temperaments as regards driving and their technique has improved enormously during the last year or so. They are definitely top-class men.'

At Goodwood on Easter Monday I drove for Cooper and BRM. In the Formula Two Lavant Cup both Jack Brabham and I drove Coopers with the new and much more powerful twin-cam Climax engine. Although Coopers were to dominate Formula Two in 1957 and the new front-engined Lotus proved unreliable, we had a lot of problems with the Climax twin-cam engine in the early races of the year. We had not realised just how hard the new engine needed revving, for it had a completely different power band from the single-cam engine, all our gear ratios were wrong and we were plagued by clutch and valve problems. Initially we were no faster than with the single-cam engine and at Goodwood I fought for the lead with Tony Brooks (single-cam Cooper) until I retired with clutch failure.

Not much progress had been made with the BRM by the Richmond Trophy Formula One race at Goodwood. We had suffered brake problems during testing and we had them again at Goodwood. I spun at the chicane in practice when one of the front brakes locked on and this caused Jack Fairman, following me closely, to go off the road with Rob Walker's Connaught. On the warming-up lap one of the brakes stuck on again and it took five marshalls to push the car to the grid where the mechanics freed the brakes. Exactly the same thing happened on the first lap of the race, the brakes locked at Woodcote and I was left straddling the road with the following cars dodging left and right to avoid me. The brakes were stuck on so tightly that we could not push the car and the

Drifting the twin-cam Cooper-Climax in the Chichester Cup at Goodwood in April 1957. I retired with engine trouble, but with the consolation of having set fastest lap (Louis Klemantaski).

marshalls had to hump it off the track. Ron also had sticking brakes, but his were not staying jammed on, and in a race depleted by retirements he finished third behind the Connaughts of Lewis-Evans and Fairman. It was without doubt my least successful appearance at Goodwood, for I always enjoyed racing there and usually won at least one race at each meeting.

After the race I discussed the problem at length with Ray and, as always, he promised that he would deal with it and ensure that Peter Berthon allowed only Lockheed to work on the brakes. It was, of course, all hot air, but Ray was so persuasive that I almost believed him!

Our next race with the BRMs was the Monaco Grand Prix. Monaco, because of its many tight corners, is a circuit where complete confidence in the car is essential. As soon as I drove the BRM in practice, I became convinced that Lockheed had never touched the brakes and that BRM themselves had been playing with them. They were still sticking badly, but with the difference that they no longer stayed jammed on completely. This caused immense problems; for example, at Casino Square the driver brakes to steady the car on the corner into the square and then accelerates hard down past the Tip Top bar. On this part of the course I became convinced that the engine was seizing, when in fact the brakes were still sticking from the application at Casino Square.

This was happening all round the circuit and was an absolute nightmare. I was trying the brakes long before corners to make sure that there was some braking power and my times were getting slower and slower. Eventually I called into the pits and said to Ray, 'You haven't been playing round with these brakes again, have you?' He assured me time after time that the brakes were absolutely standard as provided by Lockheed, and I was foolish enough to believe him. I lost confidence altogether because I thought that the problem was with my driving and I failed to qualify as a starter.

After the last practice session I returned to my hotel, the Hotel de Paris – it

Struggling – without success – to qualify the BRM as a starter at Monaco in 1957 (Edward Eves).

was ironic that BRM had provided me with superb hotel accommodation, a luxurious suite in one of the most sumptious hotels, and one of the most appalling cars that I have ever driven – and I fell into conversation with the Lockheed representative. He confided, rather reluctantly, that BRM had modified the braking system and that he was not happy about the modifications that had been made.

I exploded and immediately shot off to tackle Ray who on this occasion proved rather less than his normal charming self! Instead of offering any explanation why BRM had modified the brakes contrary to our specific agreement, Ray was more concerned about what he regarded as the Lockheed representative's breach of confidence. I decided to withdraw from the team immediately, but Ray urged me not to act hastily and give the decision some further thought. I had insufficient confidence in the BRM to drive it really quickly and BRM were quite unable to keep their word. I withdrew from the team and returned the balance of the retainer of £2,500, after deducting a proportion to cover the two races at which I had driven. The BRM saga had completely messed up my chances in Formula One and most of my friends thought that I should have held on to all the money. Ron Flockhart remained faithful to BRM – I think he was a real hero – although he was probably able to keep a much closer eye on his car than I could.

Over the Whitsun weekend I drove for Cooper at both Brands Hatch on the Sunday and the Crystal Palace on the Monday, but once again I was out of luck at both circuits. On the last lap of the Sports Car races at both circuits Colin Chapman with a Lotus powered by the single-cam Climax engine took the lead from me and I finished second with the twin-cam Climax-powered Cooper. These were the last races in 1957 in which I drove a Cooper Sports car and for the rest of the year the team concentrated on the single-seaters. Despite gearbox trouble all weekend with my Formula Two Cooper – when I selected third, I would more often than not find myself in neutral – I finished second in the Formula Two race at the Crystal Palace and at Brands Hatch. Both these races were won by Jack Brabham who had improved vastly as a driver since 1956 and was now driving much more aggressively and much quicker.

Because of a bad crash at Le Mans, Tony Brooks was out of the Vanwall team for a couple of races and I received a telephone call from the team manager, David Yorke, offering me drives in the French Grand Prix at Rouen and in the non-Championship Reims race. As I had been without a Formula One drive since I left BRM, I was very glad to accept. It was also a good deal financially as I was to receive the usual share of starting and prize money, and Vanwall were now attracting very high starting money. When I arrived at Rouen I learned that Stirling Moss had also dropped out of the team because of illness. His place was taken by the slim, frail Stuart Lewis-Evans who had driven for Connaught before they retired from racing early in 1957.

Because of my height I had great difficulty getting into the Vanwall's very narrow, high-sided cockpit and the mechanics had to modify the bodywork before I could get behind the wheel. I did very little practice with the Vanwall,

Left *On my way to fifth place with the Vanwall in the 1957 Reims Grand Prix* (Roy Salvadori collection).

Right *In the Formula Two race at Reims Jack and I had a magnificent dice with Trintignant's Ferrari. After valve failure I pushed my Cooper across the line into fourth place* (Charles A. Sytle Jnr).

chassis number VW1, but soon found that I liked it immensely, especially its very powerful and punchy engine and its excellent roadholding. I was unable to exploit the full performance of the car, as I was not completely happy with the way it was set up; I would have liked a little more understeer that would have allowed me to throw the car around rather more – so far as I was concerned it needed only minor suspension adjustments, to the anti-roll bar or the shock absorbers or, perhaps, a change of tyre pressure. If I had been able to drive the car more, I would probably have adjusted to its characteristics. In practice I was sixth fastest in 2 min 25.1 sec and Lewis-Evans was tenth fastest with a time of 2 min 27.6 sec.

On only the second lap of the race as I was going through a fast corner at around 130 mph, the revs shot up – just as if the clutch had gone – and I only managed to keep the car under control with great difficulty; as soon as I accelerated, up went the revs again. I went straight into the pits where the familiar Vanwall oil breather trouble was diagnosed. The car had been spewing oil over my back tyres and on to the course. I later learned that oil dropped by the Vanwall had caused Ron Flockhart to have a bad crash with his BRM. I rejoined the race after oil had been syphoned out of the tank, but the problem was still there and I retired on lap 26. Stuart Lewis-Evans went extremely well with the other Vanwall, but retired because a cracked cylinder head had allowed engine compression to expand the radiator header tank and foul the steering column. All through their racing career the Vanwalls had been terribly unreliable and the Rouen result was only too typical of their history so far. The race was won by Juan Fangio in one of the finest drives of his career.

At Reims the following weekend it was clear that the Vanwalls were more powerful than the Ferrari and Maserati opposition and there was every prospect that we would make a good showing on this very fast circuit. Stuart went exceptionally well in practice, taking a place on the front row of the starting grid with a time of 2 min 23.3 sec, only two-fifths of a second slower than Fangio. I was rather slower in 2 min 31.2 sec and there were good reasons for this.

The car which I drove at Reims was so different from my Rouen mount that I could have believed that it was a completely different design. It was oversteering appallingly and, as a result, weaving so badly on the straights that I was almost too frightened to move the steering wheel. The trouble may have been

caused by the fact that my car was running on large, 17-in wheels, whereas I believe Stuart's car was running on smaller wheels. I mentioned to David Yorke that the car was weaving badly, but I was merely told that most cars weaved on fast circuits (which to a certain extent is true) even in the slightest wind. I realise that I should have been more assertive and tried much harder to get my car sorted out, just as Stirling most certainly would have done.

I had a very unhappy drive in the race and I probably should have retired. I had the speed to pass other cars but I had to choose the widest part of the course, for I could not be sure where the car was going! As *Autosport* commented, 'Salvadori's car seemed to be very "weavy", even in a straight line.' I finished fifth after a quick refuelling stop, while Stuart drove brilliantly, leading the complete field for much of the race, but falling back to take third place because of an oil leak that spread over his goggles. Tony Vandervell was disappointed with the results, as he was expecting a Vanwall to win, but in fact it was the first occasion in Vanwall's history when both entries completed a full-length Grand Prix.

Tony Vandervell was so impressed with Stuart's driving – and he had put up a brilliant show – that he fielded an extra team car for him in the remainder of the 1957 races and throughout 1958. If I had known that there was even the slightest possibility of a regular place in the team, I would have made a really determined effort to get my car sorted out at Reims so as to put up the best possible showing, rather than meekly accepting what I was told about its handling characteristics.

My drives for Vanwall were the high point of my 1957 season. Although my time with the team was too short for me to get to grips with the cars or get to know the people, I was very impressed with David Yorke's organisation and ability – he had the running of the team very much under his control. Tony Vandervell himself was so wrapped up in his obsession to win the World Championship and hid himself so carefully behind a gruff, forbidding exterior that he was almost impossible to get to know.

Immediately before the Reims Grand Prix I drove a works twin-cam Cooper in the 191-mile Formula Two race. The Cooper team had also brought an experimental car that was based on the sports car. I was very quick in practice with my usual car, making fastest lap, but even quicker with the streamliner which seemed ideal for the high-speed Reims circuit. It was, however, going to be a very long and hard race run in hot conditions and I decided against using the streamliner as I doubted whether the brakes, shrouded by the bodywork, would last the distance. My doubts were proved during the race when I found that even the exposed brakes of the normal Formula Two car were overheating. Jack thought much the same way and did not even bother to practise with the streamliner. Cooper said that they were lending the streamliner to Bill Whitehouse, a fairly experienced amateur driver, but it was such a handful that I was not very happy about this and said so. John Cooper reassured me by saying that Whitehouse was only going to do a couple of laps to collect the starting money.

The race proved a magnificent fight between Maurice Trintignant (Ferrari V-6), Jack and myself. We battled for lap after lap, the lead sometimes changing three times a lap and we were often racing three abreast. We progressively lowered the Formula Two record and when Jack retired with valve trouble on lap 24, I managed to hold on to a narrow lead over Trintignant. Although I was nursing my engine, it began to run rough five laps from the finish and it dropped a valve three laps later, so I coasted down to Thillois and pushed the Cooper across the line into fourth place. It seemed that the valve trouble was a basic problem that Coventry-Climax were having some difficulty in solving. Of our performance in this race, Denis Jenkinson wrote in *Motor Sport*, 'Although Ferrari had won, Cooper could rest happy that they had shaken the Rampant Horse very severely and almost managed to tweak its tail.' Unfortunately the race had been marred by tragedy. Bill Whitehouse lost the streamlined Cooper on braking for Thillois (maybe this caused a tyre to burst) and he suffered terrible injuries to which he succumbed. Works Lotus driver, Herbert Mackay Fraser, was also killed in this race. Reims was a very dangerous circuit because the corners were so fast and if you left the road, you were likely to end up in a ploughed field which more often than not caused the car to flip over.

For the European Grand Prix at Aintree the following Saturday Cooper provided me with a Formula Two car powered by the enlarged 1,960 cc version of the Climax engine, while Jack drove a similar car entered by Rob Walker. In the race I was able to mix it with some of the Formula One cars, I had a long dice with Trintignant's Lancia-Ferrari, pulling out a lead over the Italian car, and I was holding a comfortable fourth place towards the end of the race. Out in front Stirling Moss, who had taken over Brooks' Vanwall, was on his way to taking the Acton team's first-ever World Championship race victory. Five laps from the finish I found that I was having difficulty in changing gear and I pulled into the pits. The gearbox had split its casing and lost all its oil. I restarted and cruised round to the finishing line. After Stirling had taken the chequered flag, I pushed the Cooper across the line into fifth place to score the first-ever World Championship points with a rear-engined car. Whilst Stirling and the Vanwall were, rightly, the heroes of the day, Cooper also got a very good press.

Within a few days the Cooper team was off to compete with the 2-litre cars in the Caen Grand Prix. The main opposition came from the BRM team which had entered a single car for Maserati works driver Jean Behra, but it became a two-car entry when Harry Schell's old Maserati 250F broke in practice and he was offered the spare BRM. Jack and I were driving the works Coopers and Tony Brooks was entered with Rob Walker's 2-litre Cooper.

The BRMs led away at the start, followed by the Coopers of Tony Brooks, Jack and myself. We were expecting the notoriously unreliable BRMs to break, but unexpectedly Behra's BRM held together and he went on to win the race after a very smooth and steady drive. Jack and Tony retired their Coopers, and Schell's BRM broke its engine. I finished second, about 12 seconds behind, well satisfied with the performance of the Cooper.

At the German Grand Prix we both ran in the Formula Two category, me with a works car and Jack with a new car entered by Rob Walker. For several laps I diced with Edgar Barth who had defected from East Germany and was now driving for Porsche instead of AWE! I led him for most of the time, despite trying to avoid the bumpier parts of the circuit because I was worried that something on the car would break. In fact the rear suspension collapsed at three-quarters race distance and I had to retire, but with the consolation of having set a new Formula Two lap record. Jack retired early in the race.

That evening we had the usual chase across France to catch the ferry in time to compete at Brands Hatch the following day. Jack and I were competing with Formula Two Coopers in the two-part Rochester Trophy, but I was soon out of the first part of the race because of clutch trouble. Jack won both parts.

Cooper entered two of the Formula Two cars in the Pescara Grand Prix, an addition to the World Championship series for that year only and held on August 18. Because I was road-testing a Hillman Minx convertible for *Sporting Motorist* magazine, Jack and I decided to drive to the race in this, taking John Cooper along as passenger. The drive was rather disastrous because Jack, in contrast to his circuit driving, was a very civilised driver, while I always drove much too fast. All the time I was driving, Jack was criticising me in his slow drawl and all the time he was driving, I was urging him to go faster and sometimes stretching my foot across to push the accelerator down. All this led to a somewhat strained atmosphere between us!

The Pescara circuit was a very difficult 16-mile road course, very fast, loose at the edges and with the famous long straight along the sea-front. It is another road circuit that you can scratch off my visiting list for sure! The race would clearly be dominated by the Maseratis and the Vanwalls (Ferrari had sent only one car for Musso), but we hoped to last the distance and benefit by the retirement of faster cars. Neither Jack nor I were as fast in practice as we had expected and we started right from the back of the grid.

We were both well down the field in the race, but Jack was harrying me through the back section of the course; I went quicker, Jack went quicker and he was pushing me so hard that I was looking as much in the mirrors as at the road. Just as I was thinking that if we carried on like this one of us would end up in trouble, I went on to the loose stuff at the edge, clipping a concrete kilometre post and bending the front suspension, while somehow or other Jack managed to skate round me. While I nursed my car back to the pits to explain to John

Cooper how Jack had nobbled me, Jack carried on to finish seventh and last – all of three laps behind Stirling's winning Vanwall.

After the race Tony Brooks and his delightful fiancée, Pina, asked us to give them a lift to Milan. Five-up the Hillman was slow and it was even slower with Jack driving. Jack was having great difficulty in passing what seemed to be an endless convoy of military vehicles, for every time he started to overtake he was waved back by police and soldiers. We decided that this was not good enough and so Tony was delegated to drive. When Tony put on his driving gloves, we knew that he was really going motoring; he was soon ignoring police signals, passing the lorries and slipping in and out of gaps between them to avoid oncoming traffic. A police motor cyclist started to chase after us, but the roads were very slippery and Tony had no difficulty in outstripping him.

Some miles later on Jack took the wheel again and drove on in his usual plodding way. John Cooper and I, in the back of the car, were bored and fed up with the outcome of the race and the long, tedious drive. When we passed a small motor cycle, the rider and his girl pillion passenger lay flat over the tank and tried to stay with us. Encouraged by me, Cooper, who was an expert in these matters, made rude signs at them until we eventually left them in the distance. A little later on we stopped at a level crossing and I looked round to see the motor cyclist still haring after us. John and I tucked ourselves down between the seats and the motor cyclist reached us just as the barrier was rising. Throwing his motor cycle and his girl friend on the road he grabbed Tony's arm and spat at him – I am sure he was under the impression that Tony was driving. We seemed now to have the makings of an international incident! As Tony pushed the man away and pulled his arm back, Jack accelerated hard and from then on drove much more like the Jack that we knew on the circuit.

Because of the Suez crisis in late 1956 and the petrol rationing that resulted, the *Daily Express* Silverstone meeting was postponed until September 14. It attracted a very thin entry for the Formula One race apart from the works BRMs, which dominated proceedings, the works Coopers and a large entry of private Coopers. Jack drove a 2-litre car, while I drove the Formula Two car. Because of an engine power loss I fell back to finish 12th in my heat. After the heat the trouble was traced to dirt in the carburettors and the problem was sorted out before the start of the final. The Cooper was doing very well in the final and I was leading the Formula Two category when the brakes started to go. I soon had no brakes at all, but was still lapping quite quickly (it is amazing how fast you can go round Silverstone without brakes). Cliff Allison with a works Lotus caught and passed me but, fortunately for me, he was not paying as much attention to life as he should have been, and he lost the Lotus completely at Becketts and stuffed it into the barriers. As a result I won the Formula Two section of the race, finishing eighth overall. Jack retired because of an oil leak.

At the autumn Goodwood meeting both Jack and I were entered with Formula Two cars and spent the whole race in a cut-throat dice which I won by six-tenths of a second. My race average of 94.43 mph made this the fastest-ever Goodwood race.

I also drove a Lotus 11 for John Coombs in the Sports Car race. My technique of driving was to throw a car into a corner. I could never drive smoothly like Stirling or Tony Brooks – I envied them their style, but it simply did not work for me. The only way I was able to drive quickly was to force the back of the car out going into a corner, if necessary by putting on a handful of lock, so that the back broke away. I would then correct the drift, but continue with it, applying opposite lock and keeping my foot hard down so that I would drift away from the apex of the corner. This technique of driving was hard on some rear suspensions and I found this out to my cost when driving John Coombs' Lotus in practice.

All went well to begin with, but then the car started to handle very badly and in the pits it was discovered that the rear wheels were toeing in and touching the bodywork because the de Dion tube had bent. We talked to Colin Chapman about the problem and he brought a stronger de Dion tube to the circuit the following day informing us that this was one that we would not bend. By the end of that day's practice the new de Dion tube had bent. For the race Chapman brought an even stronger tube which happily did not bend until the end of the race. Throughout the race I was drifting the Lotus at extreme angles at which these cars were rarely and in fact not intended to be seen. I loved the roadholding of all Lotus cars, even if their frailty worried me.

The Gold Cup Formula Two race at Oulton Park on October 5 attracted an immensely strong entry that included Jack and myself with works Coopers, Tony Brooks with Rob Walker's Cooper and Lotus entries driven by Cliff Allison, Keith Hall and Graham Hill. In the race Jack took an immediate lead and I chased him until my engine went off-song. Cliff Allison passed me with his Lotus and I held on to third place until lap 16 when the engine was so rough that I decided to make a pit-stop. Although I rejoined the race, I retired when my engine cut out altogether. Jack won the race by the comfortable margin of 37 seconds from Allison's Lotus.

The last race on the International calendar was the non-Championship Moroccan Grand Prix held on October 27. I remember far more about Casablanca, its wonderful climate and its clubs and bars than I do about the race! Cooper entered a 2-litre car for me and Jack drove Rob Walker's 2-litre Cooper, but we were outpaced on this very fast circuit. Both Jack and I were eliminated by gearbox trouble. The mechanic sorted out Jack's gearbox in the paddock and he rejoined the race. This was a breach of race regulations and Jack was soon black-flagged. Unfortunately the flag had no number on it, so Fangio, who was lapping in close company with Jack, thought the flag was intended for him and stopped at the pits next time round. Eventually it was all sorted out and Fangio rejoined the race, whilst Jack stopped.

1957 had been a very mixed year for me, starting with my unhappy experience with the BRM team, but as the year had progressed I had become more and more involved in Formula One with the Cooper team. I was hoping for much better luck during the coming season.

Chapter 7

Cooper in Formula One, 1958

The partnership of Jack Brabham, myself and Cooper worked very well and it was almost taken for granted that we would both stay with the team in 1958. It proved an important year for Cooper, Jack and myself, an important step towards the team winning the World Championship and my first year of regular and serious Championship Formula One racing, but none of us was consciously aware of this at the time.

We had been talking to Coventry-Climax about a further enlarged version of the twin-cam engine, and Climax devised an interim 2,207 cc (88.9 × 88.9 mm) engine with a packing piece between the cylinder block and the head. This was to develop 194 bhp at 6,250 rpm on Avgas (130-octane aviation fuel) which became compulsory in Formula One for 1958. Only four of these engines were built, one each supplied to Cooper and Rob Walker and two to Lotus, and although these were rough, rather lumpy engines they more than proved their worth during the 1958 season. Because of the difficulty in obtaining suitable crankshafts in Britain in time for the start of the season, Jack and I visited the Meyer-Drake works near Los Angeles and ordered the crankshafts there ourselves while we were travelling to the Tasman races.

For 1958 Cooper adopted double (instead of single) wishbone suspension front and rear, with coil springs at the front, but retained a transverse leaf spring at the rear (now flat and not curved). Girling disc brakes were used for the first time on the single-seaters, the cars handled much better on the latest Dunlop R5 tyres, the bodywork was wider with a more comfortable cockpit and the works cars were distinguished by a vestigial tail fin.

Maserati withdrew from racing at the end of 1957 and in 1958 Formula One racing was a closely fought duel between the Vanwalls and the Ferraris. The BRMs proved fast, but were still unreliable and the Cooper, Rob Walker and Lotus teams were all hoping to mix it with the faster, heavier cars on the tighter circuits and pick up some good places on the faster circuits through retirements.

The motor racing establishment was still not taking seriously our lightweight, rear-engined Coopers, but it was severely shaken in January 1958 when Stirling Moss drove Rob Walker's 2-litre Cooper to victory in the Argentine Grand Prix (a race not entered by Vanwall), defeating the full Ferrari team and a strong entry of private 1957 ex-works Maseratis. It was a win that gave us all at

Cooper high hopes of doing really well in the 1958 European Grands Prix.

While Stirling was competing in the Argentine, I was in New Zealand driving a Connaught for Bernard Ecclestone. I had known Bernie for many years, ever since he had raced a Cooper 500. He was a born dealer and would buy and sell almost anything. When he bought two of the B-series Formula One cars at the auction of the Connaught works team and equipment in October 1957, it was his intention to re-sell them and there was no better place to do this than New Zealand.

It was a great shame that Bernie was unable to come to New Zealand himself, for not only was he great fun to be with, but he was a very good organiser. I drove a standard 'Syracuse' B-series car, while the rather more radical, so-called 'toothpaste tube' car with wedge-shaped body was driven by Stuart Lewis-Evans, who was very much Bernie's protégé.

There was only one mechanic with the cars, they were too much for one man to cope with and they ran far from well. In the New Zealand Grand Prix at Ardmore my Connaught was plagued by an engine misfire and I finished a poor fifth, while Stuart's Connaught was eliminated by loss of oil pressure. The race was won by Jack Brabham with a 2-litre Cooper-Climax. I returned home after the Ardmore race, but Stuart stayed on to compete in one more event, but was again out of luck.

Stuart, who was certainly no businessman, had been instructed by Bernie to sell the cars. Buyers seemed few and far between, but Stuart was delighted when he negotiated a deal with a foreigner who offered a stamp collection in exchange. I urged Stuart to do nothing until he had spoken to Bernie on the telephone and, of course, as soon as Bernie heard about it, he scotched the deal. The cars were shipped back to England and Bernie entered them in a few Formula One races in 1958 with success before they were eventually sold.

Jack, Stuart and I had flown to New Zealand together. It was Jack's practice to make a list of the drivers who would be flying and at the airport hand out a number of small but heavy packages for them to take as hand luggage. We were all quite willing to help until we tried to lift the parcels! On this trip we had the best part of a complete car broken up into parcels and for once Jack's scheme went wrong. Poor Lewis-Evans had been allotted a gearbox; he found the weight a bit much and while we were waiting to check in at Honolulu airport en route, put the parcel down while he had a breather. Unfortunately Stuart rested the parcel on the luggage weighing machine where it was spotted and checked in as luggage, and Jack had to pay about £60 excess.

During the early part of 1958 we tested the works Coopers extensively at Goodwood and one incident in particular illustrated how, as a driver, I was always at my best when the team included a real maestro like Stirling or Tony Brooks who would set a 'bench mark' for lap times at which I could aim. Neither Jack nor I were lapping as fast as we would have liked and we were wondering what the reason was – maybe it was because it was a windy day or maybe there was some mechanical reason. That dry-humoured Kansan driver, Masten Gregory who was with us, turned round and said, 'Well, it's a slow day because neither Stirling nor Brooks is here.' I reckon that Masten hit the nail right on the head.

My first British races of 1958 were at Goodwood on Easter Monday. In the Lavant Cup for Formula Two cars I drove a Cooper-Climax for Tommy Atkins, while Jack was at the wheel of the works car. I made a very good start and was leading the race on the second lap when the gearbox broke and I clouted the bank at Lavant corner. Jack won the race by the narrowest of margins from Graham Hill with a works Lotus.

There was a strong entry in the International '100' Formula One race, including Mike Hawthorn with a works Ferrari, BRMs driven by Behra and Schell, Moss with the Rob Walker 2-litre Cooper with which he had won the Argentine race and similar works cars driven by Jack and myself. Stirling's engine stalled at the fall of the flag and by the end of the first lap the order was Behra–Hawthorn–Brabham–Salvadori. On the fourth lap Behra crashed at the chicane because of brake failure (hardly a new BRM fault), Stirling came through the field to pass first me and then Jack, and when Stirling retired his Cooper with a broken con-rod, I was back in a secure third place where I finished. I rounded off the day by driving a brand-new Lotus 11 for John Coombs in the 1,100 cc Chichester Cup Sports Car race, finishing third behind other Lotus 11s driven by Campbell-Jones and Dickson.

The Aston Martin team did not need me for the British Empire Trophy at Oulton Park, so John Coombs asked me if I would like to drive the 1,500 cc Climax-powered Lotus 15 which he had just sold to Belgian Pierre Berchem who did not want to drive the car in the race himself. The car had typically superb Lotus roadholding but a rather odd Chapman-devised gearbox with all the gears in a straight line so that it was only too easy to select the wrong gear by going straight through the box, with potentially catastrophic results. John modified the gearbox by fitting a safety catch that prevented the selection of first or second gear once the driver was off the line, thus limiting the problem. I ran very well in the heat for 2,000 cc cars and finished second to Cliff Allison with a works Lotus 15 powered by a 2-litre engine. The final should have provided a battle between the big capacity Aston Martin DBR2s of Moss and Brooks and

At the wheel of Pierre Berchem's Lotus 15 in the 1958 British Empire Trophy at Oulton Park. I ran well in my heat, but retired in the final because of hub failure (T. C. March).

our smaller capacity cars, but I retired with rear hub trouble, Allison's car lost its oil pressure and so the Astons scored an easy win.

There followed two brilliantly successful outings for Cooper. In the Aintree '200' race for Formula One and Two cars Stirling Moss led throughout to win with his 2-litre Rob Walker-entered car despite clutch slip. Jack finished second nearly pipping Stirling on the line, Tony Brooks was third with Walker's Formula Two Cooper and I finished fourth with a works 2-litre car which was also plagued by a slipping clutch. My moment came in the *Daily Express* International Trophy at Silverstone where I was fastest in practice in 1 min 40.8 sec, an unofficial lap record; Jack recorded 1 min 41.4 sec, Stirling 1 min 41.8 sec and Peter Collins with a works Ferrari Dino 246 was fourth fastest and completed the front row of the grid with a time of 1 min 41.8 sec.

Stirling's engine stalled at the fall of the flag, I made a terrible start and Collins led from Behra (BRM), Flockhart (BRM), Gregory (Scuderia Centro-Sud Maserati), Jack and myself. My Cooper was vibrating badly, but as the race progressed, the vibration cleared and I started to make up ground. Jack made a pit stop because of dirt in the carburettors, Behra (who had taken the lead from Collins) stopped at the pits to change smashed goggles and, with the Cooper going better and better, I pulled myself up into second place behind Collins. I could hold station comfortably behind the Ferrari, but every time I tried to close the gap, Collins was able to find that extra bit and pull away. I finished second ahead of Gregory, Behra and Brabham. The race may have proved a triumph for Ferrari, but it was also a triumph for Cooper whose underpowered cars cost a fraction of the money expended by Ferrari, BRM and Vanwall to build, prepare and race. Cooper were gaining in prestige race by race.

At the Silverstone meeting I also drove a Lotus 15-Climax for John Coombs in the 1,500 cc Sports Car race. I was fastest in practice at 94.76 mph – two seconds faster than Graham Hill with a similar car entered by Team Lotus. In those days it was possible for a private entrant to buy a Lotus or a Cooper and not only take on the works teams, but beat them. With Coombs-entered cars I always considered that I had an advantage over Team Lotus, because Coombs'

On my way to second place behind Peter Collins' Ferrari with the 2-litre Cooper-Climax in the 1958 Daily Express *Trophy at Silverstone* (John Ross).

standards of preparation were higher than the works – although it did not work out that way in this race. On the warming-up lap my engine was misfiring badly and the Coombs mechanics changed the plugs on the starting line. I made a terrible start because the engine was still hesitating, but it seemed to clear on the second lap, I moved up into second place behind Keith Hall with a works Lotus and took the lead on the next lap. Hill closed up and passed me. I repassed him and just when I thought I was all set for a win, my engine petered out. The Team Lotus cars of Hill, Stacey and Hall took the first three places.

We now embarked on the full round of World Championship Grands Prix which started in Europe at Monaco on May 18. Jack and I drew lots for the 2.2-litre engine – he won and I had to make do with the 2-litre. Maurice Trintignant drove Rob Walker's 2-litre Cooper-Climax. As this was a Championship race there were full teams from Ferrari (whose cars were rather a handful on this circuit), Vanwall and BRM. Tony Brooks with the Vanwall was fastest in practice in 1 min 39.8 sec, Behra was second fastest in 1 min 40.8 sec and both Jack and I recorded 1 min 41 sec, but as he had recorded his time before me, he was on the front row of the 3 × 2 grid and I was on the second row. The competitiveness of the Coopers on this difficult circuit is shown clearly by the fact that the Ferrari of Hawthorn and the Vanwalls of Moss and Lewis-Evans were back on the third row. The Coopers did very little practice because we wanted to conserve the cars for the race.

In the old days the start/finish line at Monaco was on the sea front and there was just a short burst before the field piled into the very tight Gasworks corner. I made a superb start, accelerated through the front row to take the lead and was going much too fast to get round the corner. As I threw the Cooper sideways to scrub off speed, I knew that I was not going to make it, so instead of spinning in front of the field, I went very wide and virtually took the road to Nice! I re-entered the traffic in about fourth place, but as I rejoined the circuit Stirling was already drifting through the corner, going very nicely, and his left-hand rear wheel tapped my right front wheel, deranging the Cooper's steering. I lost three laps in the pits while the car was repaired and eventually rejoined the race right out of the picture. I retired after 56 laps with gearbox trouble. After the retirement of Behra's BRM (which had led initially), Hawthorn's Ferrari and Moss' Vanwall, the winner was Maurice Trintignant with Rob Walker's Cooper and it seemed that with two Championship wins in succession Walker was doing more to establish the Cooper name than the works themselves. Jack finished fourth.

After Monaco we had to drive straight to Zandvoort for the Dutch Grand Prix to be held the following weekend. I hated driving on the road and always preferred to be a passenger with a good driver. I had arranged to travel to Zandvoort with Stuart Lewis-Evans, a really superb road driver, very quick and very safe, and I kept wondering how I could persuade Stuart to do all the driving. One evening, with Stuart at the wheel, as we were driving up the winding road to La Turbie for dinner, I noticed a run-off area at a hairpin bend. After dinner when I drove back, it was still fairly light. I was drifting Stuart's

At Tabac corner with the 2-litre Cooper-Climax in the 1958 Monaco Grand Prix (Bernard Cahier).

Austin Metropolitan through the bends and when I reached the bend with the run-off I was motoring so fast that there was no way that I was going to get round the corner – although Stuart thought that I was going to try. I shot up the escape road and braked heavily. What I did not know was that the escape road was only about thirty yards long before coming to a sheer drop. More by luck than anything else I managed to stop about four feet short of the drop. Stuart did not say a single word about the incident – then or later. He got out of the passenger side, walked round the car, got into the driving seat and drove back to Monte Carlo – and he drove all the way to Zandvoort.

At Zandvoort the 2.2-litre engine was fitted to my car. The Vanwalls dominated practice and all three of them gained places on the front row of the grid. Jack was fifth fastest in 1 min 38.5 sec and I was on the fourth row of the grid with a time of 1 min 39.2 sec. We thought that we had a good chance of success at Zandvoort and so it proved in the race.

I soon moved up into fifth place and stayed there for most of the race, despite the fact that my Cooper was handling terribly and was all over the road. If I had not been so well placed and going even faster than I had in practice (which meant that there could not be too much wrong with the car!), I would have pulled into the pits to have the problem investigated. In fact the problem – as I learned later – was the strong wind blowing off the sea. Tony Brooks was so disturbed by the effect of the strong wind on his Vanwall that he made a pit stop to have his car checked over. When Lewis-Evans retired his Vanwall I moved up to finish fourth behind Moss (Vanwall), Schell and Behra (BRMs), but ahead of Mike Hawthorn (Ferrari).

It was Jack's turn to have the 2.2-litre engine at the Belgian Grand Prix so I had a 2-litre engine. We expected to be outpaced on the very fast, very difficult

Spa circuit, but although we were slower than the Vanwalls and Ferraris, we were very much in with a chance. Hawthorn took pole position with his Ferrari Dino in 3 min 57.1 sec, Jack was on the third row of the grid with a time of 4 min 5.1 sec and I was on the fifth row with a time of 4 min 5.6 sec. Whilst the Coopers lacked the sheer power of the Vanwalls and Ferraris, we found that we were able to take parts of the course flat out where the drivers of the faster cars were lifting off, and we were able to save time in this way.

The Spa race witnessed a virtuoso display of driving by Tony Brooks at his best and on a circuit on which he was superb. He caught and passed the Ferraris of Collins (who subsequently retired) and Hawthorn to win at a record speed of 129.92 mph. Third came Lewis-Evans (Vanwall). I passed Jack early in the race, I diced with Cliff Allison (2.2-litre Lotus), passing him to take fourth place on lap 11, but he closed up again as my clutch began to slip and went ahead again on lap 14. As the race progressed, so the Cooper's clutch slipped more and more and I fell further and further back to finish eighth, the sole Cooper finisher.

At Reims Cooper competed in both the Formula Two Coupe Internationale de Vitesse and the French Grand Prix, but our cars were outpaced. Jean Behra with a streamlined, single-seater Porsche dominated the Formula Two race and the Coopers driven by myself, Jack and Stirling (Walker entry) all retired with mechanical problems. The Grand Prix was dominated by the Ferraris which initially held the first three places; Collins spun and dropped back. Musso crashed with fatal results at the 130 mph bend beyond the pits and Hawthorn went on to win from Moss' Vanwall. Jack finished sixth, but my car developed clutch slip yet again and I fell back to finish 11th – 13 laps behind the winner. It was clear that the Cooper twin-plate clutch was simply not up to the job and after this race Cooper, like all other Climax engine users, adopted a triple-plate clutch which gave no further trouble.

For me the British Grand Prix was one of my best ever Formula One races. I was third fastest in practice with the 2.2-litre Cooper in 1 min 40 sec, compared with 1 min 39.4 sec by Stirling (Vanwall) and 1 min 39.8 sec by Schell (BRM). Jack was on the third row of the grid with a time of 1 min 42 sec. I was faster than Brooks, Lewis-Evans, Hawthorn and Collins amongst others and I was obviously in with a very good chance.

Inevitably, with full tanks, I made a fairly gentle start with the Cooper and held seventh place behind the battling Ferraris, Vanwalls and Schell's BRM. Jack was with me all the way, we were scrapping with von Trips (Ferrari) and Behra (BRM) and passed Tony Brooks. Schell's BRM had dropped right back, Stirling's engine blew up, and spurred on by the chance of real success I closed up on and passed Lewis-Evans (Vanwall) which put me in third place. Out in front were the Ferraris of Collins and Hawthorn and there was no way that I could catch them, but after scrapping furiously with Lewis-Evans I managed to pull away.

As the race progressed, the Cooper's air intake sucked in a lot of loose paper that was blowing round the circuit, the air intake became partly blocked off and this caused the water and oil radiators to overheat. I was also getting hotter and hotter and very exhausted from the heat of the oil and water pipes running through the cockpit. Stuart, urged on by the Vanwall pit, started to catch me again. Although the finish looked close, I had the situation under control, even though I was being sprayed by hot oil from a leak during the closing laps, and I was able to stave off the Vanwall. All the time that this dice was going on, Charles Cooper, who was quite a good friend of Tony Vandervell, was ribbing him about the vast expense of building his Vanwalls compared with the cost of the Coopers. Later he even offered to sell Vandervell a couple of Coopers. I doubt very much whether anyone else could have got away with talking to Vandervell like this. After the race I was driven to Northampton General Hospital for treatment for the oil burns, but fortunately on this occasion I was not detained!

For me third place with the Cooper was a magnificent triumph and Jack's sixth place consolidated the Cooper performance. In *The Motor* Rodney Walkerley wrote, '. . . the man of the hour of the Grand Prix was Roy Salvadori with the just over 2 litres works Cooper. The results speak for themselves: third in practice, third in the race by only 50.6 seconds in 225 miles and with an average of 101.39 mph. What does not emerge from the statistics is his astonishing cornering and the way he saved his engine while keeping ahead of Lewis-Evans' Vanwall.'

I restricted my practice for the German Grand Prix because the Nürburgring is a circuit on which it is so easy to bend or break the car. I was driving the 2.2-litre car at the insistence of the organisers who thought that I was better known than Jack. This rather upset the whole Cooper team, including myself, and it was decided that both Jack and Bruce McLaren should drive Formula Two cars for which there was a separate award. Mike Hawthorn was fastest in practice in

I drove this Lotus 15 entered by John Coombs into second place and a class win at the 1958 British Grand Prix meeting at Silverstone (T. C. March).

9 min 14.0 sec, next came Tony Brooks (Vanwall) in 9 min 15.0 secs, Stirling Moss (Vanwall) in 9 min 19.1 sec, Peter Collins (Ferrari) in 9 min 21.9 sec and von Trips (Ferrari) in 9 min 24.7 sec. Vanwall entered only two cars in this race. I was sixth fastest in 9 min 35.3 sec and Maurice Trintignant with Rob Walker's 2.2-litre Cooper was alongside me with a time of 9 min 36.9 sec. The grid summed up the 1958 Formula One season – a titanic struggle between Vanwall and Ferrari which culminated in victory in the World Championship for Hawthorn by one point from Moss, but with the Coopers firmly in the background ready to pick up places and getting stronger as the season progressed.

My story of this race was a steady progression through the field from ninth place at the end of the first lap when I was holding comfortable station behind Allison's 2.2-litre Lotus which I was pretty sure would break. Stirling Moss, the real master of the Nürburgring, led initially, broke the circuit record on lap three and promptly retired with magneto failure. Collins now led from Hawthorn, but Tony Brooks closed up on the Ferraris with his Vanwall, took the lead on lap ten, lost it and on the same lap went in front again; on that lap Collins, trying too hard to stay with the Vanwall, overdid it at a right-hand bend through the Pflanzgarten and crashed, suffering injuries that proved to be fatal. Mike Hawthorn, his closest friend and right behind, was naturally shocked by what he had seen and slowed off. On the following lap, much to Mike's relief, his engine blew up. Already the BRMs of Behra and Schell were out of the race and, although I did not know it, Allison's Lotus was slowing because of overheating problems.

As I passed Mike, who was walking back to the pits, he gave me a two-finger sign – not the rude gesture at which he was so good, but a signal to indicate that I was now in second place – and gave me the same 'hold it' signal I was to receive from the Cooper pit. I slowed down at some of the more dangerous parts of the circuit, avoiding the worst bumps and driving steadily to finish three-and-a-half minutes behind Brooks. Jack had retired at the end of the first lap after a collision with Bonnier's Maserati and Bruce McLaren, fifth overall, won the Formula Two category. The death of Peter Collins, who had been one of my earliest colleagues in the Aston Martin team and a good friend, took away all the satisfaction and pleasure that I would have derived from my performance at the Nürburgring.

Jack and I swapped engines again at the Portuguese Grand Prix which was held on the Oporto street circuit and, unusually, run in an anti-clockwise direction. I was slow in practice and in the race and settled for merely finishing. It all seemed so very different from when I had raced the sports Cooper there and cheerfully thrown it round the circuit and I really could not understand why. Jack made a better job of it than me, but not much better and finished seventh to my ninth and last after a pit stop to change a wheel which I had buckled against a kerb. Most definitely a race which I would prefer to forget.

After I had finished seventh because of mechanical problems in the Kentish '100' Formula Two race at Brands Hatch at the end of August (Jack finished

After I had won the Unlimited Sports car race at Oulton Park in September 1958 with John Coombs' Lotus 15, the trophy was presented by Colin Chapman (Roy Salvadori collection).

second), the Cooper team trekked off across Europe again to compete in the Italian Grand Prix run, thankfully, on the road circuit only at Monza and excluding the banking. I reckoned that it was a good circuit, to my mind much more like the sort of aerodrome circuit that I preferred, and if I could convince myself that I liked the circuit, then I would go well! It was of course a very fast circuit and we were outpaced by the sheer bhp of the Vanwalls, Ferraris and BRMs. We were also beaten in practice at Monza by the Lotus 2.2-litre car of Graham Hill and this had been going faster and faster as the season progressed.

I ran steadily in the race but had to make two long pit stops because of overheating which was eventually sorted out when it was found that the radiator header cap was not sealing properly. As more and more cars fell by the wayside, I moved up the leader board to finish fourth, elevated one place by the disqualification of the Maserati 250F entered by the American Buell team for Masten Gregory. Tony Brooks (Vanwall) was the winner at Monza and Hawthorn and Phil Hill with Ferraris finished second and third. Jack Brabham had retired on the first lap as the result of a collision with Gendebien's Ferrari.

At the International meeting at Oulton Park on September 20 I switched marques again to drive a Lotus 15-Climax 2-litre for John Coombs. There was a strong entry from Team Lotus and Lister. In practice we had mechanical trouble and I was well down the grid with a time of 2 min 15.0 sec compared with the fastest time of 2 min 7.0 sec recorded by Ivor Bueb with a works Lister-Jaguar. By the start of the race the Coombs' mechanics had sorted out the problem and I soon shot through the field to take the lead from Bueb under braking for the Esso bend on lap three. Thereafter I was unchallenged, I set a new lap record for sports cars of 86.28 mph and while I was contentedly motoring on to victory, 'Noddy' (that was John Coombs' nick-name) was holding out a variety of pit signals ranging from the polite 'Ease up' to 'Time for a Shag' (which I am told were seen in the television broadcast of the race).

This Oulton meeting was the occasion of a particularly riotous party at the Chester Country Club. John Coombs, Nick White (who often helped us at Oulton) and I booked a large bedroom with three beds and decided to have a reasonably early Friday night. John Coombs, as usual, tried all the beds and chose the most comfortable which was near the door. Only a few minutes after we had gone to bed and put out the lights, the door opened and someone walked into the room. Coombs switched on his bedside light to reveal a most attractive girl whom we knew as Anthea wearing a very scant bikini and apparently sleep-walking, with arms stretched out. She made for the bed occupied by Nick and climbed under the sheets. Nick, who had difficulty in believing his luck, half sat up in bed, as a man rushed into the room with a camera and flash, shouting, 'You'll be hearing from my solicitors.' The photographer was Geoffrey Budge, whom we knew well, and Anthea was his girl friend. Geoff Uren, the manager, followed and behind came various members of the motor racing fraternity, including Dick Jeffries of Dunlop, Dennis Druitt of BP and several drivers. Fortunately they had brought their own bar, as there were no drinks provided by the hosts.

People were continually coming and going, but at one time I counted 36 men and five girls in the room. The form seemed to be that with each arrival the lights were turned off and Noddy's bed turned end over end with him underneath. For Coombs the final straw came when one of the manufacturers' representatives pushed the lavatory cleaning brush well down the pan and anointed Coombs with it. Coombs was livid, complained violently about the smell, refrained from hitting the representative because he was so much bigger and retired to the shower with plastic curtains in the corner of the room. There he casually showered himself, not bothering to close the curtains.

At about 2:00 am there was a loud banging on the wall, followed by a female voice that we recognised complaining that if we did not stop the noise she would call the manager; her husband was racing that day and needed some sleep. Nobody took any notice, a little while later there was more banging and we were informed through the wall that the racing driver in person was coming to sort the matter out. Shortly afterwards there was a knock on the door and in came Graham Hill in his pyjamas, looking absolutely furious. When he saw who was holding the party Graham's anger disappeared, he had a drink and began enjoying himself. At this time Graham was only just starting his professional racing career and we did not know him very well – but the party helped to change that. The next communication through the wall from Bette was a plea to Graham to go back to bed and get some sleep. At breakfast the following morning Bette looked very subdued, but at one point she turned to Graham and said, 'I sometimes wonder why you married me.' Graham thought for a moment and replied, 'Well, Bette, it seemed a good idea at the time.'

Our final race of the year was the Moroccan Grand Prix at Casablanca which counted as a round in the World Championship in 1958 only and was the final decider as to whether Mike Hawthorn or Stirling Moss won the Driver's Championship. I was entered with the 2.2-litre Cooper-Climax, Jack Fairman drove the 2-litre car because Jack Brabham wanted to drive a Formula Two car to clinch the Formula Two Championship and a second Formula Two car was entered for Bruce McLaren. It was through me that Jack Fairman got this drive with Cooper. He had been urging me to put forward his name at Cooper for some time and I had said to him, 'Jack, you're a womaniser, you're a drinker – and you know that Charles Cooper disapproves of such behaviour. If you want to improve your chances of driving for Coopers, you will really have to pull your socks up and change your way of living.' So far as I was concerned, it was all a joke. Some time later he said to me, 'Salvadori, I have considered what you said and I'm now living in a way that Cooper would approve of. Will you talk to Charles and see if you can get me a drive?' I assured him, 'Of course I will, Jack. I will recommend that he considers you as a driver.'

The situation was getting out of hand and I was trying to think of a way out of what now seemed to be a thoughtless joke. The answer came when Charles Cooper said that he wanted a reliable driver for Casablanca, someone who would drive for a modest sum and look after the car. Jack was the perfect answer and that was how he got his drive.

At Casablanca I shared a room with Jack Fairman. Each year a number of drivers were invited to go to the palace at Rabat to meet the King of Morocco. One morning before the race, John Cooper telephoned me to say that I had been nominated to meet the king. I replied, 'There is no way that I'm going to drive through the desert all day and miss practice.' During our argument Jack Fairman woke up and I rapidly changed my tack, saying, 'Yes, Jack Fairman is a senior member of the BRDC and he should meet the king – Oh, the king has asked to see him, has he?' John responded with, 'What the hell are you on about Salvadori,' but soon caught the drift of what I was saying. I told Jack that the limousine was waiting and that there was no time for breakfast. Jack protested about the lack of breakfast and I told him that I had some energy chocolate that would keep him going. While Jack was dressing, I took a slab of Ex-lax from my toilet bag and stuffed it in Jack's mouth.

When Jack returned from Rabat, he looked absolutely ghastly. He said that he had had a dreadful day and had to stop the limousine in the desert four times on the way to the palace. I was terrified that Jack would discover what had caused his 'squitters', but I managed to persuade him that the local water was to blame.

Casablanca was a very fast circuit and our only hope was to finish. The team orders were just to keep going and hope that some of the faster cars blew up, but unfortunately that did not happen! We were both fairly slow in practice and I plugged on to finish seventh and Jack Fairman was eighth. Jack and Bruce took the first two places in the Formula Two category. Stirling won the race and set fastest lap, while Mike Hawthorn finished second which was sufficient to give Mike the World Championship with 42 points to Stirling's 41. Tony Brooks

Casablanca, 1958, with, left to right, John Cooper, Ron Flockhart, myself, Stuart Lewis-Evans, American serviceman and Jack Brabham (Roy Salvadori collection).

was third with 24 points. I was fourth in the Championship with 15 points.

During the latter part of 1958 I learned that Aston Martin would be competing in Formula One the following year with their front-engined car which had existed for a couple of years. Reg Parnell, who was now the Aston team manager, wanted both Jack and I to drive for the team and he was particularly interested in Jack because of his abilities as a test driver.

What happened next is a story that has been incorrectly reported on many occasions. Coventry-Climax informed Coopers that for 1959 they were developing a 2,495 cc twin-cam engine and if it was successful, then Cooper would have an excellent chance in the 1959 World Championship series. By this stage Jack and I had orally agreed terms with Aston Martin. When John Cooper heard about this, he telephoned Reg Tanner to see whether Tanner could persuade us to change our minds. I already had a substantial personal contract with Esso, but Reg arranged a contract that would provide additional money to persuade Jack to stay with Cooper. Money was not a factor in my choice of team for 1959.

Jack telephoned me and said, 'Roy, I think we have a chance of doing really well with the new Climax engine if we stay with Coopers. I intend telling Reg Parnell that I'm remaining with Coopers. We get on well driving together and I think that we should go on doing so.' I told Jack that I would like to stay with Cooper if I could. I had been driving for Aston Martin since 1953 and I had been happier in that team than any other. I had very close relations with John Wyer and Reg Parnell and I thought that it would be very difficult for me to get out of my agreement with them. I talked to Reg Parnell and made the point that without Jack to test, the chances of success would be much reduced and it would be better if I stayed with Coopers. Reg persuaded me that Aston Martin had a high budget for Formula One and a good development track record. He appealed to my loyalty to the team – after all, they had shown faith in me in my early days and I should have faith in them now. I stayed with Aston Martin and had a rather unsuccessful 1959 season in Formula One.

It is, however, interesting to speculate what would have happened if I had stayed with Coopers. Up until that time I had been the number one Cooper driver, but it is likely that in 1959 Jack and I would have had equal status. If I had stayed the team's efforts would have been divided, even to sharing the first 2.5-litre engine, and Jack would have had much less support. Over the previous couple of years Jack had improved immensely as a driver, but I was still competitive on many circuits. In 1959 he was to win the Driver's Championship by a margin of only four points. I am not suggesting that if I had stayed I would have won the Championship, but inevitably at some races I would have finished higher up the results and I could very well have prevented Jack from winning the Championship. My decision to stay with Astons proved good for both Coopers and Jack and because of my feelings for that team I was not unduly distressed!

There was no worthier winner of the World Championship than Jack. When Jack first came to England, he already had superb engineering and mechanical ability, but he did not get his driving act together until much later. As the Australians aptly put it, he started 'coming good' in mid-1956, although he was experiencing more than his fair share of mechanical failures. At the Gold Cup race at Oulton Park that year he had a fantastic dice with Tony Brooks, only to have his fuel pump let him down. After the race he was so despondent that he decided to return to Australia. I spent hours trying to convince Jack that his luck must change and John Cooper supported my arguments. Jack did of course stay and from the start of 1957 his luck changed, his driving ability improved greatly and he moulded himself into a truly great World Champion. It was a great pleasure to be in the same team as Jack. He was exceptionally helpful, he had immense integrity – a quality not always in abundance in motor racing – and if Jack could not help you, he would never do you down.

Chapter 8

Aston Martin, 1957–59: the DBR1 and DBR2 era

1957

Throughout 1956 I carried out a fair amount of testing with the new DBR1 that was to be the Aston Martin team car from the start of the 1957 season, although of course the majority of the testing was done by Reg Parnell. My testing ability was affected because of my loss of hearing in my right ear and the fact that I wore wax substitute ear plugs meant I could not hear the car properly – all I heard was a rumbling noise and it was not possible for me to identify and locate strange noises or a change of engine note. I lived by the tachometer. My job in testing was simply to do what I was asked and to stick to the lap times of which we knew the car to be capable. If I could do that, then I knew that the car was all right. It was not for me to suggest, for example, modifications to the suspension, although of course I could discuss handling characteristics. Unless you have a superb tester like Jack Brabham in the team, you are probably better off with a tester who simply does what the engineers tell him.

The DBR1 was a completely new car in almost every respect. There was a new longer wheelbase, multi-tubular space-frame chassis with front suspension similar to that of the DB3S, but at the rear, whilst there was still a de Dion tube located by trailing links, a Watts linkage had replaced the sliding guide and the torsion bars ran fore and aft instead of across the frame. Initially the engine capacity remained the same as for the DB3S (83 × 90 mm), it used the same twin-plug head and as before three Weber 45 DCO twin-choke carburettors were fitted. From 1958 the crankshaft ran in seven main bearings and there was

dry sump lubrication. The engine built for the 1956 Le Mans race had a capacity of 2,493 cc (83 × 76.8 mm) and as raced in this form in the first couple of events at the beginning of 1957 power output was 223 bhp at 7,200 rpm; the usual 2,922 cc version developed around 240 bhp at 6,250 rpm. Transmission was by a new David Brown five-speed 'crash' gearbox in unit with the final drive known as the CG537 and inspired to a certain extent by the design of the Maserati 250F gearbox/final drive which I borrowed from the Gilby team for Aston Martin to use for design study purposes. The gearbox proved to be the least satisfactory feature of the DBR1. The restyled bodywork was panelled in 20-gauge aluminium alloy and it was much lighter than the DB3S body.

The DBR1 was in almost every respect a vast improvement on the DB3S. Basically the DB3S handled superbly, it was an understeering car that the driver had to throw around to get the best out of, it was very safe but very 'skatey' in the wet when it would use a lot of road. By 1956 it suffered from a severe power disadvantage compensated for, to a certain extent, by its excellent handling, its superb brakes and its positive if not particularly strong gearbox.

In contrast the DBR1 had nicely neutral handling with a slight tendency to understeer that I liked very much, it was much more stable than the DB3S, and it had even better brakes. The increased power output made it so much more competitive, especially from 1958 onwards when there was a 3-litre capacity limit in the Sports Car World Championship. The one weakness was the gearbox which had a heavy change and a tendency to stick and jam; perhaps it would have operated more smoothly if we had risked losing time by double de-clutching, but in racing our main aim was to get into the next gear as quickly as possible and we never bothered with such niceties.

Our first outing in 1957 was in the British Empire Trophy at Oulton Park. Because of the Suez crisis and the petrol rationing that followed, the 1957 race was shortened to three 25-lap heats and no final, so that the winner was the

Below left *Words with Aston Martin tester Roy Parnell before the 1957 British Empire Trophy at Oulton Park* (Roy Salvadori collection).

Below *Still chatting on the grid at Oulton Park. Just behind me Duncan Hamilton is making himself comfortable in the cockpit of the HWM-Jaguar under the watchful eye of George Abecassis.* (T. C. March).

At Deers Leap during the 1957 British Empire Trophy at Oulton Park with the 2.5-litre Aston Martin DBR1. I finished second, unable to match the speed of Archie Scott-Brown with the new Lister-Jaguar (T. C. March).

fastest driver regardless of the heat in which he ran. The DBR1 was still in 2.5-litre form and I drove this while Noel Cunningham-Reid was entered with a DB3S fitted experimentally with CAV fuel injection. The real opposition came from Archie Scott-Brown with the new Lister-Jaguar, and my prospects of beating the lighter, much more powerful Lister were slim. I led initially, but Archie soon forged ahead and, slowed by gearbox trouble, I had to settle for second place. Cunningham-Reid finished fifth.

It was on my way to Chester on the eve of the race at the wheel of a hotted-up Morris Minor – a car taken from stock at Elmbridge Motors as I did not own my own road car – that I caught up Archie's distinctive Ford Zephyr painted green with a yellow stripe, just like the works' Listers. I chased him really hard and we had a hair-raising dice down the dark Cheshire roads, as I struggled to pass Archie and he fought off the unknown driver at the wheel of the Minor. Eventually I managed to scrape past by using the grass, sliding wildly, almost losing the Minor and leaving Archie to sort himself out. When we stopped at some traffic lights in Chester, Archie got out of his car, came to the driver's window of the Minor and said, 'You are an absolutely fantastic driver — you got out of line once, but you sorted it. You ought to try motor racing.' I replied, 'But, Archie, that's what we shall be doing all weekend.' When he realised who was driving, Archie was absolutely livid.

It was much the same story in the Sussex Trophy at Goodwood on Easter Monday. We were still having trouble with the gearbox, for it would stick in gear and the gears were either difficult to free or would jam completely. Even when these problems were sorted out the gearbox still gave trouble, not so much changing up but changing down and it was necessary to synchronise the engine speed and the change so precisely that almost inevitably drivers ended up by grating and crashing the 'box. It was a bad gearbox that proved the weak point of the DBR1 throughout its racing career. Although I had to give best to Archie with the Lister, finishing over 20 seconds in arrears, I was well ahead of Tony Brooks with a works 3-litre DB3S and it was clear that Aston Martin development was going in the right direction.

It was decided to run two DBR1 cars, now with the full 3-litre engines, in the Sports Car Grand Prix at Spa on May 12. John Wyer thought that the cars would go well there, but Tony Brooks and I had our doubts because it was such a fast circuit. Surprisingly we were fastest in practice – Tony was a complete revelation and turned in a lap of 4 min 21 sec (121 mph), whilst I lapped in 4 min 28 sec and knew that I would have to give best to Tony on this circuit. Spa was a circuit with a succession of fast bends that demanded absolute precision. If you got out of line on just one corner, you were in serious, quite possibly fatal, trouble. I liked Spa very much, but it was a circuit on which I felt that I wanted to go only as fast as I had to – I had a better sense of self-preservation than most people thought.

At the start of the race Tony and I held the first two places, but torrential rain started to fall and although the DBR1 was a very good car in the wet, we had a problem caused by rain getting into the car and under our visors. This made it impossible for us to see the road clearly and I was passed by Henry Taylor (D-type), who was a superb wet-weather driver, and by the Belgian Rouselle with another D-type, and Henry closed right up on Tony.

Fortunately the rain eased, visibility improved and I was able to speed up and repass the two Jaguars for second place. If the rain had continued, the Aston Martins could have been trounced – despite Tony's superb driving. It was a problem caused, I believe, by the aerodynamics of the car, that was cured back at the works and never recurred.

The Nürburgring 1000 Kms race was dominated by the DBR1 of Tony Brooks and Noel Cunningham-Reid who led almost throughout despite a very strong entry of Ferraris and Maseratis. At this race I was partnered by Les Leston who was having his first drive with the Aston Martin team. We went quite well in practice, but Leston, who was much more used to light rear-engined cars, had great difficulty in adjusting himself to both the circuit and the car. The race was a plain struggle for both of us, for the car stuck in fourth gear for the last eight laps, and a broken chassis ruined the handling. We finished sixth while the third entry, a DB3S driven by the Whiteheads, took tenth place.

After this race we had to drive to Monte Carlo for the Monaco Grand Prix and I was due to share a works-loaned Aston Martin DB2/4 with Tony Brooks. I managed to persuade Reg Parnell that he should instruct Tony to drive all the way. Tony protested to me that it was a thoroughly stupid idea because the distance was so great. My argument was that Reg clearly had much more trust in Tony and, on the contrary, it was a thoroughly good idea! We lost two hours on the way when we were detained by the police after Tony, at my instigation, had overtaken on double-white lines and he was far from happy when we

MINTEX
ENERGOL
ENERGOL
LUCAS
19

arrived at Monte Carlo. He was even less happy when he learned that I had arranged the driving with Reg!

Le Mans proved another disaster for Aston Martin. I was teamed up again with Les Leston who was beginning to get used to the car but was still lapping slower than most of the other Aston drivers. Whilst I did not necessarily expect us to win, I thought that we would finish well up the field. We lapped strictly in accordance with the target times set for us by John Wyer. After six hours' racing we were fifth and Brooks/Cunningham-Reid, who were going very strongly, held second place behind the Flockhart/Bueb D-type Jaguar of Ecurie Ecosse which was to win the race. Almost inevitably our DBR1 developed gearbox trouble, the lever stuck immovably in fourth gear and we staggered on until early on the Sunday morning when an oil pipe broke while Leston was driving and the loss of oil damaged the engine. Not long afterwards Tony Brooks crashed at Tertre Rouge when struggling to free a gear on his DBR1, but he was not too badly injured and was racing again within a month. The third Aston entry in this race was the new 3.7-litre DBR2 driven by the Whitehead brothers, and this also retired with gearbox problems.

Top left *Reg Parnell holds a pre-practice drivers' meeting at La Chartre before the 1957 Le Mans race, with, left to right, Tony Brooks, myself, Reg, reserve driver Henry Taylor, Graham Whitehead, Peter Whitehead* (Roy Salvadori collection).

Left *Another shot taken at La Chartre in 1957 with, left to right, Les Leston, Tony Brooks, myself, Noel Cunningham-Reid and Henry Taylor* (Roy Salvadori collection).

Below left *At Le Mans in 1957 with the DBR1 that I shared with Les Leston. We retired because of a broken oil pipe* (Roy Salvadori collection).

Below *On the starting grid with the DBR1 at Aintree in July 1957* (Peter Elinskas).

The Aintree Sports Car race was my first race in England with the 3-litre version of the DBR1. We were a little disappointed that the DBR1 was not as fast as Archie Scott-Brown's Lister-Jaguar, but we were probably expecting too much as we were giving away nearly a litre. In practice his best lap was in 2 min 6 sec, while I recorded 2 min 6.8 sec. The race, run in pouring rain, proved a two-car duel. I was in second place all the way, catching Archie in the last couple of laps, mainly I think because he was having difficulty in seeing in the rain and we made joint fastest lap in 2 min 11.8 sec (81.94 mph).

We were back at Spa on August 25 for the Belgian Sports Car Grand Prix where DBR1s driven by Tony and myself and a DBR2 for Noel Cunningham-Reid faced stiff opposition from Gendebien's 4.1-litre Ferrari and Gregory's similar 3.5-litre car. Cunningham-Reid shunted the DBR2 too badly in practice to run in the race, Tony's DBR1 was plagued by low oil pressure and I had the almost inevitable gearbox problems. Despite his practice problems Tony led throughout to win from Gregory, Gendebien (who had tyre trouble) and myself. I lost the use of first and second gears early in the race and then towards the finish the gearbox stuck in fourth yet again. I feel bound to comment that when some of my finishes were fairly poor, it was often because I had struggled on with a sick car, as I would always rather finish well down the field than retire. There were different schools of thought with regard to this. If Tony Brooks had a problem with his car he would stop at the pits to investigate it. If nothing could be done and the car was not capable of finishing well up the field he would retire. I always remember Tony telling me that the maximum effort should be made in practice to establish a good lap time. Then, if you retire in the race, at least you have shown your capabilities and it will stand in the records. Tony was very positive about his motor racing and it was worthwhile hearing his views. Here we had a magnificent driver who would drive only so long as it suited him, after which he intended to remove himself from the scene and concentrate on his business and private life – a rather balanced and intelligent approach to motor racing – and this is exactly what he did.

In September Aston Martin entered four cars at the postponed Silverstone meeting, DBR2s driven by Cunningham-Reid and myself and DBR1s driven by Brooks and Lewis-Evans. Aston were determined to win this race and that meant beating Archie who had been dominating British sports car races all year with the Lister-Jaguar. Obviously our chances of achieving this goal were greater now that we were racing the DBR2, but it must be remembered that this 3.7-litre car with the Lagonda multi-tubular chassis was less powerful than the Lister and was also a heavier and much more substantially built car primarily intended for long-distance racing. The lightweight Lister was built specifically for British 'sprint' races and its record in endurance racing was to prove pretty dismal. Another shortcoming of the DBR2 was its lack of development testing, the result of the heavy racing programme with the DBR1. It was a very pleasant car to drive, with the much easier and more reliable five-speed gearbox in unit with the engine, and it was possible to turn in really quick laps without feeling the car was being pushed too hard. With the later and much more powerful 4.2-

At the September 1957 Silverstone meeting with the 3.7-litre DBR2. I managed to beat Archie. The angle of the Lister's front wheels in this photograph taken at Copse shows just how hard Archie used to try (T. C. March).

litre engine it was capable of beating almost anything and this should have been developed much earlier.

I was fastest in practice by 0.6 sec, but that did not mean much as Archie could always be relied on to find that extra something in the race. I was away first at the Le Mans start, with Brooks right behind me and Archie in third place, but by the fourth lap Archie had pushed through to the front. I was confident that I could go faster than in practice, although my car was a little over-geared and a lower axle ratio should have been fitted after practice – I was using only third and fourth gears in the five-speed 'box and at a couple of points round the circuit was lifting off slightly rather than wasting time changing up into fifth and down again. This was a situation that I hated because of the temptation to over-rev. It was quite a race. I pressed the Lister very hard and I passed Archie going into Stowe on the fifth lap. I went on to win by a margin of two seconds, having set a new sports car lap record of 98.48 mph (1 min 47 sec). My average speed of 96.0 mph was the fastest ever recorded in a British sports car race. Noel Cunningham-Reid finished third, Brooks fourth and Lewis-Evans sixth. It was a day for celebration.

1958

In December 1957 we took a DBR1 to Monza for testing in the hope that the weather would prove more favourable than English weather usually is at that time of year. The main purpose of the test was to do a full 24 hours' run on the combined five-speed gearbox and final drive in anticipation of the Sebring race in March. Reg Parnell was in charge and the drivers were Masten Gregory and myself. We were there for nearly a week, but hit a patch of bad weather with rain and fog. At one stage we were having to lap steadily with road cars to clear snow before we started testing. We then drove at racing speeds on the narrow strip which we had cleared. We never did complete a full 24 hours' run and all our testing was in cold weather. The heat of Sebring in March soon revealed the transmission shortcomings that had remained undiscovered at Monza!

A major change for 1958 – and one, of course, that favoured Aston Martin – was the introduction of a 3-litre capacity limit in World Championship Sports Car racing. By this time Maserati had withdrawn from racing for financial reasons, the 3-litre version of the Jaguar engine proved unreliable and racing turned into a duel between Aston Martin and Ferrari with the V-12 'Testa Rossa' cars. Stirling Moss was once again a member of the team, the other regulars were Brooks and myself and other drivers were brought into the team for various races. For 1958 the DBR1 had a new cylinder head, first tried in 1957 at Spa, with the valves at an angle of 95 degrees and an increased power output of 255 bhp at 6,000 rpm. A slightly larger bore 2,992 cc (84 × 90 mm) engine was adopted at the Tourist Trophy.

At Sebring two DBR1s were entered for Moss/Brooks and myself/Shelby. The Astons were quick in practice – Stirling was fastest of all, setting a new unofficial lap record of 91.99 mph – and our chances of success seemed very good indeed. As was the usual Aston plan, Stirling went out to break up the opposition, while Carroll and I held back, lapping consistently in accordance with John's target time.

After about three hours' racing I was in third place when I handed over to Carroll who joined the race after a fairly lengthy pit stop while all four tyres were changed. At this stage in the race everything looked rosy for the Aston team. Not long afterwards Shelby came into the pits, complaining of gearbox trouble; the mechanics worked on the car and he rejoined the race, but was soon back to report that he could get no gears at all. The problem was in fact caused by a broken chassis and the car was retired. The Moss/Brooks DBR1 stayed in the lead until a pit stop, dropped back to second place and Stirling carried on making up lost ground – despite the bonnet blowing off, breaking the windscreen and chipping his visor – until the gearbox went after 90 laps. It was a great shame because this was a race that Aston could have won. Ferraris took the first two places.

At Aintree on April 19 both Tony Brooks and I were entered with DBR2s fitted with enlarged 3,910 cc engines. The strongest opposition came from Archie with the works Lister-Jaguar and that very quick sports-car driver Masten Gregory, entered with a Lister by Ecurie Ecosse, who took the lead at the start. I managed to pass Masten and I chased after Archie, while Tony went on tangling with Gregory until the final drive started to give trouble and he retired the DBR2. In my chase of Archie I set a new lap record of 2 min 3.6 sec (87.38 mph), but I never quite managed to catch him because of lapping slower traffic. If I had been able to have a clear run right from the start, the result *might* have been different. Masten Gregory finished third despite an enormous spin at Tatts.

There was a strong entry of Astons at the *Daily Express* Silverstone meeting in May, with DBR2s driven by Brooks and myself, while Stirling Moss had chosen to drive an experimental car based on the DBR1 but designated the

DBR3 and powered by a DB4 engine reduced to 2,992 cc (92 × 75 mm). The opposition included Archie and Gregory with Listers, and Ferrari sent an experimental 3-litre V-6 car for Mike Hawthorn to drive. Practice was dominated by the Listers, for Archie lapped in 1 min 43 sec and Gregory recorded 1 min 44.6 sec, while Stirling lapped the DBR3 in 1 min 45 sec. Of the DBR2 drivers Tony Brooks was faster in 1 min 46.2 sec, and I recorded 1 min 46.6 sec. In the race we simply could not stay with the Listers and Mike passed me so that the finishing order was Gregory, Scott-Brown, Hawthorn and myself fourth ahead of Tony Brooks. It was a poor day for Aston Martin.

On the day of the Spa race, May 18, when two DBR2s driven by Shelby and Frère faced the Listers of Scott-Brown and Gregory, I was competing with a Cooper in the Monaco Grand Prix. Archie was chasing Gregory in the damp when he lost control and crashed – the works Lister burst into flames and poor Archie suffered the most horrific burns which proved fatal. I believe that Ecurie Ecosse in terms of power had the slight edge, as Wilkie was an expert in engine development with years of Jaguar experience, and Archie was trying too hard to make up the difference. Archie was consistently brilliant on British circuits and had marvellous car control, but, as I have mentioned, an accident at Spa could very well prove fatal. He was a great sportsman who would never baulk you, he was completely trustworthy to race against and he lived for his motor racing. Archie and I had been fighting our duels since 1954 and I felt his death more than with any other driver with the possible exception of Peter Collins. If you motor race you must accept that it is a dangerous sport, and the intelligent driver knows that he cannot expect to go through a career of motor racing without a brush or two with death. Archie was one of those unfortunate drivers who did not have luck on his side and, believe me, that is all that it is.

The Nürburgring 1000 Kms race provided a magnificent victory for Stirling Moss and Aston Martin. Stirling drove for 36 of the 44 laps, leaving his co-driver, Jack Brabham, with a mere eight laps to cover and, apart from a short time while Jack was at the wheel, led throughout. I co-drove with Carroll Shelby and we had a thoroughly miserable race. I was in fifth place on the first lap and retired with gearbox trouble at the end of the second lap. The other DBR1 at this race was driven by Brooks/Lewis-Evans and was in fourth place two laps from the finish when Tony went off the road after tangling with a saloon car entry.

It seemed that, unlike other regular team members, I was always swapping co-drivers and I am not sure that I know why. At Le Mans I was partnered with Stuart Lewis-Evans who was six or seven inches shorter than me and we only managed to share the same seating position with considerable discomfort. Stuart never shaped up as an Aston Martin driver and it was inexplicable that he was so fast with the Vanwall Formula One car, yet could not turn in competitive lap times with the DBR1. The other DBR1s were driven by Moss/Brabham and Brooks/Trintignant.

Le Mans was another disastrous race for Aston Martin as Moss/Brabham were out after only 30 laps because of a broken con-rod and we survived only until the fifth hour of the race when in eighth place Stuart crashed at the corner after the pits. The Brooks/Trintignant DBR1 retired because of gearbox failure and the sole Aston finisher was the private DB3S of the Whitehead brothers which took a fine second place behind the Ferrari of Gendebien/Phil Hill.

There were no Ferraris entered in the Tourist Trophy at Goodwood on September 13 and the opposition to the Aston Martin DBR1s came only from the Listers and the Jaguar D-types. Three DBR1s were entered for Moss/ Brooks, Shelby/Lewis-Evans and myself/Brabham. The best practice times were recorded by Stirling in 1 min 32 sec, myself in 1 min 32.2 sec and Brooks in 1 min 33.2 sec. Ivor Bueb with a works Lister-Jaguar also recorded 1 min 33.2 sec. Stirling took the lead, I was in second place trying to maintain contact with him. While I was overtaking Greenall's Lotus at Madgwick, the two cars collided and I spun; Greenall spun in trying to avoid me, as did Bueb who went off the road. Both Bueb's Lister and the Lotus were out of the race, but I was able to rejoin after a long pit stop, very furious with myself. We eventually moved back into second place and the Aston team took first three places in the order Moss/Brooks, myself/Brabham and Shelby/Lewis-Evans in a race that the Aston team had thoroughly buttoned up. Aston Martin finished second in the Sports Car World Championship with 18 points to the 32 of Ferrari.

I drove for Aston Martin in one more race in 1958. Joe Lubin, who had bought the two 3.9-litre DBR2s and was racing them in the United States, asked John Wyer to send over a DBR1 to compete in the United States Grand Prix for Sports Cars held at Riverside Raceway, California, on October 11. The DBR1 was shipped out on the Queen Mary, while I flew over. The opposition included two of the two 5.5-litre Scrabs with Chevrolet engines, Phil Hill with a new 4.1-litre Ferrari, Dan Gurney with a 4.9-litre Ferrari and several other very competitive Ferraris and Jaguars. Joe Lubin was expecting great things from the DBR1, but was to be sadly disappointed. I tried terribly hard with the car and I did well to qualify eighth fastest. The race was run in appallingly hot

In 1958 I drove a DBR1 in the United States Sports Car Grand Prix. Before the race I was involved in a public relations exercise on behalf of the David Brown Group. However this resulted in an Aston Martin confidential racing report to the effect that my socialising adversely affected my driving (Foto-Treichler).

conditions and the fuel of the DBR1 was vapourising, a problem that the locals solved by using dry ice for cooling. Throughout the 203-mile race the DBR1 was misfiring, hesitating all along the straight; I spun the car while trying to stay with Jean Behra's Porsche and finished sixth. Much later I read an official Aston Martin confidential report that I had not given of my best in this race because I had spent too much time socialising. It is true that Lubin had laid on a wonderful round of parties, but I had put everything into the race and that report was not justifiable.

1959

Because of Aston Martin's preoccupation with the Formula One cars, it was originally intended to compete with the DBR1s at Le Mans only in 1959. In fact the programme expanded considerably and I drove the cars in three races.

A single car for me and Carroll Shelby was sent to Sebring and this was only because the organisers were prepared to meet all expenses of the team. I was first away at the Le Mans start, but Gurney (works Ferrari) passed me on the second lap and I let him go, as I was driving to strict target lap times. Behra's Ferrari also passed me and then I was challenged by Pedro Rodriguez (Ferrari), and I must admit that I could not resist involving myself in a fight. We were battling all the way round the circuit and I remember that we were kicking up so much dust past the pits that the organisers moved the straw bales back to give us more road. The dice ended when Pedro went off the road, damaged his car and had to stop at the pits for repairs. Soon I had problems with the DBR1; it developed electrical trouble and an oil leak. By the time I handed the car over to Shelby we were well down the field, and it was not long before Carroll was back in the pits waving the gear-lever which had broken off. The car was withdrawn. The winners were Hill/Gendebien with a Ferrari 'Testa Rossa'. Again Aston sent a single car for Moss/Fairman to the Nürburgring 1000 Kms race and they scored an Aston hat-trick with a fine win; once again Stirling did nearly all the driving.

For Le Mans, the one race which Aston had originally planned to do, there was a full team of three cars driven by Moss/Fairman, myself/Shelby and Trintignant/Frère. A lot of development work had been carried out on the cars, all of which had slightly modified rear bodywork with spats over the rear wheels, and extensive testing had ensured that the gearboxes, if still not pleasant to use, would prove reliable. The Moss/Fairman car was fitted with a slightly more powerful engine.

We kept down the amount of practice and on the Wednesday I covered only seven laps with a best time of 4 min 12 sec which was a quick and competitive time. Shelby did ten laps and recorded a best time of 4 min 21 sec. Moss was the fastest of the Aston drivers with a lap in 4 min 11 sec and he had covered 20 laps. These times are from the official Aston Martin records. Shelby and I were so satisfied that we decided not to practise at all on the Thursday to save the car.

Although the Ferraris were slightly faster than the DBR1s, it seemed that Aston Martin had a really good chance of winning the race. For my own part I knew that Carroll and I had the right mental approach for winning and I discussed with Carroll how we should drive: we agreed to put all our effort into late braking and fast cornering so as to save the engine and gearbox as much as possible. Instead of taking the car up to 5,700/5,800 rpm in the gears we would change at 5,400/5,500 rpm and try not to make snatch changes. There were two corners on the course where it was desirable to use first gear, Mulsanne and Arnage, but I was anxious that we should not use first gear at all. To take the corners in second, especially with a full tank, it was necessary to use a very light throttle out of the corner – if you booted the car, then the engine would splutter. In fact, driving smoothly was probably as quick as booting the car out of the corner and letting it go sideways! The result of our confidence was that Carroll and I were able to stay at the hotel while everyone else was at the circuit, and play endless games of gin rummy.

I started the race and although I was away quite quickly, I was determined to keep out of the initial 'Grand Prix' and at the end of the first hour was in eighth place. I was driving at about 4–5 seconds faster than my target lap time, but the pits were not giving me any 'slow' signals and by the end of the second hour I

Left *Carroll and I playing the inevitable gin rummy. Joakim Bonnier is taking a keen interest in Carroll's cards – all eleven of them!* (Yves Debraine, Roy Salvadori collection).

Below *Just before the start, Le Mans, 1959* (Roy Salvadori collection).

Below right *Being passed by Behra's Ferrari 'Testa Rossa' during the opening laps of the 1959 Le Mans race and remembering my instructions not to get involved in the first 'two-hour Grand Prix'.* (Roy Klemantaski).

was fifth. I got into a tussle with Innes Ireland (Ecurie Ecosse D-type) which was good clean fun, but managed to exercise restraint and kept the car within the intended rev limits. Stirling had been fighting it out with the Ferraris and was leading the race, although the car lost ground while Fairman was at the wheel, and shortly after Stirling took over again he brought the car into the pits to retire with engine failure. Stirling had done a magnificent job as pacemaker for the team and had probably lured the Ferrari team into over-stressing their cars. The leading 'Testa Rossa' of Behra/Gurney had lost its oil pressure and was lapping slower and slower; it made several pit stops, and a little after six hours' racing I moved up into the lead, ahead of Ferraris driven by Gendebien/Hill and Behra/Gurney.

We held the lead for about four hours until our DBR1 developed a rear-end vibration and I stopped at the pits for the problem to be investigated by the mechanics. They could find nothing wrong and I was told to continue. I did another two laps, came back in again and was told to carry on for another five laps until the car could under the strict race regulations be refuelled. The vibration was now so bad that I thought the rear end was about to fall off and I lapped at a crawl. When I finally stopped to refuel, the car was jacked up and Reg Parnell got underneath and discovered that the offside rear tyre had been damaged, probably by a bit of metal dropped by another car and this had cut away part of the tread. In all we must have lost 12–15 minutes during these laps.

Shelby took over after the pit stop, by which time our DBR1 was in second place, three laps behind Gendebien/Hill and two laps ahead of the other Aston driven by Trintignant/Frère. Reg criticised me fiercely on the grounds that I should have known that the problem was a tyre. This upset me terribly because I had been driving very quickly but sensibly, we had never had trouble with the Avon tyres which were run at very high pressures (50 lb psi at the front and 55 at the rear) and it had seemed that the vibration was much more likely to be associated with the transmission which was always the weakness of the DBR1. I suppose that Reg was merely venting his bad temper because we had lost the lead and reflecting the very tense atmosphere in the Aston Martin pit. It was John Wyer who talked to me at length, calming me down and saying, 'Roy, we don't want you and Reg upset – everybody's a little heated at the moment, so

just let things calm down and the race will go right. There's no need for either of you to lose confidence.' He continued, 'The race is far from over, have patience and you'll get yourself first on the leader-board yet.' He added that the Ferraris were dropping out like flies, there was no reason to suppose that the race leader, the Phil Hill/Gendebien car, was going to be any different and the plan should be to keep the maximum pressure on the Ferrari. While John helped enormously, I was still rather hurt by Reg Parnell's lack of confidence in me.

When I took over the car again I started to motor fast to make up lost ground, but all the time I was trying hard to conserve the car, getting down to very late braking points that I would not have thought feasible, changing gear as smoothly as possible, keeping the revs down and gradually, but consistently, whittling down the lead of the Ferrari by one to three seconds a lap. Even so, there was no way that we were going to make up the lost three laps on the Ferrari which was still being driven very hard. We did close up to within just over a lap when at 11:00 am on the Sunday morning we had the luckiest possible break. The Ferrari came into the pits steaming, did another lap and was retired soon afterwards. We were back in the lead with Trintignant/Frère second.

I eased back and began to imagine all the moans and groans from the engine and the whines from the transmission, and this worried me a great deal. I tried to make myself forget all the noises, real and imaginary, and we carried on to score what was probably Aston's greatest victory. With cars in first and second places I think that we could have risked keeping up the speed and if we had, we would have won the Index of Performance as well. In all I drove for the maximum permitted under the Race Regulations. Before the race Carroll had suffered from a stomach bug and had been very sick so we were always worried whether he would last the distance. Stirling made the fastest Aston lap time in the race in 4 min 3.0 sec and I was only about a second and a half slower – we were much faster than the rest of our team. I had burnt my right foot very badly from the heat of the exhaust of the DBR1 which for this race had been re-routed under the car and overheated the footwell (I still have the scars) and I was so tired that all I wanted to do was to sleep, so I deliberately missed the presentation at the circuit. It was all very much of an anti-climax.

Originally Aston Martin had no intention of competing in the Tourist Trophy at Goodwood in September, but with victories at the Nürburgring and Le Mans the team was poised for victory in the Sports Car World Championship and on points Aston, Ferrari and Porsche were all pretty well level-pegging. Three cars were entered, but after the first day's practice it was decided that I should partner Stirling as John Wyer had decided to put the two fastest drivers together and the other DBR1s were driven by Shelby/Fairman and Frère/Trintignant. At this race all the cars were fitted with built-in jacks operated by compressed air. Aston Martin brought along a spare car fitted with a Maserati gearbox which we all preferred to the normal David Brown unit. We all tried this and set faster lap times than with the cars having the normal gearbox, but as we had no race experience with this car, it was not used.

Ferrari had sent a trio of 'Testa Rossas' to be driven by Brooks/Gurney,

Right *We returned to England by Silver City Airways, completely exhausted after Le Mans* (Roy Salvadori collection).

Below *With Reg Parnell before the Tourist Trophy at Goodwood in 1959* (Roy Salvadori collection).

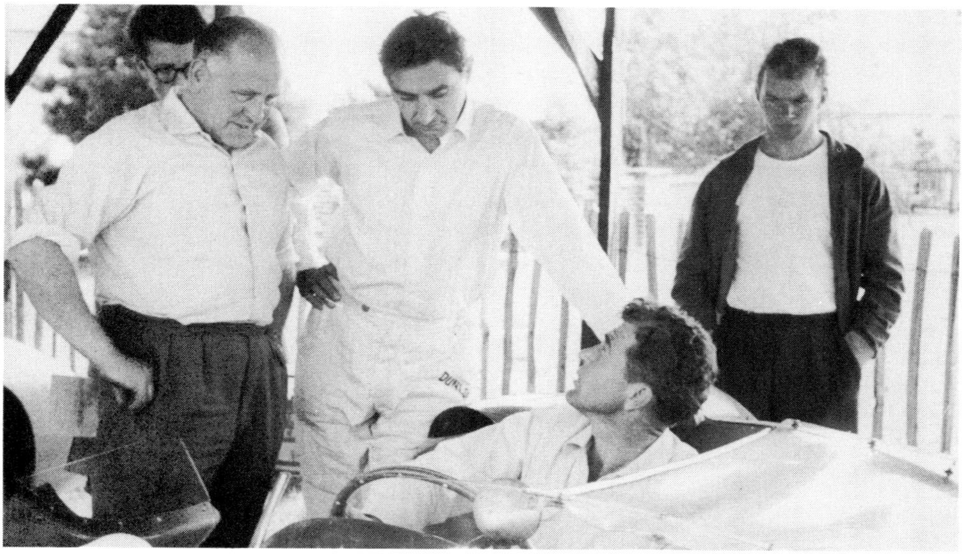

Cabianca/Gendebien and Allison/Phil Hill, but in fact the team swapped drivers a lot during the race so these pairings did not mean very much. There was also a strong Porsche entry. Practice and the race were tense because even if an Aston won, Ferrari could still clinch the World Championship provided they finished second. Stirling was fastest in practice in 1 min 31.1 sec, I was slower in 1 min 32.6 sec and Dan Gurney turned in the best Ferrari lap, second fastest, of 1 min 32.0 sec. The Ferraris were not handling very well at Goodwood and we knew that we should have the legs of them in the race. I was particularly confident because I was co-driving with Stirling and Goodwood was a circuit on which I always went well.

Stirling took the first spell at the wheel and when he handed over to me after

47 laps, he had a substantial lead. I covered the same number of laps, building up a lead of over three minutes from team-mates Shelby/Fairman, and it was beginning to look as though Aston Martin had the race in the bag. When I came into the pits, I was a little slow in getting out of the car as I wanted to leave it in first gear all ready for Stirling. As I climbed out I felt what seemed like water on my back – in fact it was fuel gushing out of the refuelling pipe – and suddenly the whole car was alight. Although I am not particularly athletic, I was out of the car like lightning with my overalls on fire; I jumped high in the air and over the head of the mechanic who was taking off the left-hand front wheel, kicking him in the ear as I passed him, rolled on to the grass that divided the pits from the circuit and rolled down the strip to try to get the flames out. Fortunately a very alert St John's ambulanceman immediately took off his overcoat and put it round me, extinguishing most of the flames. However, my hand was still alight, so he wrapped his cap round my hand to put out the flames. I was taken to the first-aid tent where my burns were treated and then made my way back to the pits where I hoped to carry on driving the Shelby/Frère car. Stirling had already taken this over and was going so well that there was no need for me to partner him even if Reg Parnell had allowed me to. Whilst I have a terrible fear of fire, the full implications of the situation did not dawn on me at the time and it is only now when I see photographs of the flare-up that I realise just how lucky I was. There was simply no time to be scared.

Stirling went on to win the race by a clear lap from the Porsche of von Trips/Bonnier and clinched the World Championship for Aston Martin with a total of 24 points to the 18 of Ferrari. The sole surviving Ferrari, shared by

Left *The ill-fated pit stop in the 1959 Tourist Trophy. The fuel can be seen pouring out of the re-fuelling pipe and within moments the car was ablaze* (Motor Sport).

Right *After the Goodwood fire, wondering whether I would be allowed to drive again in the race* (Roy Salvadori collection).

Brooks, Gendebien, Cabianca and Allison finished third ahead of the other Aston of Trintignant/Frère. The Tourist Trophy proved a magnificent climax to Aston's last season in sports car racing, and at long last the team had fulfilled David Brown's two great ambitions – to win Le Mans and win the Championship. While the drivers were delighted with their contribution to the team's success, I know that we all realised that we owed an immense debt to David Brown, John Wyer and Reg Parnell, who supplied the expertise, the organisation and the management (together with a superb team of mechanics) that made victory possible. This was the genuine feeling of the drivers who believed that the Aston Martin team was something special.

Although the works withdrew from sports car racing, it was not the end of my career with the DBR1, for the team cars were sold to private owners and I drove them again at Le Mans.

Chapter 9

Grand Prix racing with Aston Martin, 1959–60

I have described in Chapter 7 how it was originally intended that both Jack Brabham and I should join Aston Martin's Grand Prix team in 1959. When Jack decided to stay with Cooper, Reg Parnell had to start looking for another driver for the Aston Martin Formula One team; the very experienced Carroll Shelby, who was already a member of the Aston Martin Sports Car team and had gained Formula One experience with Maseratis in 1958, was a natural choice.

The first DBR4/250 Formula One car had been built in 1957 and tested by Tony Brooks at MIRA in December of that year. It was untested and unraced throughout 1958 because Aston Martin had wanted to concentrate all their efforts on the Sports Car Championship. The DBR4 could have been a race-winner in 1958, probably capable of beating that year's front-engined Ferraris and Vanwalls, and it was competitive in the early part of 1959, but rapidly lost ground as the Coopers and other cars were developed during the season.

In chassis and engine design the DBR4 was derived from the DBR1 sports/racing car. It was based on a multi-tubular space-frame, at first with the wishbone and longitudinal torsion bar front suspension used on the experimental DBR3 raced by Moss at Silverstone in 1958, but wishbone and coil spring front suspension was substituted by the time the car was first raced. At the rear there was a de Dion rear axle suspended on longitudinal torsion bars, basically the same arrangement as on the DBR1. The engine was a 2,493 cc (83 × 76.8 mm) version of the DBR1 running on three twin-choke Weber carburettors and developing 250 bhp at 7,800 rpm. Transmission was by the same CG537 combined gearbox and final drive unit as fitted to the DBR1. In appearance the DBR4 was superb, with sleek, purposeful lines.

During the early part of the year we tested the cars extensively, mainly at Goodwood, and I soon found that it was an absolutely fabulous car to drive, perfectly balanced and with roadholding to match any of its rivals. It drifted beautifully and it had superb brakes. As we were soon to learn, its shortcomings were its power deficiency compared to its front-engined rivals such as the Ferraris, which in 1959 were developing 285 bhp, and its much greater weight compared with the Coopers and Lotus. In addition it was plagued by bearing troubles that took most of the season to cure, and as a result throughout 1959 we were limited to around 7,250 rpm, which made the cars even less competitive.

Even so, we went to our first race of the year, the *Daily Express* Trophy at

Silverstone, in an optimistic mood and our performance proved good enough to mislead us as to our prospects for the rest of the year. Fastest in practice was Stirling Moss with the pale green British Racing Partnership-entered BRM in 1 min 39.2 sec (Stirling had struck his own deal with Alfred Owen to run a BRM outside the works team), and alongside him was Tony Brooks (works Ferrari) in 1 min 40.0 sec. I was third fastest in 1 min 40.4 sec, a time matched by Jack Brabham with the works 2.5-litre Cooper. Carroll was on the second row of the grid with a time of 1 min 41.8 sec.

Jack Brabham led right from the start of the race, followed by Moss, myself and Shelby. Stirling took the lead on the second lap, but spun off at Copse only three laps later when he lost his front brakes (it seemed that nothing changed with BRM). I chased after Jack, setting fastest lap, but as the race progressed I gradually lost ground to the Cooper and at the finish I was just over 17 seconds behind. Carroll fell back to hold a steady sixth place until his DBR4 broke a con-rod shortly before the finish.

Below *On the starting grid for the debut of the Aston Martin DBR4 at the 1959* Daily Express *Trophy at Silverstone* (Roy Salvadori collection).
Bottom *The DBR4 went really well at Silverstone and I took an excellent second place behind Jack Brabham's Cooper-Climax* (T. C. March).

It was a most encouraging first appearance for the DBR4 and *Autosport* noted, 'Greatest talking point after the BRDC International Trophy meeting at Silverstone on Saturday was the outstandingly good performance of the new Formula One Aston Martins – one of the most encouraging debuts ever made by a British Grand Prix contender. Salvadori's car was consistently reliable, showing up even better in the race than it had during practice, and equalling the circuit lap record of 1 min 40 sec (105.37 mph). The second car, driven by Carroll Shelby, was said to have lost top gear early in the race. Nevertheless, it kept with the leaders until only a lap from the end, when the engine failed after 150 miles of in-the-gears-racing. Both cars were impressively steady, although Jack Brabham's winning Cooper was a match for Salvadori's car in sheer speed.'

Our first World Championship race (and the first of the European season) was the Dutch Grand Prix at Zandvoort on May 31. It was now that reality struck and in practice the cars proved disappointingly slow. Even with the benefit of hindsight it is difficult to explain why the cars had gone so well at Silverstone! Joakim Bonnier (BRM) and Jack Brabham recorded joint fastest time of 1 min 36.0 sec, while Shelby's time of 1 min 38.5 sec put him on the fourth row of the grid, and after mechanical troubles throughout practice I was on the fifth row with a time of 1 min 39.7 sec. I was out of the race after only four laps and Carrol lasted only another 22 laps before he too retired. In both cases the cause was bearing failure. We were bitterly disappointed. The race was won by Joakim Bonnier, scoring BRM's first-ever World Championship race victory.

Aston Martin did not race the Formula One cars again until the British Grand Prix at Aintree on July 18. The team had carried out a lot of development work, but we were still not sure that the bearing trouble had been finally cured. Reg Parnell told us not to worry about the bearings in practice and to concentrate on recording good times. On the Friday I had been bedding in the brakes and then decided that I would try for a really quick lap. The car felt superb and I turned in a lap of 1 min 58.0 sec which was joint fastest with Jack Brabham (Cooper). Carroll Shelby's 1 min 59.6 sec was sixth fastest.

Just before the start of the race Reg told us that we would find that the odd drop of fuel would be splashed around with the cars running on full tanks. We had not tried the cars in practice with full tanks – a mistake – so we were not quite sure what to expect. Neither Carroll nor I made a good start (the DBR4 was very slow off the line with full tanks) and I soon found that I was being saturated by fuel. I could not believe that it was merely spitting from the overflow and I thought that the tank had split. Because of the same worry Carroll stopped at the pits at the end of lap two and I stopped at the end of lap three. While the mechanics checked the car, Reg was shouting at me, 'You bloody fool – I told you that the fuel was going to seep.' Although I was back in the race within a minute, I was now way down the field and out of touch with the leaders. I accepted Reg's explanation, but the car continued to splash fuel for lap after lap, I was sitting in a pool of petrol and my overalls were soaking. The car was going really well, the brakes were superb and even though the Aston could not match the acceleration of the lighter cars, I was soon making up lost ground.

I caught up Graham Hill (Lotus) in eighth place and although he was faster than me out of corners, I was braking much later and he was holding me up into corners. I nudged and bumped the tail of the Lotus a couple of times just to remind Graham that I was still around, but it took me five laps to get past. I then caught Masten Gregory's works Cooper and had the same trouble in getting past him. Once I was past, I showed just how much quicker I was by opening up a good advantage. I then spun at Anchor Crossing and had to start all over again catching the Cooper. I re-passed Gregory shortly before the finish to take sixth place behind Brabham (works Cooper), Moss (BRM), McLaren (works Cooper), Schell (BRM) and Trintignant (Walker-entered Cooper). But for the pit stop I would have finished much higher up the field. Shelby retired because of magneto failure.

Of my drive with the DBR4 at Aintree *Sporting Motorist* commented, 'In watching the progression of the Aston Martin it was truly remarkable to see its tremendous braking power and stable cornering. Indeed had its acceleration matched its deceleration there would have been no holding the new Feltham bolide. On lap 14, for instance, Salvadori lapped a slower car and passed Hill's Lotus from being some 20 yards behind both on the approach to Tatts Corner. As they accelerated away Hill was able to re-pass the Aston Martin quite comfortably.' In my view this is a pretty fair summary of the Aston's superb brakes and lack of acceleration. Aintree was one of my most satisfactory outings with the DBR4.

We next raced the DBR4s in the Portuguese Grand Prix held on the Monsanto circuit at Lisbon on August 23. In practice the best I could manage was 12th fastest and Shelby was 13th fastest so we were near the back of the starting grid. It was much the same story in the race which was dominated by Moss (Cooper-Climax). I finished sixth and Shelby was eighth. The writing was

This photograph of the DBR4 in the 1959 Italian Grand Prix shows off the superb lines of the Aston Martin Formula One contender (Fotocars).

I retired at Monza because of valve trouble with the DBR4 (Motor Sport).

on the wall. The day of the conventional, front-engined Grand Prix car was over and the Coopers were likely to prove increasingly dominant.

Our problems continued in the Italian Grand Prix at Monza, where I drove a new car, DBR4/3, with the centre-section of the body integral with the chassis and with a new one-piece de Dion tube. I was not in very good shape because I was still suffering pain from the burns on my face, my right wrist and arm sustained during the Goodwood fire. In practice I lapped in 1 min 44.7 sec, 17th fastest, but good by Aston standards on such a fast circuit and I was pleased with my performance. Shelby lapped in 1 min 46.4 sec. In the race I went well, working my way up to seventh place and with good prospects of improving my position when the engine broke a valve. Shelby finished tenth.

Aston Martin were not simply running for starting and prize money and throughout 1959 had been content to miss races so as to concentrate on development. Although these efforts had come to nothing the team planned a much lighter and more compact car for 1960; more power was to be extracted from the engine and the bearing problem had been cured. As events were to prove, the biggest mistake was to be the retention of the front engine when both BRM and Lotus were following Cooper's example and adopting a rear-engine layout.

The 1960 car, known as the DBR5, featured a much lighter, multi-tubular space-frame chassis. Aston had reverted to longitudinal torsion bar front suspension and at the rear there was a one-piece de Dion tube running in front of the gearbox. The team adopted a much lighter Maserati gearbox and final drive unit in place of the David Brown unit and the engine had been modified. There was a new cylinder head with the valves at an angle of 80 degrees and in this form the engine developed 260 bhp at 7,500 rpm. However, as John Wyer has recounted in *Racing With The David Brown Aston Martins*, because of a design fault the engine misfired at part-throttle openings on the Weber 50 DCO carburettors which it was intended to use, and Lucas fuel injection was hurriedly substituted. This resulted in a reduction in power to 244 bhp which was less than we were getting in 1959.

For 1960 the team was joined by that very charming and experienced French driver, Maurice Trintignant. It was almost taken for granted that I would stay with Aston Martin and I certainly did not contemplate leaving the team. We all had our doubts about the outcome of the 1960 season, but if the technical developments worked out, there was cause for some optimism. I knew that we were not on to a winner, but the cars should have proved fairly competitive. It was a sad disappointment that they turned out to be even slower than the 1959 cars and unfortunately there was no opportunity for a back-to-back comparison – Reg had sold the first two 1959 cars to buyers in Australia.

Our first outing was at the *Daily Express* Trophy at Silverstone where I was entered with DBR5/2 on carburettors and Trintignant drove DBR5/1 on fuel injection. At the start of practice, before the Astons had even turned a wheel, Stirling Moss was going through the pit lane with the Rob Walker-entered Cooper when he lost control on a large puddle and slid into the side of my DBR5 which was parked in front of the Aston Martin pit. My car was far too badly damaged to be repaired in time to run in the race and back at Feltham the engine and gearbox were hastily transferred to DBR4/3. The replacement car arrived late on the Friday and although I had very little time for practice which was held in the wet, I did get in a few laps and recorded 1 min 57.6 sec (10th fastest). Moss was fastest with a Walker-entered Cooper and alongside him was Joakim Bonnier (BRM). Reg Parnell asked the BRDC if they would permit a further timed practice session and they agreed, provided that all entrants signed their consent. I trailed along the pits with a slip of paper, asking everyone to sign, and they all agreed with the exception of Raymond Mays and Rob Walker. They were not willing to run their cars in another timed practice session and risk losing their first and second places on the grid.

I am not sure that it would have made any difference because my car developed a misfire and I retired after only four laps. Trintignant finished tenth. It is perhaps a little ironic, in view of the attitude of both Ray and Rob, that Stirling and Bonnier retired in the race. Maybe they would have found the solution to their problems with extra practice! The winner was Innes Ireland, scoring a superb first victory with the new rear-engined Lotus 18.

A sad happening at Silverstone had been the death during Friday's practice of Harry Schell who had hit the retaining wall at Abbey Curve and had been thrown out of the car. Harry Schell was the number one character in motor racing; he spoke many languages, he was tall and good-looking, he had tremendous wit and charm. He was a very inconsistent driver but on occasions his driving would hit tremendous form, such as at Reims in 1956. On this occasion he was lapping his Vanwall faster than Mike Hawthorn and when Harry retired, Mike was called in so that Harry could resume the battle with the Ferraris. Harry's death was a tragic loss to motor racing.

Aston Martin entered only a single car for me at the Dutch Grand Prix at Zandvoort. It was running on fuel injection and it was very slow. Stirling had a drive with the car during practice, but was unimpressed – this did nothing to restore my confidence. Only 20 starters were allowed and of these only the fastest 15 received starting money. My fastest lap of 1 min 37.8 sec was good enough to scrape in on the back of the grid, but out of the money. There seemed to be no point in racing such an uncompetitive car and we all returned to England.

Aston Martin were still struggling to make the DBR5 race-worthy and we did not run again until the British Grand Prix at Silverstone in July. Both cars were back on twin-choke Weber carburettors and my car, DBR5/2, was fitted with torsion bar independent rear suspension. My car handled atrociously and although Silverstone was a circuit which I really liked and I tried very hard, my best lap of 1 min 39.4 sec was only 13th fastest. Trintignant could do no better than 1 min 43.8 sec. I never rose above 12th place in the race, I spent a long time in the pits while the mechanics tried to sort out the steering and I retired after 45 laps. Trintignant finished 11th.

It was only too obvious that the Aston Martin development programme was not making any real progress. There was talk of building a new rear-engined car, but it came to nothing and the team decided to withdraw from racing altogether. Although I drove a Cooper-Climax for Tommy Atkins in non-Championship races, Aston Martin's withdrawal disrupted my Formula One season. I had backed the wrong horse, but I enjoyed racing with the team so much that I did not regret my two seasons with the Aston Martin Formula One car too much.

Handling problems caused my retirement with the fully independently sprung DBR5 in the 1960 British Grand Prix at Silverstone. This was the last appearance of a works Aston Martin Formula One car (T. C. March).

Chapter 10

Racing for private owners, 1959–60

Introduction by John Coombs, Racing Entrant

'It is strange the way the passage of time tends to distort one's views. We now seem to accept as normal that a racing driver specialises in one particular class or formula of racing. This was certainly not the case in the 1950s and 1960s. "Versatility" is the word I think of first with regard to Roy Salvadori. It was not unusual for a racing driver of that era to drive a number of different cars in different classes during a season, but I can't think of any one else who drove so many with such wide-ranging success.

'Roy and I met in 1952 at Thruxton. We were introduced by John Young, a mutual friend, who was acting as Roy's mechanic at the time. We had both won our respective races, Roy in a sports car and myself in a Formula Three Cooper. My reward was a small silver trophy and a cheque for £5. How things have changed! This was the beginning of a strong friendship both on and off the track. Little did I realise at that time that Roy was going to be not just one of my closest friends, but the most successful of my drivers in later years.

'Unwittingly I was responsible for Roy's first works drive. I was invited to test drive at Snetterton for the Connaught Formula Two team. The late Rodney Clarke, Managing Director, also asked if I could recommend anyone else. I suggested Roy. He had little problem in being the fastest of six selected drivers and as a result joined the works team. Equally as unwittingly, Roy was responsible for my decision to give up the role of racing driver and become an entrant. During a test session at Goodwood in identical cars I realised I couldn't stay in front of a driver of his calibre. From 1958 to 1973 I ran teams of sports, saloon and Formula Two cars. Out of 22 drivers, including 12 Grand Prix winners and three World Champions, Roy was the most successful of my drivers in terms of wins.

'Roy's first drive for me was in a 1½-litre Lotus at Goodwood in 1957. We soon decided we wanted to win races rather than classes. He suggested that I invested in a Cooper Monaco for 1959. We bought the car, but minus an engine. We wanted the most powerful engine we could fit in. At that time the most obvious decision would have been a 2-litre Coventry Climax. However, there was a 2½-litre Maserati which was proving successful and we managed to obtain one.

'Roy, a true professional, arrived punctually and eager to get started. It's an indication of my enthusiasm that for once I was punctual too. The mechanics unloaded the car and fired it up. It sounded fabulous. Roy was seated in an instant and ready to go. I asked him to do one lap and return to the pit for the mechanics to do a routine check. This was done. I then asked Roy to do a few more laps fairly gently . . . five laps later he had broken the outright Sports Car lap record at Goodwood by some two seconds! When he came back into the pit, before I could ask him how the car felt, Roy said "Boy, this is bloody quick!" We had obviously made a good decision. It was the only car I have ever had the experience of building which, apart from tyre pressures and the odd minor adjustment, had no other alterations made at all during the test period. This was most unusual. The combination of Roy as driver, the engine and the car was a fabulous threesome.

'This was proved at Silverstone in 1959 when Roy drove the Cooper-Maserati against a works Aston Martin DBR1 driven by Stirling Moss. Roy immediately went into the lead, pulling away from Stirling with apparently very little effort. Halfway through the race he started to indicate to the pit and gesture towards the back of the car. This was interpreted as being a problem with the rear of the car. My immediate concern was that Reg Parnell, the Aston Martin team manager, would have seen Roy's gestures. He would probably have assumed that Roy had problems, and tried to speed up Stirling. However, in spite of slowing slightly and losing a small amount of ground, it was Roy who won the race.

'After the slowing-down lap Roy came to the finishing line to receive his reward. I went to the rostrum to congratulate him. When he got out of the car he said, "It's been a bloody hard drive. The car has been one hell of a handful." The mechanics found that the linkage which held the top spring in position had broken. This meant that the wheels had no vertical support, and the car would have had unbelievable oversteer on both left and right hand corners. When Roy saw this he said, "Thank God! I thought it was me!" I was amazed at his coolness, and the easy manner in which the whole thing was dismissed.

'The next year was even more successful with a similar car; this time it had a Climax 2½-litre engine. We won five out of five events entered. We also had a fabulous run in Jaguar saloons and E-types.

'Wherever Roy drove, there was rarely an event in which he failed to bring the crowd to their feet with sheer excitement. He is an outstanding example of a racing driver who could effectively race anything. He had the marvellous ability to keep on trying – exploiting the cars' good points and adapting to the bad ones – and this applied as much to a five-lap race at Goodwood as to the 24 hours at Le Mans. There were better racing drivers than Roy – just a few – but I can't think of anyone else who had so much talent in so many different cars. He did not have endless opportunity for practice in any one of the machines he raced, but he produced the very best out of them wherever the flag fell.'

* * *

1959

Throughout 1959 and 1960 I raced for private owners John Coombs and Tommy Atkins. John Coombs was a very experienced racing entrant fully supported by Esso, but for Tommy, who was far less experienced in the business side of motor racing, I helped to arrange the sponsorship. This involved a deal with Reg Tanner of Esso and, on the basis that I drove for Tommy, they provided a sum of money that more than paid for the cars. Esso paid Tommy on January 1 in each year and this obviously helped him a great deal in sorting out his racing finances.

Tommy ran a specialist engineering business, High Efficiency Engineering, at Tolworth, but kept his competition cars in a block of lock-up garages opposite Jack Brabham's garage at Chessington. The cars were looked after by first-rate mechanics headed by ex-racing motor cyclist Harry Pearce. Tommy's cars were always superbly prepared and immaculately turned out. In 1959 he entered a brace of single-seater Coopers, a 2.5-litre four-cylinder Maserati-powered car that I drove in Formula One races when I was not needed by Aston Martin, and a Climax-powered Formula Two car.

John Coombs was another motor racing fanatic, a very forceful and very determined character whose car preparation was second to none. He had close links with Jaguar via his company, Coombs of Guildford, and he coerced them into giving him exceptionally good deals. In 1959 Coombs was racing Jaguar 3.4-litre saloons. Tommy Sopwith's Equipe Endeavour team were our main rivals and Jaguar were exceptionally fair to all the leading entrants – if they brought out a new modification, then every team would get it. Sometimes Jaguar's fairness worked against us, for John Coombs was very friendly with 'Lofty' England of Jaguar and kept him informed about all the 'mods' that he had made to his Jaguars. John's successful modifications would soon be seen on most of the Jaguar entries. Mike Parkes, who was development engineer and tester to Equipe Endeavour, devised quite a number of modifications to that team's Jaguars, but I believe that they tended to keep information to themselves. I should add that Jaguar supported Coombs only in terms of special deals on the cars and technical information. Coombs also entered me with a Maserati-powered Cooper-Monaco sports car.

My first races of the year were at Goodwood on Easter Monday and I drove in a total of four events, two for Atkins and two for Coombs. I was fastest in practice for the Formula Two Lavant Cup, a race in which I faced stiff opposition from works Coopers driven by my former team-mate Jack Brabham and from a full works Lotus team amongst others. Unfortunately I made an appalling start and it took me until lap five to get to grips with race-leader Jack Brabham who was using all the road – and sometimes the grass – and showering me with mud and stones; Brabham was not to earn his nick-name 'Black Jack' for nothing! On lap seven I made an opportunity and forced my way past but Jack passed me again on lap nine and had no intention of letting me past again. So despite driving as hard as I knew how and really chancing my arm in my efforts to get past Jack, I still had to settle for second place, two-fifths of a second behind, but with the consolation of having set fastest lap of 95.79 mph. This proved to be the fastest Goodwood lap of the year for which I was later awarded the Scott Gaze Challenge Trophy. It was a magnificent solid silver trophy in the shape of a Spitfire, and was presented by the family of Pilot Officer I.S.O. Gaze who had failed to return to Westhampnett Airfield (as Goodwood was known when it was an operational airfield) after a mission in 1941. It was the one trophy that I would really have liked to keep and Tommy ordered an exact replica for me from the original silversmiths. It is one of my most treasured possessions.

The rest of the day's racing proved less satisfactory. In practice for the Sussex Trophy for Unlimited Sports Cars I had been fastest by a comfortable margin, but the race was run in torrential rain, and after an enormous spin between Woodcote and the chicane I finished fourth with Coombs' Cooper-Maserati. I had lapped in 1 min 42 sec in practice for the International '100' Formula One race, second to Harry Schell with a works BRM (1 min 39 sec). However, the race was also run in the wet and I was back in fifth place when I spun at Lavant. I managed to get my goggles covered with mud and after stopping at the pits to change them for a clean pair I finished seventh. Frankly, it was a race in which I lost interest at an early stage and I would have pressed on with dirty goggles (or no goggles) if I had been better placed. I rounded off the day with second place with Coombs' Jaguar to Bueb's Equipe Endeavour car in the Saloon Car race.

It rained again at Oulton Park on April 11. I had been fastest in practice again for the Formula Two British Empire Trophy, but I never managed to get up with the leaders on the wet track, spun off on lap five and spent the remainder of the race working my way back through the field to finish sixth. I led the Unlimited Sports Car race with Coombs' Cooper-Maserati, but I was passed on lap eight by Jim Russell driving exceptionally quickly with a Climax-powered Cooper, and finished second. Russell was running on Continental tyres which proved faster in the wet than the Dunlops used by most competitors and just as fast in the dry. We bought some Continental tyres and fitted them if rain was threatening, until Dunlop brought out an improved tyre not long afterwards.

At Aintree a week later I again finished second in the Saloon Car race to Bueb with an Equipe Endeavour car (and I set a new class lap record of 76.70 mph) and won the Sports Car race fairly easily from Graham Hill (Lotus). In the '200' Formula One race I started from the third row of the grid with a time of 2 min 2.8 sec which I regarded as satisfactory, as our Maserati engine was rather less powerful than the equivalent Coventry-Climax with inferior torque characteristics. Maserati claimed 210/215 bhp, but whenever you put an Italian engine on the brake, its power never matched the claims made and this Maserati engine was developing less than 200 bhp. In the race I held fifth place until trouble with the Colotti gearbox forced me to retire. The race was won by Jean Behra (Ferrari) from his team-mate Tony Brooks.

At the *Daily Express* meeting at Silverstone on May 2 I raced both for Aston Martin and against them. As I recounted in Chapter 9, I finished second with the DBR4 in the Trophy race, but I also won the 3,000 cc Sports Car race with

Coombs' Cooper-Maserati from Stirling Moss at the wheel of a rather special Aston Martin DBR1. Obviously the DBR1, designed for endurance racing, was not the ideal car for a short British event and, equally obviously, I was rather disappointed at not being offered an Aston drive. I appreciated, of course, that if Stirling was available it would be stupid not to use his services, but I would have thought that Aston could have prepared two cars and entered me as well. However, as soon as John Coombs heard that I was free to drive, he rushed to get the Cooper-Maserati ready in time for the race.

I was fastest in practice in 1 min 43.4 sec (101.91 mph) and led the race initially. I was passed by Graham Hill (2-litre Lotus) on lap two, repassed him, and Stirling with the Aston moved up to second place as the result of mechanical problems suffered by Hill, Brabham (Coombs-entered 2-litre Cooper Monaco) and Stacey (who crashed his Lotus when the steering broke). I won the race by a margin of 4.6 seconds from Stirling, but fastest lap (and a new class lap record) went to Jack Brabham. As the race progressed, so the handling of my car deteriorated; it was shuddering badly under braking and darting all over the track. When Coombs looked round the car after the race, he found to his horror that the rear suspension had broken.

At Silverstone I drove in two other races. The first race of the day was a 12-lap Grand Touring race. Aston Martin entered a DB4 for Stirling, who scored an easy win, and I held second place throughout with Coombs' Jaguar, gradually falling back as the race progressed, but well satisfied with my performance. Aston Martin racing manager Reg Parnell was apprehensive that because the organisers had accepted the DB4 entry even though the model was not yet homologated, John Coombs might well make a protest stick. John had in fact no intention of making a protest. I also finished second in the Touring Car race with Coombs' Jaguar.

Much of my 1959 racing season was commited to the Aston Martin Formula One team, but I fitted in a fair number of Formula One and Two drives for Tommy Atkins. The weekend after Silverstone I drove his Cooper-Maserati in

With Atkins' Cooper-Maserati in the 1959 Monaco Grand Prix. The gearbox packed up and I pushed the car across the line into sixth place (Motor Racing).

the Monaco Grand Prix. Although the car was less powerful than the Climax-powered entries, it was nicely set up for the circuit and I was eighth fastest in practice which was very pleasing. I drove a steady, sensible race holding sixth place and by lap 70 (out of 100 laps) was fourth ahead of Trintignant. Trintignant managed to pass me again and on lap 82 my Colotti gearbox packed up. I pushed the car across the line to finish sixth and last. Monaco was a long, slow race that thrashed a car's gearbox and brakes and finishing well up the field was really a matter of survival. If I had lasted the distance, I would probably have finished third.

At the Crystal Palace on Whit Monday I won two races and finished second in another. I won the London Trophy Formula Two race with Atkins' Cooper-Climax and the Unlimited Sports Car race with Coombs' Cooper-Maserati, but my hardest drive of the day was in the 1,500 cc Sports Car race run in two heats and a final. I drove a Climax-powered Cooper Monaco for Coombs and I tried everything to stay with Innes Ireland who was one of the quickest of the Lotus drivers. I was using the road, the grass, the kerbs – almost everything – and was throwing the car all over the circuit. I lost the Cooper at the back of the circuit, dropped to fourth place and in my fight back to second place set a new class record of 80.45 mph. Despite my desperate, maybe dangerous driving that day, the Crystal Palace was a circuit that I usually treated with respect because the consequences of a mistake were likely to be serious.

I drove for Atkins at a number of races later in 1959. At Reims in July the Cooper-Maserati was uncompetitive in the French Grand Prix and I retired after a succession of pit stops, while mechanical trouble eliminated me in the Formula Two Coupe de Vitesse. I finished second in the Formula Two John Davy Trophy at Brands Hatch on August Bank Holiday Monday and a not so satisfactory sixth at the same circuit at the end of that month. With the Cooper-Maserati I took a fourth place in the Gold Cup race at Oulton Park, but I retired in the Silver City Trophy at Snetterton in October.

1960

I still drove for both Coombs and Atkins in 1960, but both had now abandoned the use of Maserati engines. In 1959 they had opted for Maserati engines because it would be some while before the full 2.5-litre Climax engine would be available to private owners. While Climax 2.5-litre engines were in short supply and most people were using the 2 and 2.2-litre Climax engines, we were just about, but only just, competitive. As 2.5-litre engines became more numerous, so we became uncompetitive. The Maserati engine was also much more difficult to maintain and many of the components had an exceptionally limited life. Another problem was that it was necessary to use Colotti gearboxes and these gave endless trouble. The 2.5-litre Climax engine was proving so successful and so reliable that there was no question of using any other engine in 1960.

In 1960 Formula Two racing was even more competitive because Lotus were now racing their rear-engined 18 car that was to prove so very successful in both Formula One and Formula Two, and Porsche were racing a much improved

On my way to third place with Atkins' Formula Two Cooper-Climax in the 1960 Oulton Park Trophy (T. C. March).

single-seater Formula Two car, an example of which was loaned to Rob Walker for Stirling Moss to drive. In all the circumstances I was more than satisfied with the third place that I took in the Oulton Park Trophy, my first race of the year, behind Ireland (Lotus) and Surtees (Cooper).

Goodwood on Easter Monday provided me with a typical, busy day's racing. During practice I crashed Tommy's Formula Two Cooper at the chicane when a Jubilee clip jammed the accelerator and caused the throttles to stick wide open. The engine was still revving flat out after the crash, the ignition switch did not work and I had to yank off the plug leads. The result was that I suffered shock from the shunt and a shock of a different kind from the Cooper's electrics. We rushed the car back to Coopers where Harry Pearce managed to rebuild it in time for the race, the Lavant Cup, and I again finished third behind Ireland (Lotus), who was in terrific form that day, and Moss (Porsche). I followed this up with a win in the Sports Car race with Coombs' new 2.5-litre Climax-powered Cooper Monaco and set a new class record of 96.43 mph. At the end of the day I finished second with Coombs' saloon Jaguar to Stirling's Aston Martin DB4GT in the race for closed cars.

There was an immensely strong entry in the International '100' Formula One race and I was fifth fastest in practice with Atkins' 1959 ex-works Cooper behind Bristow, Moss, Schell (all with Coopers) and Ireland (Lotus). In the race Dan Gurney (works BRM) and I were having a tussle for fourth place when we collided on lap four. Dan tried to pass me on the outside at Lavant in a rather desperate move and I was disinclined to cede the corner. In fact Gurney's driving at this race reminded me of a driver I used to know well, Roy Salvadori! Gurney hit the bank and retired; I carried on, only to be eliminated by gearbox trouble. Dan was rather upset about the accident because he thought that I should have given way to him. It was, however clearly my line into the corner and I rather think that Dan had his head down and was pushing too hard.

Gurney had largely forgotten about the incident when we all attended the usual cocktail party held by the Duke of Richmond and Gordon after the day's racing. Unfortunately John Coombs, who is one of the world's most professional stirrers, said to Dan, 'Oh, Gurney, I hear that you tried to carve up my old mate, Salvadori. It's a bit much you know!' Dan stood up – and Gurney really is a big chap – looked me in the eye, prodded me in the chest with his finger and said, 'Roy, remember this, I never turn the other cheek.' I believed him and afterwards I always treated Dan with the respect that a guy as big as he is deserves!

As the season progressed, the Coombs' Cooper Monaco-Climax proved itself to be the fastest sports car in the country and I won races at Aintree at the end of April, at Silverstone in May (and set a new class lap record) and at Brands Hatch on August Bank Holiday Monday. I also did very well that year with the Coombs Jaguar 3.8 with wins at Silverstone and Brands Hatch.

My victory in the Production Touring Car race at Silverstone in May was particularly satisfying. To try to make sure of beating the Coombs team, Equipe Endeavour had persuaded Stirling to drive one of their cars and the race devolved into a duel between us. I led initially, but then Stirling passed me and as I followed him round the circuit, I realised that I was quicker through Stowe and that it was the one point on the circuit where I could really make up ground. Unlike Stirling, who was changing down into third for Stowe, I was hanging on to top gear all round the circuit except for Copse and Beckett's and I suspect that that was why I was slighly quicker. Two laps from the finish I took Stirling on the inside at Stowe and managed to hold him off until the finish. I was delighted with this win because quite apart from beating 'The Maestro', I had driven a very sensible, cool, neat race and I had set a new class lap record. Coombs was euphoric about the win because the rivalry with Equipe Endeavour was getting more and more intense.

Our performances with the Atkins single-seater Coopers tended to be rather patchy. In Formula Two I retired at Aintree in April, won at Oulton Park the

At Silverstone in May 1960 Equipe Endeavour entered Stirling Moss with a Jaguar 3.8 in an effort to beat the Coombs entry. We had a magnificent duel and I won by a very narrow margin (T. C. March).

following month and retired again at Brands Hatch late in August. It was much the same story with the Formula One car. At the end of May I drove the Cooper-Climax in the Monaco Grand Prix. I qualified 12th fastest in 1 min 38.7 sec and Stirling took pole position with the Walker Lotus in 1 min 36.3 sec. I reckoned that if I could keep going steadily I would be sure of a place in this race in which there is always such a high level of retirements. I worked my way up to hold a promising eighth place, only to spin at the Gasworks hairpin on lap 28 when rain started to fall. The circuit was well covered with oil by this time and very slippery, so I did not blame myself too much. I restarted, but my engine was beginning to overheat and I retired two laps later.

I drove the Formula One car in three other races in 1960. On August Bank Holiday Monday at Brands Hatch I ran in the Silver City Trophy, a strongly contested race with works entries from BRM, Cooper, Ferrari and Lotus. I was seventh fastest in practice and held fifth place in the race, delayed for some time as I tried to lap Ginther's Ferrari which was occupying all the road. Eventually I got past, but I was eliminated when Piper spun his Lotus in front of me at Bottom Bend and there was no way that I could avoid a collision. In September I finished fourth in the Lombank Trophy at Snetterton and I retired in the Gold Cup race at Oulton Park because of steering problems.

Whatever the results at Oulton Park, they were always occasions to remember because of the continuous parties at the Chester Country Club. The party on the eve of this meeting in 1960 nearly ended in disaster. We were all gathered in one room in the early hours of the morning and for some reason Graham Hill was lying on his back on the floor. Innes Ireland, taking the view that Graham looked rather untidy, decided to dust him down with a Hoover. Unfortunately the suck of the Hoover nearly did Graham a grave personal injury, but he was saved when somebody pulled out the plug – Innes had no intention of letting him escape.

In 1960 I received an invitation to drive in two races for Jock McBain's Border Reivers team. The Border Reivers ran an ex-works Aston Martin DBR1 which was usually driven by Jim Clark, but of course a co-driver was needed for

At Brands Hatch in 1960 with, left to right, Olivier Gendebien, Joakim Bonnier and Stirling Moss. In the right of the photograph are two of the very quick Porsche Formula Two cars. (Roy Salvadori collection).

endurance events and this is where I came into the picture. Jimmy was still very much a 'coming' man, but his potential was immense. Already he was very quick, very safe and with excellent temperament and judgment. Our first race was the Nürburgring 1000 Km in May and Jimmy, who was quickest of all off the mark at Le Mans starts with the possible exception of Stirling, took the first turn at the wheel. He had worked his way through to fourth place by lap four when the DBR1 broke a valve and we were out of the running without me even getting a drive.

My second drive for the Border Reivers was at Le Mans and obviously we had hopes of repeating my 1959 victory. One result of this was that the team had support from the personnel at Aston Martin, and their efforts were justified. We did not have the fastest car, but we were in the hunt throughout the race and finished a good third. Both Jimmy and I drove really well and the car was still in first-class condition at the end of the race, indicative of just how sensibly we had driven it. I enjoyed driving for Border Reivers. I felt completely at home with the team and at this stage in Jimmy's career I had a slight edge in lap times.

In August I drove an Aston Martin DB4GT for the John Ogier team in the Tourist Trophy, run as a Grand Touring Car race at Goodwood. A second DB4GT was driven by Innes Ireland. The Ogier team was fully works-supported and Reg Parnell and the Aston mechanics were at the race. The main opposition came from Stirling Moss with a Ferrari 250GT entered by Rob Walker. Stirling was fastest in practice in 1 min 35.6 sec, but I was second fastest in 1 min 37.0 sec and Innes was 1.4 seconds slower than me. In private practice I had lapped close to 1 min 35 sec – and Reg had urged us to keep something in hand in practice.

My instructions from Reg were to stay with Stirling and push him – in other words do to Stirling what Stirling usually had to do to the opposition when he drove for Aston Martin. My car was expendable and all being well Innes would be behind me ready to take the lead. Of our prospects in this race, Keith Challon wrote in *The News of the World*, 'Recently Salvadori in a DB4 consistently lapped the tough, twisting Goodwood circuit at just under 90 mph. At the Easter Goodwood meeting Moss' fastest lap in Sopwith's DB4 was 87 mph. Salvadori is the master of racing saloons and I even think he is the equal of Moss. I can pay Salvadori no higher compliment.'

Although it was a Le Mans start I was away very quickly and for the first 20 laps I was right up Stirling's chuff. On lap 20 I managed to pass Stirling at Madgwick, but he was back in front again two laps later. When Stirling stopped for tyres, I led again briefly, but then I stopped; the pit stop took some six seconds longer, but I was still very much in contention and in a race of this length, not too concerned about the time loss. As I have mentioned previously, my style of driving threw an immense strain on the car – at Goodwood the spokes went on a rear wheel of the DB4GT, the tube punctured, the wheel collapsed and I crawled back to the pits on the brake disc. I was back in third place behind Innes Ireland after my pit stop and chasing my team-mate. Part of

The left-hand rear wheel collapsed on my Aston Martin DB4GT in the 1960 Tourist Trophy at Goodwood. I finished second to Stirling Moss (Ferrari) and set fastest lap (Roy Salvadori collection).

Innes' exhaust system broke away, he was black-flagged for repairs and I moved into second place again. There was now no hope of catching Stirling so Reg slowed us down and we finished second and third. Initially fastest lap was credited to Stirling, but after Reg had checked with the timekeepers a correction was issued crediting me with the fastest lap in 1 min 36.2 sec (89.81 mph).

Of this significant race *Autosport* commented, 'These DB4GT machines ran like clockwork, and either of them could have disputed the issue with Moss, had Salvadori not lost time after a puncture caused by a faulty wheel, and Ireland by reason of his exhaust pipes coming adrift.

'In point of fact, the entire race centred on tyre changes and the times taken for pit stops. Moss lost only 2 min 35 sec, as against about 4 mins by Salvadori and over 4 mins by Ireland. . . .'

In October I was invited by David Murray of Ecurie Ecosse to drive the team's Cooper Monaco-Climax in two races in the United States at Watkins Glen and Riverside Raceway. It was an opportunity too good to miss. When I arrived at Watkins Glen I found that it was impossible for me to get into the Cooper, which was usually driven by Tommy Dickson who was considerably shorter than me. I am 6 ft 2 in and with my long legs I was rarely comfortable in the cockpit of any racing car, but I simply did not fit the Ecosse Cooper at all. This involved 'Wilkie' Wilkinson in extensive surgery to the Cooper, and he cut away the bodywork until I was able to fit in the cockpit.

Ecurie Ecosse had no spare engine and we had to conserve the engine so that it would last both my races and also a third event at Laguna Seca where I was not driving. Another problem was that the fuel tank was too small for us to run through the 203-mile Watkins Glen race without a pit stop. Watkins Glen was a Formule Libre race and in the face of very strong single-seater opposition I drove a very good, steady race to finish third, some way behind the winning Cooper Formula One car of Stirling. The Riverside race was for sports cars and our chances of success there were much greater. After Watkins Glen Wilkie changed the axle ratio for Riverside, but in practice we found that I was over-revving on the straight and because we were worried about breaking the engine, he had to change the axle ratio once again, which meant an overnight stint. I made a very good start in the race and was well up with the leaders on the first lap, but it got rather crowded at one corner, I was reluctant to give way but somehow was outfumbled, went off the road and stalled the engine. I could not start the engine because the carburettors were flooding and it took me ages to get going. When I did start I was last and from then on it was a flat-out grind to the finish. I was finding it harder and harder to pass the very fast opposition as I worked my way back through the field, but Phil Hill (Ferrari) generously waved me by on the lap before the finish and I finished a strong sixth.

From Riverside I flew back to Europe to compete in my last race of the year, the Paris 1000 Kilomètres at Montlhéry near Paris, run on a combined road and track circuit. I was again driving for the Ogier team and shared a DB4GT with Innes Ireland. The team's second car was driven by Jim Clark and Tony Maggs. At this time GT racing was in the ascendant and the race attracted a strong entry of Ferrari 250GTs. I was the fastest Aston driver in practice, but slower than some of the Ferraris.

With 'Wilkie' Wilkinson and the Ecurie Ecosse Cooper Monaco before the start at Watkins Glen in 1960 (Roy Salvadori collection).

The 1960 BRDC dinner (left to right) John Coombs, John Young and Graham Hill. We had just received the bill for dinner! (Roy Salvadori collection).

The race started before the morning fog had cleared from the circuit and on a damp track. I started the race and went really well, although unable to stay with the faster Ferraris, until the Aston started to understeer badly as I went into a fast ess-bend. I managed to get round the bend and stop the car to discover that a front wheel had collapsed. I had made up my mind to abandon the car when I heard a voice, 'Roy, Roy – get the car to the pits.' I looked round to see Marcel Blondeau, the French Aston Martin agent. It was a long way back to the pits and I would have to drive round the banking on what was left of the wheel and the disc brake. Blondeau kept urging me on and I eventually drove the car back, thinking, 'Oh my God, I don't fancy putting on another wheel and charging round the banking again – it's far too chancey.' I was no sooner in the pits than the mechanics had the car jacked up and the wheel was being changed. While all this was going on, Innes arrived in the pits, buckling on his crash helmet and asking what had happened. As soon as I saw Innes, I was out of the car in a flash and jumped to the other side of the pit counter. Innes looked at the car, looked at the remains of the damaged wheel – by this time I was already unbuckling my helmet – got in the car and reluctantly went off to finish the race. In the closing stages of the race the Aston developed a leaking exhaust manifold and although poor Innes was badly affected by fumes he gamely kept going to finish sixth. The Clark/Maggs car retired at the end of Maggs' spell when the engine went on to five cylinders.

At Montlhéry the atmosphere between Jimmy Clark and Innes Ireland that had persisted all season was frostier than ever. Both were members of Team Lotus where the problems had originated and there was immense rivalry between them over places in that team. I found that I was being dragged into the dispute and urged to take sides – which I strenuously avoided. Jimmy was already a brilliantly smooth and fast driver and conspicuously easy on his cars, whilst Innes at that time was certainly as quick, but not as relaxed and possibly harder on his cars. Both had the qualities which are essential in the make-up of a World Champion. Eventually, although Innes had won the 1961 United States Grand Prix, Chapman retained Jimmy in the team. There was no place for Innes who was forced to race for private entrants, so we never knew just how well he could have done.

Chapter 11

Formula One with Yeoman Credit, 1961

At the end of 1960 Reg Parnell had left Aston Martin to run the Yeoman Credit team and had taken with him some of the Aston Martin racing personnel, including the mechanics and the Competitions Secretary, Gillian Harris. The Yeoman Credit team was run by the finance company of the same name controlled by the Samengo-Turner brothers. Reg asked me if I would join the team and offered a substantial retainer together with the usual split of starting and prize money. I was very pleased to accept the offer, not only because it was a good offer, but also because I liked Reg. I had some reservations about Reg's management ability which had proved fine under John Wyer's guidance, but he was now on his own, although of course he had the support of Gill Harris who was a first-rate organiser. In some ways the team was home from home for me as I knew so many of the ex-Aston personnel. The other driver was John Surtees who was very quick, but was having his share of shunts. Most experienced observers, especially Reg, had high hopes that John was a World Champion in the making and there was probably too much pressure on him, forcing him to drive faster than he should have at this stage in his career. There was no number one driver in the Yeoman Credit team as such, but it was understood that if a chassis or engine was particularly good it would be given to John. John was the coming man and really pushing, while my career was tailing off. I admired John, we got on well and we had no personal differences during the two years we worked together.

For 1961 there was a change in the Grand Prix Formula to 1,500 cc. This resulted in rather underpowered cars and the 1961 British cars were uncompetitive, as all the constructors were relying on the stop-gap FPF Mark II four-cylinder Coventry-Climax engines until the new V-8 designs from Climax and BRM were ready. The year's racing was dominated by Ferrari, save at Monaco and the Nürburgring where Stirling with Rob Walker's Lotus thrashed the Maranello entries and at Watkins Glen which Ferrari did not enter. Yeoman Credit pursued a particularly active competition programme, competing in the Tasman races at the beginning of the year and Inter-Continental Formula races as well as Formula One. All the British constructors had opposed the new Grand Prix Formula and at their instigation a lot of British races in 1961 were held to the so-called Inter-Continental Formula for cars of between 2 and 3 litres which meant, in reality, the previous year's Formula One cars.

I continued to drive for John Coombs in 1961 at the wheel of a Jaguar 3.8 saloon, the new Jaguar E-type and a Cooper Monaco-Climax. The Monaco was one of the new Mk III cars with redesigned chassis, double wishbone and coil spring rear suspension, new bodywork with twin tail-fins and the 2.5-litre Coventry-Climax engine.

At the end of 1960 the Yeoman Credit team flew out to New Zealand for the Tasman races. We flew to New Zealand via Los Angeles, where I stayed for three days with Lance Reventlow in his magnificent house, stopped over for a couple more days in Honolulu and flew to Auckland on New Year's Eve. A long flight is not the best way to spend New Year's Eve, but the hostesses were doing their best to create a party atmosphere and were plying us with drink. When the Captain rang for coffee, Innes Ireland persuaded one of the hostesses to take off her uniform. Innes slipped the uniform on and with suitable padding and make-up looked absolutely superb. When Innes took the coffee through, we thought that it was a magnificent joke, but the Captain failed to share our sense of humour and rollicked the hostesses over the intercom. Innes can be a great diplomat on occasions, and it took all his powers of diplomacy to smooth out this situation!

John Surtees was still under contract to Lotus, so Reg Parnell brought into the team Jo Bonnier. We took with us three 2,500 cc Formula One cars, two Coopers and a Lotus 18. One of the Coopers was to be hired to Denis Hulme and I would have preferred to drive the other Cooper because I expected it to be more reliable. Jo, however, was very keen to drive the Cooper and because I did not want to make an issue of it, Reg let him have it.

I soon found that the weakest point of the Lotus was the gearbox and this caused my retirement in the first three races of the series. I had virtually no practice for the fourth race, the Invercargill Trophy, held at Teretonga on February 4. My mechanic, Peter Bryant, was out on the town on the evening before practice; we could not find him in the morning and I had to wait until he eventually arrived and reassembled the Lotus gearbox. What practice I did manage was very fast and Jo Bonnier, who had been doing well with the Cooper, realised that I was likely to give him a lot of trouble in the race. Jo told me that he thought that it would be stupid for us to fight each other in the race and suggested that we came to an arrangement. Not unexpectedly, Jo's idea of an arrangement was that I should let him win! I turned down Jo's suggestion and so he went off to bend Reg's ear. I then had to contend with Reg who argued, 'Look, Roy, we've been doing very well in this series of races. It's stupid to go out and break each other up!' It all sounded quite sensible – Reg usually made good sense – and he went on to say that Jo was willing to split the prize and bonus money. It was Jo's last race with the team and he wanted to win. I said, 'Jo's a newcomer to the team and he's trying to dominate the situation and make his own terms. It should be for me to have any advantage, not a newcomer who's only in the team for a few races.' Reg appealed to me on the basis of our long association and stressed how good for the team it would be if we finished first and second. Eventually I gave in, as I always did with Reg, even though I was very unhappy with the arrangement.

Just before the start of the race Reg told me that Jo only wanted to split the prize money if I finished second – after all, my car was unreliable and I might very well retire. I thought that Jo's behaviour left a lot to be desired, but I decided that there was not much point in arguing. Reg told me that if I was leading on lap 40, I must let Jo go ahead on that lap. I had to start from the back of the grid because of my almost complete lack of practice, but I rushed through the field and was in second place not far behind Jo by lap eight. On lap 13 I took the lead at one of the corners and pulled well away, making fastest lap. I kept my word to Reg, but made it as obvious as possible that the race was fixed. As I passed the pits on lap 40, I slowed right off to let Jo pass, gave Reg a very dirty look and then accelerated hard.

After we had finished the main race, we both competed in the very short, so-called 'Flying Farewell' race for the fastest eight cars. I suggested to Jo that we should let Denny Hulme (a future World Champion), who had been driving very sensibly and very well, win this race. Jo's answer was, 'No. We can't let an unkown driver beat us.' I was staggered, especially as Jo had only just shown himself to be one of the most able fixers in motor racing, and I stressed that he should clearly understand that this race was *not* fixed. We started the race very determined to beat each other. I managed to just nose in front of Jo at the start; he was all over me on the first lap, and at the loop on the second lap I left my braking very late and only just scrambled round. Jo went straight on and hit a tree, wrecked the Cooper but, fortunately, did not hurt himself too badly. Afterwards Jo said, not entirely convincingly, that the throttle had stuck wide open. While I was sorry that Yeoman Credit had lost a car, I was hardly in the mood to cry crocodile tears for Jo. After this incident I won the race easily.

After the Invercargill races we flew back to England, but I was soon off again to compete in Australia. Jack Brabham was taking a couple of Coopers to Longford in Tasmania and Albany and he asked me to drive one. We routed via Karachi where the aircraft stopped over for a couple of hours and I think that it was there that I picked up the most terrible bug. By the time we arrived in Tasmania, I was running a high temperature and feeling dreadful. I went to bed at once and I was not fit enough to do more than a couple of laps in practice for the first race at Longford.

The Longford meeting started with a short race which Jack won with his new-type Cooper; local driver Patterson was second with a special 2.36-litre Cooper-Climax and I finished third with Jack's older Cooper. Another short race followed in which I kept up well with Jack in the opening laps, but a stone broke my goggles and cut my eye. Despite being able to use only one eye I managed to make a race of it with Jack; we swapped the lead a couple of times and I finished second. Immediately after the race a local doctor removed several pieces of glass from my eye – I think that I had only managed to keep racing because of the effect of the drugs that I had been given previously for the 'bug'. In the final Jack put on another good show, making it look like a real tussle (at this stage in his career I doubt whether I could have beaten him in a straight fight with a Cooper) – I led on a couple of laps and to the spectators it all looked very convincing. When Jack retired because of a broken universal joint, I went on to win at 104.50 mph. We had not planned anything before the race and when I suggested to Jack afterwards that he was playing with me, his reply was, 'You know, Roy, that I would never play with you.' To race with a gentleman like Jack (albeit a very hard one when the chips were down) made a refreshing contrast with my experiences of racing with Bonnier in New Zealand. The following weekend we competed in a series of races at Albany which brought me a win, again by courtesy of Jack, and two second places in minor races, plus fourth place in the main race after a collision with Bib Stillwell's Cooper which put me right back down the field. I enjoyed competing in Australia immensely, partly because the starting money was the best that I ever received (Jack proved the most generous entrant that I ever drove for), but also because the Australians were such good company and so very hospitable; they took their motor racing very seriously and the local-entered Coopers were superbly prepared, very quick and very well driven.

At the end of March we started the long European season with a race meeting every weekend (and occasionally two). The first meeting was at Snetterton, and in the Lombank Trophy for Formula One and Inter-Continental Formula cars I drove one of my best races for a long time. After two pit stops for carburation adjustments to my 1,500 cc Cooper I battled with Jim Clark (works Lotus), who had also lost time in the pits, on the limit all the way round the circuit and eventually passed Clark to finish third in the Formula One class behind Surtees and Trevor Taylor (works Lotus). I set a new Formula One lap record of 99.55 mph.

Reg Parnell was obviously delighted with the way that the Yeoman Credit team had performed at Snetterton and further success was gained at Goodwood on Easter Monday. My day at Goodwood did not, however, start too well. In the first race, the St Mary's Trophy for Saloon Cars, run on a wet track, I was chasing Parkes' leading Jaguar and was hotly pursued by Bruce McLaren who was racing a Jaguar saloon for the first time; Bruce took St Mary's much too fast, lost control of the Jaguar and cannoned into the back of my car. Bruce carried on to finish fifth, but one of the rear wings of my car was rubbing on the tyre and I cruised round to the pits to retire. After the race Bruce apologised: he had thought that the handling of the Jaguar was so good that he could take St Mary's practically flat out, was amazed when the car went straight on and was very thankful that my car was in the way because it prevented him from having a nasty shunt! I finished fifth for Yeoman Credit with the Lotus in the Inter-Continental Formula Lavant Cup (John Surtees finished third) and I took third place with a Cooper in the Formula One Goodwood Trophy after a spin (John won the race).

Shortly before the Oulton Park meeting on April 15 the Coombs team and Equipe Endeavour took delivery of the first E-type Jaguars. There was no opportunity to sort the cars at all and in practice Hill (with the Sopwith car) and I were plagued by the engines cutting out on left-hand corners. John Coombs

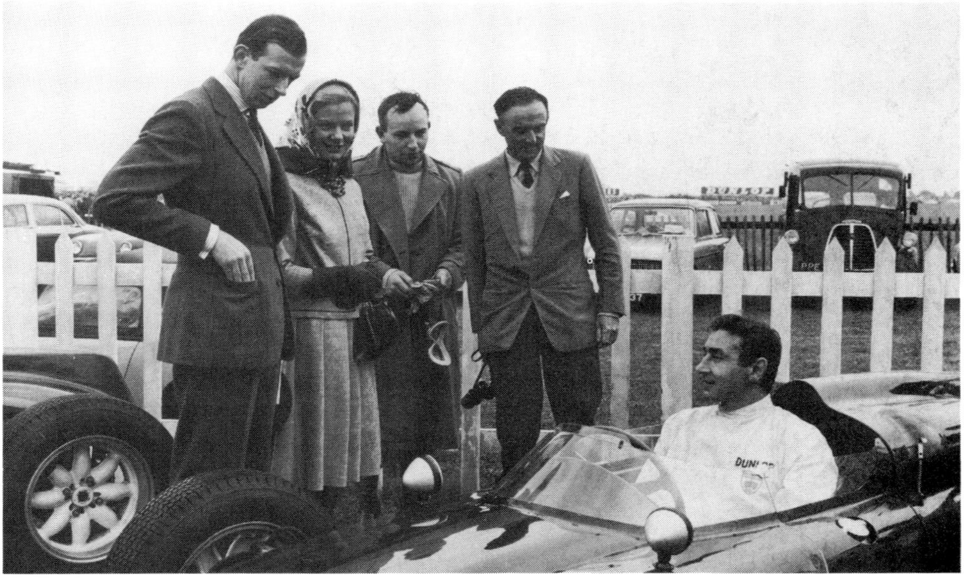

At Goodwood in 1961 with the Yeoman Credit Cooper and, left to right, the Duke and Duchess of Kent, John Surtees and the Duke of Richmond (Dunlop).

cured this by fitting the complete fuel system from the 3.8 saloon and Lofty England suggested that Equipe Endeavour did the same thing. Between practice and the GT race the cars went back to the Jaguar factory. Both the brake discs and pads were changed on Hill's car, but there was time only to change the pads on my car. The result was that the discs, which were in poor condition, cut up the pads during the race.

I thought that the E-type was magnificent, very quick, with superb roadholding, very comfortable and very easy to drive; the steering was pretty neutral with a slight understeer, but the brakes were rather indifferent. At this time the cars which we raced were very close to production form, although later during the year a lot of development work was carried out. I led from Graham until my brakes went and I finished third behind Hill and Ireland (Aston Martin DB4GT). Graham and I shared the fastest lap and a GT record at 84.69 mph.

Our next two race meetings followed in quick succession. At Aintree on April 22 I finished a poor eighth with my Yeoman Credit Cooper-Climax in the Formula One Aintree '200' race after a pit stop to try to sort out exhaust problems. After Aintree there was a frantic rush to get to Sicily for the Siracusa Grand Prix held only three days later. All the British team cars were flown to Catania in Bristol Freighters chartered by Webbair and the drivers flew by Dan-Air Elizabethan.

Siracusa was not a circuit that I liked because the roads were very narrow, the cambers were bad and the surface was appalling. Most of the British cars were not at their best, as there had been no time to work on them after the Aintree race. The foreign entries were limited to the works Porsche team with cars for Gurney and Bonnier and a works Ferrari driven by the young Italian Giancarlo Baghetti; this V-6 Ferrari was officially on loan to a private team, but it was supported by the Ferrari team manager and the works mechanics. Baghetti was second fastest in practice and came through to win the first Formula One race in which he had ever driven from Gurney and Bonnier. I had quite a good race, being eighth fastest in practice and fifth finisher after a long battle with Trintignant (Cooper-Maserati).

At the International Silverstone meeting on May 6 I appeared with Coombs' new Cooper Monaco. The car was very new, still unpainted and we had a host of problems in practice. I was third fastest in practice behind the UDT-Laystall-entered Lotus 19s of Moss and Allison. I worked with the Coombs mechanics late into the night before the race and our efforts were rewarded. Although the Lotus 19s displayed a tremendous turn of speed in the race and Stirling was the winner, I managed to keep within striking distance and snatched second place from Allison in the closing laps.

In 1961 the International Trophy was held as an Inter-Continental Formula race. For this event my team-mate John Surtees had been released to drive Tony Vandervell's rear-engined 2.6-litre Vanwall (making what was to be its only race appearance), and as the works Coopers missed this race, Reg brought Jack Brabham into the team. During practice I had a very nasty moment when I came through Maggotts close to the limit to find John pushing the Vanwall across the track after the engine had stopped. John kept on pushing and I just drifted past on the outside! I made sixth fastest practice time in 1 min 36.2 sec (McLaren with Tommy Atkins' Cooper was fastest in 1 min 34.2 sec). The race was run in the wet and for once I was in good form on a wet track. Just about the only drivers not to spin were Stirling, Jack and myself and we took the first three places; some of the more press-on drivers spun two or three times!

My final race of the day was the Saloon Car event which was dominated by Dan Gurney's enormous Chevrolet Impala until it lost a wheel. The Jaguars scurried behind in pursuit, I was second until I was black-flagged because the boot lid was flapping, and I rejoined the race in fifth position. Soon afterwards my engine began to smoke and I decided to call it a day (it proved to be only an oil leak).

Because Yeoman Credit was a private team, it was guaranteed only one entry at Monaco and the second driver would have to qualify. So while John Surtees ran at Monaco I competed in a minor Formula One race held at Naples the same day. The Posillipo road circuit at Naples had high kerbs all the way round, it was lined by trees, badly surfaced and the marshalling was inept. I was fastest in practice – admittedly the opposition was mediocre apart from the inexperienced Baghetti with the much more powerful Ferrari that was expected to win the race.

I made a good start, took the lead from Bandini (Cooper-Maserati) and was then myself passed by Baghetti. I decided to follow the young Italian and hustle him in the closing laps when his inexperience would probably give me a chance to pass. This never happened, for I began to feel the car handling rather oddly and it started to use a lot of road. I decided to call into the pits, but before I got there I lost the Cooper on a long, left-hand bend, went off the road backwards and ended up with the car neatly parked between a couple of trees. I managed to get back to the pits where a punctured rear wheel, the cause of the accident, was changed and I rejoined the race to finish eighth – a great disappointment in a race which I had an excellent chance of winning. Peter Bryant, my mechanic, had noticed that the tyre was deflating as I passed the pits, but there was no chance to warn me.

The qualification problem occurred again the following weekend at the Dutch Grand Prix, so John ran there while I competed at the Crystal Palace and managed to win a total of four races with four different cars – every race in which I was entered. They were all short races, so the question of tiredness did not arise, but the real problem was that there was not enough time in practice to get all the cars set up to suit the circuit. I won the Norbury Trophy for GT cars with Coombs' E-type, the MGM Green Helmet Trophy for Sports Cars with Coombs' Cooper Monaco and the London Trophy Formula One race with a Yeoman Credit Cooper. The last race of the day was for saloon cars and on the starting line John Coombs came over to me and said, 'The plan is that Parkes is going to try to get ahead and Sears is going to look after you.' While there was nothing surprising about this, I was not sure whether John was being very nice and urging me to take the race easily or whether he was trying to stir me up and get me in a fighting mood. He certainly succeeded in the latter! I was so steamed

At the Crystal Palace on Whit Monday 1961 I drove Coombs' E-type Jaguar to a win in the Norbury Trophy (Anthony J. Bond).

up that I got away badly in third place at the start and at the end of lap two I thrust past Sears at Tower corner, bumping over the grass and the kerb and taking him on the inside. Jack held his line, the Jaguars collided and whilst I went off on my way, he went into the railway sleepers lining the corner. I chased after Parkes, not expecting to get a chance to pass him, but he lost a wheel on lap six going into Ramp corner and I was able to stroll home.

After the race John seemed to be disowning me and was consoling Tommy Sopwith, but I did get a 'thumbs up' from John when Tommy was looking the other way. It had really been a very bad day for Tommy, for in addition to the two Jaguars shunted in the Saloon Car race, Parkes had crashed Sopwith's Ferrari 250GT in the GT event. The rivalry was really only between Sopwith and Coombs, for I always got on splendidly with the Equipe Endeavour drivers Parkes and Sears. For me it had been a magnificent day and also very lucrative – quite possible the best that I ever had in England.

For the Le Mans race I was invited to drive John Ogier's Aston Martin DBR1 with Tony Maggs as co-driver. Our car was works-supported with a works-prepared engine and with works mechanics at the race. The Ferrari team were almost certain winners and we looked on the Border Reivers DBR1, driven by Clark/Flockhart and also works-supported, as our main rivals. Maggs was a very good driver, we got on well together and we thought that we had all the ingredients for a good race. Jimmy and I had a scrap in the opening laps, but for most of the time we led the other DBR1 which retired with engine trouble. We

In all I won four races with four different cars at the Crystal Palace. Here I am on my way to victory in the London Trophy Formula One race with my Yeoman Credit Cooper-Climax (Roy Salvadori collection).

were holding fourth place in the 18th hour of the race when I had to bring the car into the pits because of a bad fuel leak. It was a dangerous situation because the tank was split and petrol was dripping on to the very hot gearbox/final drive unit; there was no alternative but to withdraw the car. Works Ferraris took the first three places.

By this stage in my career I had mastered the art of the 24 Hours race, that combination of stamina and fairly hard driving which tries not to take too much out of the car. I think that I was already a past number in Formula One (although it gave me all the benefits of large retainers and high starting money) and it was on long-distance racing that I should have concentrated my efforts.

My single-seater results over the next few races were uninspiring. I had a rather uneventful race in the French Grand Prix to finish eighth, although it was in fact a very eventful race, run in incredibly hot conditions, with the road surface breaking up in the heat and three of the four Ferrari drivers retiring (including Phil Hill who spun on wet tar in front of Stirling and eliminated them both). The race was won by Baghetti's nominally private Ferrari. Six days later I drove a Yeoman Credit Inter-Continental Cooper in the British Empire Trophy race at Silverstone and finished sixth after the loss of two gears. The Touring Car race at Silverstone proved a complete disaster, for it started to rain just before the start and I was caught out with completely wrong tyres – they were scrubbed and lacked pattern at the edges, just the way I liked them when I was racing at Silverstone in the dry. The wheels were slipping even as I drove to the start line and common sense dictated that I drove a very cautious race. Instead I pushed the car hard until I aquaplaned into the bank at Club corner on lap four. Bruce McLaren, a very good wet-weather driver, did exactly the same thing at the same corner soon afterwards and the race was won by Mike Parkes who had cannily managed to fit a set of Dunlop SP road tyres just before the start.

The following weekend I was in action again with a Yeoman Credit Cooper-Climax in the British Grand Prix at Aintree. The race was run in the wet and now Dunlop had introduced a new wet-weather tyre that suited me very well. I worked my way up to fifth place and for the first time in my life I was disappointed when the rain eased. As the track dried, some of the more powerful cars were able to pull away from me and I lost a place to Bonnier's Porsche to finish sixth, but ahead of Gurney, McLaren, Brooks and Ireland. I also gained my first World Championship point of the year.

At the August Bank Holiday weekend the Yeoman Credit team split its effort between the German Grand Prix on the Sunday and the International Brands Hatch meeting the following day. The German race at the Nürburgring saw the first and none too successful appearance of the new V-8 Coventry-Climax engine in the Cooper driven by Jack Brabham. Jack took the lead at the start, but crashed after only a few kilometres, and Moss soon went ahead to score one of the finest wins of his career, defeating the much more powerful Ferrari team. It was a victory aided by Moss' decision to run on the latest Dunlop D.12 rain tyres – the Ferrari team opted for dry-weather tyres – and this enabled him to

A splendid photograph of the Aston Martin DB4GT Zagato which I drove into third place in the 1961 Tourist Trophy behind a brace of Ferraris (B. F. E. Clarke, Roy Salvadori collection).

consolidate his lead in the closing laps of the race when heavy rain fell. John Surtees finished fifth.

I had a thoroughly miserable race. I started off driving fairly steadily, holding ninth place, but then speeded up. I lost the Cooper at the Karussel, stalled it and, rather dangerously, blocked the road at its narrowest point until I could lug the car clear. Apart from a bashed nose, the Cooper seemed all right; I eventually restarted and carried on to finish tenth, slowing considerably in the heavy rain towards the end of the race.

The main race at Brands Hatch the following day was the 201-mile Guards Trophy for Inter-Continental Formula cars and after the Nürburgring none of the drivers was at his best. I drove a steady race, but like several other drivers I spun on oil dropped by Munaron's Cooper-Maserati. Jim Clark had a quick spin and carried on without stalling his engine; I stalled my engine and lost time restarting, and poor John Surtees stuffed his Cooper into the bank. I climbed back through the field to finish fifth behind Brabham, Clark, Graham Hill and McLaren. At the start of the day I had driven the Coombs E-type in the GT race and led initially, but finished third because of plug trouble. I rounded off the day by finishing second in the Redex Trophy, splitting a pair of Equipe Endeavour Jaguars and setting a new class lap record of 78.97 mph. *Autosport* wrote, 'Parkes won by 3.4 seconds from Salvadori, who looked absolutely exhausted after his four races in two days.' There was already a rule preventing a driver from competing in another race the same day as a Grand Prix, but it was only later that a longer interval between races was imposed. It was a change much needed to protect drivers from themselves!

For the Tourist Trophy, a three-hour race for Grand Touring cars at Goodwood, I was invited to drive one of three Aston Martin DB4GTs entered by the Ogier team. Jim Clark and I drove Zagato-bodied cars, while Innes Ireland had a standard-bodied car, and as in 1960 it was a works-supported effort. The race was really between Stirling with a Ferrari 250GT entered by Rob Walker and Mike Parkes with the similar Maranello Concessionaires' car, whilst we were in with a chance only if something happened to the Ferraris; our cars were not as fast as the Ferraris and suffered heavier tyre wear. Parkes took pole position with a time of 1 min 34.4 sec, Stirling had recorded 1 min 34.8 sec, I was third fastest in 1 min 36.6 sec and my team mate Jim Clark lapped in 1 min 37.6 sec.

At the Le Mans start Parkes was away first, Jimmy (always very quick at Le Mans starts) got away second, I was third, followed by Moss who took a couple of laps to pass the Astons. I passed Jimmy on lap three, Stirling took the lead on lap eight and when Innes came through to hold station behind Jimmy the finishing order for the race had already been established! Not only were we using tyres at a faster rate than the Ferraris (during the race I changed 14 tyres), but our pit stops were slower. Places changed temporarily as a result of scheduled – and unscheduled – pit stops; Jimmy lost time while a flapping boot lid was secured and Parkes' Ferrari spent over a minute in the pits while the Maranello mechanics struggled to remove a damaged, trailing aluminium sump guard. In the closing laps of the race I closed to within five seconds of Parkes, but he put on speed and I had no real hope of catching him. Stirling averaged 86.62 mph, compared with my average of 85.70 mph.

On the evening of the Goodwood race many of the drivers, including me, flew to Sweden to compete in the so-called Kannon Loppet, a series of races held on a 1.863-mile course at the Karlskoga Motor Stadium and for the first time run for Formula One cars. I finished fourth, pushing my car across the line after the engine blew up a lap before the finish. A sad aspect of this race was Geoff Duke's bad crash with Fred Tuck's Cooper. When John Surtees and I went to see him in hospital, the extent of his injuries worried us a great deal and we were very

Concentrating hard with the Yeoman Credit Formula One Cooper-Climax in the 1961 Modena Grand Prix. I retired because of engine trouble (Attual Foto).

relieved when we heard that he was making a good recovery. Geoff's injuries effectively ended his chequered attempt to make a career in motor racing that dated back to 1952. I had learned from my Aston Martin team-mates that although they considered Geoff had the talent to become a World Championship contender, he really needed a basic training programme with a good team before graduating to International Sports Car racing.

The following weekend we competed at the Roskilde Ring in Denmark where I was third on the aggregate of two heats behind Moss and Ireland. Yeoman Credit then travelled to Italy for the Modena race and the Italian Grand Prix. Both John and I were out of luck at Modena and retired with engine problems. The Italian Grand Prix was held on the banked track and road circuit at Monza, a combination that favoured the very powerful Ferraris even more than at most circuits. Ferrari entered four cars and there was an additional, nominally private entry for Baghetti. The Ferraris dominated practice and the fastest British runner was Graham Hill with a BRM-Climax, sixth fastest in 2 min 48.7 sec. Both John and I were right out of the picture and the reason is not difficult to pinpoint. Reg Parnell was always inclined to carry out modifications to the Climax engines and for Monza he had been persuaded to make a number of changes that destroyed the cars' straight-line speed. I was 17th fastest in 2 min 55.2 sec and poor John who was usually so very quick at Monza, was even slower: 20th fastest in 2 min 55.6 sec.

The race was marred by the collision between Clark's Lotus and von Trips' Ferrari which cost the life of the young German driver and fifteen spectators; three other Ferraris retired and Phil Hill clinched his World Championship by winning with the surviving Maranello car from Gurney (Porsche), McLaren (Cooper) and privateer Jack Lewis who had driven a fine race with his Cooper. My brief for the race was to keep going steadily and this I did, completing a rather bumpy, boring race to finish sixth.

The Yeoman Credit team travelled straight from Monza to Zeltweg in Austria for a Formula One race the following weekend. I was fifth fastest in practice, well up with the leaders in the race and having a good dice with Jack Brabham. As we approached the hairpin bend on lap 11, Pirocchi with a Cooper-Maserati took a left-hand line into the corner, apparently letting me and Jack through on the inside. I had left my braking very late, so that there was no room for error, and when Pirocchi cut across the corner in front of me I hit him and went straight over the top of the Cooper-Maserati; my car was launched about ten feet in the air, cleared the straw bales lining the circuit and landed on its nose. Both cars were write-offs and I was incredibly lucky to escape without injury. Afterwards Jack Brabham told me that I braked so late that even if I had not hit Pirocccchi, it was unlikely that I would have got round the corner.

My final outing of the year was in the United States Grand Prix at Watkins Glen, a race that Ferrari missed now that the Championship was in the bag. The British teams, Cooper, Lotus, BRM and Yeoman Credit, together with Porsche, were out in force and there was a large number of private entries. Neither Surtees nor I were particularly quick in practice, but Watkins Glen was a circuit that I liked very much and I really got going in the race. I held eighth place in the opening laps but worked my way through to fifth, and I was really motor racing (a contrast with some of my Formula One performances earlier in the year!). Moss retired, I passed McLaren and Gurney, and when Graham Hill stopped at the pits because of a loose magneto I moved up into second place. With five laps to go to the finish I was only five seconds behind race-leader Innes Ireland (works Lotus) and gaining every lap, but as I came up to lap his team-mate Jimmy Clark (who had problems earlier in the race), I found that I was being held up on corners and on that lap alone I lost two seconds. It seemed that Jimmy was trying to preserve Ireland's slender lead. On the next lap I managed to squeeze past coming out of one of the corners, but only a few yards later there was a loud bang as my engine broke and I was out of the race. I believe that I had over-revved my engine in my desperate attempt to get past Jimmy. It was a very disappointing conclusion to a year in which I had driven in more Formula One races than any year previously in my racing career, and a very disappointing end to my best race of the year.

Chapter 12

Finale in Formula One, 1962

Reg Parnell asked me to stay with the team for 1962 and it was agreed that Surtees would definitely be the number one driver and I would play 'second fiddle'. There would be insufficient of the new V-8 Coventry-Climax engines and Reg could not effect as good service arrangements as Cooper and Lotus, so I would use engines with which Surtees had practised and raced once. This meant that I always had a tired engine and had to nurse it in races. I agreed to all this even though I did get rather upset about the arrangement during the course of the year.

The Yeoman Credit company had been sold to Bowmaker, another big finance company, and the team raced initially under the name Bowmaker-Yeoman Racing and later simply as Bowmaker Racing. Perhaps the most important development was that the team had made arrangements for its own Formula One contender to be designed and built by Eric Broadley who had achieved phenomenal success with his front-engined Lola sports cars.

The Lola was based on a very small and very slim multi-tubular space-frame chassis constructed from mild steel tubing with front and rear suspension by double wishbones, short transverse links and long fore-and-aft radius arms. The engine was the Coventry-Climax FWMV V-8 developing around 180 bhp and this was used in conjunction with a Colotti five-speed and reverse gearbox. It was a neat, simple and very effective car of immense promise, but it was probably too much to hope that the cars would be right in their first season and we were to have many disappointments.

Initially the chassis was insufficiently stiff, there were suspension breakages, the gearbox was less than ideal and we suffered more than our fair share of engine failures. It proved very much a year of development with changes made to the cars on a race-by-race basis. I raced a special Cooper during the early part of 1962. This was based on the smaller, more compact Cooper Formula Junior chassis, with Formula One suspension and brakes and modified Formula Junior bodywork, and had been raced by John a couple of times in 1961. I was never much in favour of 'specials' and would have preferred to race the standard Cooper product.

When I started to race the V-8 Lola, I found it a pleasant car to drive, but I do not think that it was a car that inspired me. The steering was superb, light and positive, the Girling brakes were powerful and reliable, and the car had good

John Surtees, Reg and myself in New Zealand in 1962 (Roy Salvadori collection).

adhesion. The V-8 Coventry-Climax engine was, of course, much more powerful than the old four-cylinder, although it must be remembered that we were racing cars substantially less powerful than at the start of the 2,500 cc Grand Prix Formula eight years previously; the latest 1,500 cc cars were of course much lighter, much more compact and to a degree easier to drive.

At the beginning of the year Bowmaker-Yeoman competed in New Zealand and Australia with their 1961 Inter-Continental Formula cars. Our first two races were cut short because of rain storms and I took a fourth in the New Zealand Grand Prix and a fifth in the Hudson Memorial Trophy. In contrast the following weekend's Lady Wigram Trophy was held in stiflingly hot conditions and I again finished fifth.

Bowmaker-Yeoman skipped the last of the New Zealand races to give themselves plenty of time for shipping the cars and preparing them for the International '100' race at Warwick Farm in Australia on February 4. At Warwick Farm we were using an improved Dunlop tyre and although Surtees and I each had a set for the race, we had to share a set in practice. Surtees came back into the pits near the end of practice and the mechanics had a frantic rush to transfer the wheels from his car. I had made a very quick time on the harder tyres and was keen to improve this on the softer compound.

I charged off from the pits, joined the long straight and was approaching the hairpin bend that followed very quickly. As to what happened next I have to rely on what I was told, as I remember nothing of the accident. As I braked for the hairpin, my car turned sharp right into a flag marshalling area protected by sleepers and hit this at around 100 mph. I suffered head injuries, a broken cheekbone and severe facial cuts, the car was a write-off and two marshalls were injured. I was unconscious until the following day; after a spell in hospital I spent a few days recovering at the home of a friend and I was later flown back to England for further medical treatment. I had plastic surgery carried out by a very fine surgeon Robin Beare, who built up my eyelid and the area round my eye that had been badly damaged in the accident. My theory as to the cause of the accident is that we had failed to pump up the brakes (a procedure peculiar to the Cooper after a wheel-change) and then as I pumped them up quickly for the corner, the right front brake locked.

I flew back to Australia for the Sandown Park Trophy on March 11/12 and in this race I drove a 2.5-litre Cooper-Climax that Jack Brabham had sold to Lex Davison to replace the Cooper that he had crashed at Longford. I was far from fit and it was a very stupid thing to do, although it seemed a good idea at the time! I was slow in practice and in the race and retired because of mechanical trouble.

When I returned from Australia I contacted John Coombs to sort out details for the coming season. Our original deal had been that I would drive a Jaguar E-type and a 3.8 saloon for him, but later he had discussed a deal with Graham Hill which would have brought John Coombs additional sponsorship. Coombs asked me if I would go along with this. If Graham joined the team, Coombs would be racing five cars, two 3.8 saloons, the E-type and a DB4GT Zagato and a Ferrari 250GTO which were about to be ordered. There would be more cars than the team could cope with and I was convinced that one of the drivers would suffer. John said that it would mean a great deal to him to sign up a driver of the calibre of Hill, but I would remain number one driver with a choice of cars. I was not at all sure that Graham would accept an arrangement like that, and for my own part I was not prepared to treat Graham, a good friend, in this fashion. Accordingly I suggested that both Graham and I went to a circuit for testing at the beginning of the season and we would each choose a Jaguar 3.8. If we could not agree who would drive which car, then we would spin a coin. This did not of

Below left *Discussing pre-race tactics with team-mate Graham Hill of the Coombs organisation* (Roy Salvadori collection).
Below right *A publicity photograph taken for Dunlop at Goodwood in 1962* (Dunlop).

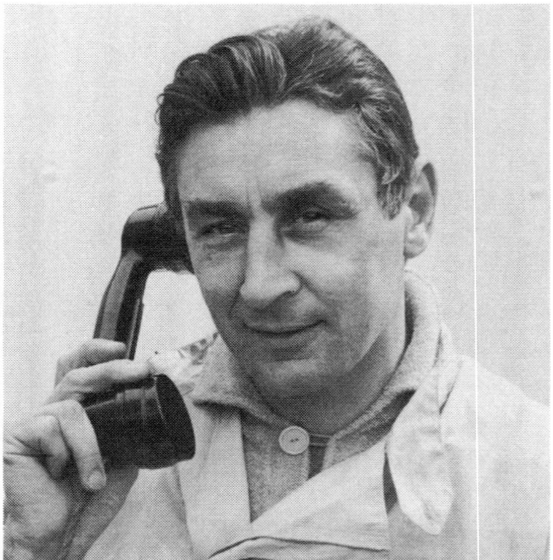

course solve the problem of Coombs having too many cars to prepare, but it did seem a reasonable compromise. John accepted this idea, although I have no idea of what Graham thought because Graham never mentioned his views to me. With hindsight it would have been better for the three of us to have had a meeting to sort out the situation.

I discovered that Graham had already done the testing, set the cars up to suit his driving style and made his choice! When I did drive my 3.8, I found that it was most disappointing. It proved a dreadful handful when I first raced it at Oulton Park on April 7, finishing sixth in the GT race; I rolled it in practice at Snetterton on a fast corner which should have been flat out and after the bent panels had been beaten out drove it in the race to finish fourth; later I finished second to Hill at Goodwood and Aintree and I retired with clutch trouble at Silverstone.

The way Graham set up a car, very stiff with a hard anti-roll bar, did not suit me at all and I made my views very clear to John. I suggested that if Graham could achieve a competitive lap in my 3.8, I would keep quiet. Graham tried my car at Silverstone, but failed to record a really fast lap time; even so Graham thought that the car was all right. There seemed to be very little point in discussing the problem further and I rather regretted driving for John under these conditions. We did improve my car as the year progressed. This was the only car of John's that I ever had misgivings about.

Bowmaker's first European races were the Brussels Grand Prix and the Lombank Trophy at Snetterton. In both these events John Surtees drove a four-cylinder Climax-powered Lola, I drove the lightweight Cooper and we both retired. Bowmaker-Yeoman fortunes improved at Goodwood. John drove both a V-8 Lola-Climax and a four-cylinder Lola, while I had a four-cylinder Lola afflicted by the most terrible understeer. In the Lavant Cup for four-cylinder Formula One cars I finished second to Bruce McLaren (works Cooper), but only after I had spun coming out of the chicane, fallen right down the field and made up lost ground. John, leading the race, was eliminated when he tried to lap Seifert's Lotus at the chicane, bounced off the wall and tore off the Lola's nearside rear wheel.

In the International '100' race I began to master the understeer of my Lola by keeping the inside front wheel right on the grass at corners, but if I was not quick enough to catch the back end as it broke away I was likely to be in serious trouble. I have mentioned time and time again that many of the cars I drove suffered marked understeering characteristics and I suspect that these characteristics were often exaggerated by my driving style. I spun at Lavant, but finished fourth behind Graham Hill (BRM V-8), McLaren and Ireland (Lotus). Surtees was right out of the picture after two pit stops. This was the race in which Stirling crashed so badly at St Mary's that his racing career came to an end. As I passed the crashed Lotus lap after lap, it was only too obvious that Stirling was trapped in the wreckage.

Stirling was the greatest British driver of his era and, with the exception of Fangio in Formula One, the best in the world. In any type of car he could maintain a marked superiority. Throughout his career he was always at the forefront of racing and unlike many other drivers – including some World Champions – he was never off form, but consistently brilliant. When Stirling was racing, every driver tacitly accepted his superiority. There was no immediate successor to assume his mantle and it is a matter of conjecture whether there has been to this day.

My drive with the Lola in the Aintree '200' was marred by a broken piston in practice and by a broken throttle linkage in the race. A fortnight later at Silverstone I raced the V-8 Lola for the first time. I was eliminated on the first lap when Trintignant was put off the road by another car at Abbey and spun; I took to the grass and was clouted by Shelly's Lotus, also taking evasive action. Surtees finished third. In the Dutch Grand Prix Surtees crashed heavily when a front suspension wishbone broke. Reg Parnell withdrew my car as a precautionary measure. By the time the Lolas were next raced, they were fitted with much stronger wishbones.

In the face of Ferrari 250GTO opposition the E-type had much less chance of winning and I had crashed Coombs' E-type at the Easter Goodwood meeting whilst chasing Parkes' 250GTO too hard. By the Brands Hatch meeting on May 27 Coombs had taken delivery of a new Aston Martin DB4GT Zagato, but it proved no Ferrari-catcher, it needed a great deal of sorting and I finished a poor second in the Peco Trophy race to Ireland's 250GTO. The Coombs team did not enter the Aston Martin again. I was expecting an easy win in the Touring Car race at Brands Hatch, as I had been fastest in practice, but I got stuck behind Kelsey's enormous Chevrolet which was fast on the straights and slow through the corners. I lacked the speed to pass on the straight, was held up by the Chevrolet at every corner and had to settle for second place, but with the consolation of having set a new Touring Car lap record.

At Monaco both Lolas were fitted with very short noses to prevent accident damage on this tight and crowded circuit from blocking off the air flow to the radiators. My car was fitted with very soft springs which gave problems with full tanks, but we anticipated that the handling would improve as the tanks lightened. Neither of us was particularly quick in practice, John recording 1 min 37.9 sec, while I turned in 1 min 38.5 sec (Clark was fastest in 1 min 35.4 sec), but we both qualified comfortably. On the first lap of the race Mairesse (Ferrari), who had rushed through from the second row of the grid, overcooked the Gasometer hairpin (the first corner) and set off a chain reaction crash which eliminated Trintignant, Ginther and Gurney; when everyone had sorted themselves out, I came round in last position! Monaco was the one race above all others where I wanted to keep going, as there were always prospects of a good place through retirements, but my car was handling so appallingly that I eventually retired on lap 45. Surtees took fourth place.

On Whit Monday the Bowmaker team divided its efforts and sent Surtees to Mallory Park where he won the 2,000 Guineas International race, while I was entered at the Crystal Palace. The Coombs team entered Graham Hill with the E-type at Mallory Park, while I drove Graham's 3.8 in the Saloon Car race at the

Palace. I tried both his Jaguar and mine in practice, and it was obvious immediately that Graham's car was vastly superior to mine, some two-seconds-a-lap faster and with much better handling. I was fastest in practice and led throughout to win from Jack Sears and Kelsey's Chevrolet which was disqualified for having no silencer.

In the 36-lap Formula One race the main opposition to my Lola V-8 came from the UDT-Laystall-Lotus-BRM V-8s of Ireland and Trevor Taylor. Innes missed practice because he had been racing in Canada and started from the back of the grid. I led the race initially, Innes passed me on lap 3 and at the finish I was just over 20 seconds behind. I must admit that I was not putting enough into my Formula One racing. Part of the problem was that I did not really get on with the Lola and I think that I was too old to 'bend' with the car, unlike Surtees who was full of youthful enthusiasm. However, whilst I had lost my edge in Formula One, I was still very much a winner in Saloon, Sports Car and GT racing and regularly beating front rank Formula One drivers in similar cars.

Bowmaker were short of engines for the Belgian Grand Prix and ran only one car for Surtees. My next race was Le Mans where I had been asked to drive for Briggs Cunningham. It was intended that I should handle one of Briggs' Maserati Tipo 151 coupés, but when I tried the car I found that I could not get into the cockpit. Briggs had also decided to run a Jaguar E-type, something of a late decision, and a car had been quickly prepared by the factory. I tried this and it proved to be the most comfortable competition car that I ever drove. Cunningham was proposing to drive this car himself and said to me, 'You don't want to co-drive with me, do you?' I told him that nothing would please me more. I drove fairly hard in the race, while Briggs in his usual style took the race rather more cautiously, and as faster cars retired we gradually moved up through the field so that by 10:00 am on the Sunday we were holding fifth place behind the rather faster, more heavily modified E-type of Sargent/Lumsden. Our car was running superbly, as fit as ever, and when the Sargent/Lumsden car was slowed by a collapsed rear engine bearer, I was able to speed up and catch it two laps from the end so that we moved up to finish fourth and win our class behind a trio of Ferraris. For the third time I had been co-driver for the winner of the Wolf Barnato Trophy, the award for the entrant of the highest placed British car.

After this delightful interlude it was back to Formula One with the Bowmaker team. On July 1 we ran in the Reims Grand Prix, a non-Championship race which was supported nevertheless by all the leading teams except Ferrari and Porsche. I drove a steady race, dicing with Ginther (BRM) until his gearbox broke, and finished sixth. Surtees had led the race, building up a substantial lead of 20 seconds, until a valve spring broke causing his retirement. A week later we ran in the French Grand Prix at Rouen where Porsche entered their new flat-8 cars, but Ferrari, still unhappy with his V-6 model, again gave the race a miss. I had a lousy engine, it was hesitating and pulling badly in practice and it eventually blew up. This created a problem for Reg, as the team had only a brand-new engine straight from Coventry-Climax. Reg decided that I should use this engine, do a few laps to collect the starting money and then retire. When I tried my car with this engine the following day, the carburation was dreadful and the car would simply not pull out of corners. Reg refused to adjust the engine, commenting, 'After all, you're only going to cover a few laps.' When I received a pre-arranged signal from Reg, I pulled into the pits to retire, but after a long discussion it was decided that so many cars were retiring that I ought to carry on for a bit and see whether I was likely to finish well up the field. Eventually Reg signalled me again and the whole sequence repeated itself so that I found myself back in the race once more. When I received yet another 'come in' signal from Reg, I pulled in to retire. As I was leaving the pits I met William Samengo-Turner who sympathised about my retirement and commented on my bad luck in Formula One. It was apparent that he had not been informed about the arrangement at this race and I was very embarrassed. The race was won by Gurney (Porsche); John Surtees finished fourth after delays caused by fuel starvation.

I next ran in the British Grand Prix at Aintree on July 21. Surtees drove superbly, ran second fastest in practice and finished a very strong second to Jimmy Clark (Lotus) in the race. I was running eighth when my engine started to run rough. The cause was thought to be a flat battery that was affecting the ignition and fuel pumps. However, a change of battery failed to cure the problem and there was no alternative but to retire. Surtees again finished second in the German Grand Prix run on a wet circuit, but although I ran well in practice (ninth fastest) I retired early in the race because of problems with my Colotti gearbox.

At Brands Hatch the following day I drove John Coombs' new and long-awaited Ferrari 250GTO in the Peco Trophy race for GT cars. I had been rather discontented because Graham Hill was getting most of the drives in the E-type, so John Coombs promised that I would be able to drive the new Ferrari when it arrived. The 250GTO was the most fabulous GT car that I ever raced, very powerful, with superb roadholding and great controlability on the throttle when it was drifting. The race was run in the wet, but I was in the hunt right from the start and once I had settled down with the new car I speeded up to pass the GTOs of Ireland and Surtees to finish second behind Parkes with a similar car – a marked contrast with my Formula One performances.

The following weekend Bowmaker ran at Karlskoga and, rather surprisingly, I went very quickly with the Lola V-8. I started from the second row of the grid, tangled with Innes Ireland at the first corner but managed to get going again, while he went off into a shallow ditch and lost a lot of time before he rejoined the race. I then had a race-long battle with Bonnier (Porsche), squeezed past him and managed to hold him off to the line to take second place behind Masten Gregory (UDT-Laystall Lotus). After the race Ken Tyrrell, who was at the circuit with his team of Formula Junior Coopers, congratulated me and commented, 'Roy, you've had a good innings – I reckon it's now time for you to pack up Formula One!' – in effect confirming the decision that I had already reached.

John Coombs had told me that I would be driving the GTO in the Tourist Trophy at Goodwood the following weekend, but even so I was given the E-type to drive in the race. I was very disappointed and I probably should have made a fuss. I was fourth fastest in practice with the E-type and reconciled to the fact that the Jaguar lacked the acceleration to stay with the 250GTOs. I knew that the E-type's pit stop would take longer than the Ferraris', but it proved an absolute disaster and lasted 70 seconds, compared with 37.6 seconds for Graham Hill. I drove absolutely on the limit for the full 240 miles to finish fourth behind the 250GTOs of Ireland, Hill and Parkes and my average speed of 92.95 mph was the highest ever achieved by an E-type at Goodwood.

It was across to Copenhagen the following weekend for the Formula One race at the Roskilde Ring. My race was soon over because Rhodesian Gary Hocking (Lotus) collided with me at the first corner of my heat and put me out. John Surtees was eliminated in the final when he collided with Innes Ireland. Reg Parnell was convinced that Hocking was going to make it to the top in motor racing as well as motor cycle racing, but he did not have to shunt me to prove it!

We next ran at Oulton Park where I also entered with Coombs' Jaguar 3.8 which was much improved. Both Hill and I had been going well in practice and I was trying hard to match Hill's time which was marginally faster than mine. On the approach to Cascade I braked hard for the corner, there was a loud bang as a tyre burst, the car charged straight into the bank at around 90 mph, flipped into the lake the other side and landed on its roof in about 4 ft of water – just a little farther out the water had a depth of 30 ft. It was really terrifying to see the bank coming up so quickly and to know that there was absolutely nothing that I could do about it.

I sat upside down in the water, held in place by my seat harness. Somehow, not consciously, I touched the central release of the harness and I found that I was floating inside the car. I believe that at some stage I was able to breathe and I think that there must have been some 3 or 4 in of air at the floor of the car (it was, as I have said, upside down). I am told that two minutes elapsed before I was released from the car. The pain was dreadful, I felt that my chest was exploding and I began to swallow water. It seemed a terribly degrading death for a racing driver – the last thing that a driver expects is to drown. Suddenly a hand grabbed me and pulled me out of the car. A marshall had waded into the water and pulled me out through one of the rear doors. Without a doubt that marshall saved my life because I could not have escaped from the car on my own. I suffered facial cuts and also sinus trouble as a result of the accident; this took some two years to clear up.

The Jaguar was to all intents and purposes a write-off and I was a non-starter in the Saloon Car race. Although I was badly shocked, I practised later in the day for the Gold Cup race with my Lola. I do not remember a thing about practising or a long conversation that I had with Stirling who was attending his first race meeting since his Goodwood shunt. This all sounds rather frightening, but I must have seemed relatively normal or Reg would not have let me practice and in fact I was one of the Formula One drivers who broke the lap record. In the race I held seventh place until I had throttle cable problems on lap 18. I stopped out on the circuit and borrowed a box of matches from a marshall so that I could jam a matchstick between the cable stop to give enough tick-over to crawl back to the pits.

I non-started in the United States Grand Prix because Surtees crashed heavily in practice and took over my car for the race. We then flew to Mexico City to compete in the Mexican Grand Prix, a new non-Championship race. The only important teams to contest this race were Lotus, Brabham and Bowmaker. Jim Clark was disqualified for receiving a push start, Surtees lost eight laps while the transistorised ignition was changed and I held second place behind Jack Brabham with Innes Ireland hot on my exhausts. When Ireland spun at one of the hairpin bends he hit the Lola's rear wheels, damaging the transmission and putting me out of the race. My final race of the year was the South African Grand Prix at Kyalami where I retired because of a leaking rubber bag fuel tank. It had been a thoroughly miserable year for me in Formula One, almost enough to put me off motor racing altogether, and I was only too glad when the year came to an end.

A significant event in 1962 was the Krikler Report. This was a paper published by Dr Berenice Krikler, Chief Psychiatrist at St George's Hospital, following a series of tests carried out with six Formula One drivers: Innes Ireland, Jimmy Clark, Jack Brabham, Bruce McLaren, Graham Hill and myself, spread over about a week. The purpose was to set a pattern of reaction and behaviour for Grand Prix drivers which could be used as a yardstick for Stirling Moss who was still recovering from his accident. The tests consisted of the use of a simulator, reaction tests and many adaptions of the familiar and established psychiatric tests.

After some of the tests I had the feeling that I could not cope and the simulator in particular made me feel sick. Because of the head injuries which I suffered in racing, there are certain things that I cannot cope with and it seemed that the tests were touching on these areas. I mentioned the problem to Dr Krikler and the result was that after a couple of days I was thanked for my contribution and told that I would not be needed for the remainder of the tests. Very shortly afterwards Dr Krikler wrote to me, advising that because of the head injuries that I had suffered I should give up racing and consult a neurologist. I did not agree with her view – after all, the Silverstone accident had happened 11 years previously and since then I had raced without feeling any of the stress that I had suffered during the tests. I could only assume that Dr Krikler had vastly overestimated the stress factor in motor racing.

When the report was published, it mentioned that a driver had been dropped from the tests and advised to give up racing, but no name was mentioned. I took no notice of Dr Krikler's advice – in fact I was rather amused by it – but later there was a lingering doubt as to whether I should have pursued her advice. Looking back now with some degree of detachment, I am convinced that she was wrong. I am well aware that there are certain things that I cannot do due to that accident and I adjust my life pattern to avoid these problem areas.

Chapter 13

My final racing years, 1963–65

Introduction by John Wyer

'When I left Aston Martin to join the Ford GT40 programme, towards the end of 1963, one of my first assignments was to propose the drivers for the 1964 season. As the car then existed only on paper it seemed highly unlikely, to me at least, that we would have a competitive car in 1964, so I did not have much to offer except the almighty dollar. In most cases this was to prove sufficient inducement and there was no shortage of applicants.

'As in everything else connected with the Ford GT40, politics came into the selection of drivers. Understandably, Ford wanted the emphasis to be on American drivers and I was quite happy about this because there were some very good American drivers available. We agreed upon Phil Hill, Richie Ginther and Masten Gregory. My own first choice was Roy Salvadori, who was accepted without demur, and the team was completed with Bruce McLaren, who was acceptable to everybody, and Joe Schlesser, which made Ford France happy.

'I particularly wanted Roy in the team because, in what I could see was going to be a difficult development period, I needed at least one driver who had worked with me before, with whom I could communicate and upon whom I knew I could rely to give me an objective and unbiased opinion. If, in the event, there had been any proper development period, I will always believe that Roy's association with the project would have been of the greatest value. But any hope of seriously testing the car before our first public appearance at the Le Mans Trials disappeared when Ford demanded that the first car to be completed be sent to New York for a press presentation. The results were disastrous and we went to the Le Mans Trials in a blaze of publicity with two cars which were completely untested. While showing great potential, they proved so unstable as to be extremely dangerous. Schlesser crashed very heavily, completely destroying the car but fortunately without personal injury. Roy Salvadori, for reasons which he will no doubt relate, also crashed in the braking area before Mulsanne, without serious damage.

'This was bad enough but for me worse was to follow. A few days after our return from Le Mans Roy returned the cheque for his retaining fee and said he no longer felt able to drive for us. He had completely lost confidence both in the car and in the course which the development programme was taking. With the ready support of Frank Zimmerman, our leader in Detroit, who had met Roy at the Le Mans Trials and taken an instant liking to him, I was able to persuade him to accept the cheque on the grounds that he had earned it if he never drove for us again. He also generously agreed to continue to help me with the development testing. But he was firm in his decision not to drive for us in races and I could do nothing to shake him.

'It was a very sad moment. With Roy's help I was able to establish a sensible test programme and, very largely due to his help, we were at least able to go to Le Mans in June with cars which were not only extremely fast but very stable. But we went without Roy Salvadori and I felt a great sense of loss. He was already contemplating retirement and I knew it was unlikely that he would drive for me again.

'Far from being adversely affected, our personal friendship was strengthened by the incident. I respected him for his decision, even while I found it hard to accept. Motor racing must be based upon mutual confidence between the driver and those responsible for the preparation of the car. Throughout our long association this confidence had existed between Roy and myself. Now, with the intrusion of politics and big money, there was a wind of change. Perhaps we had had the best of it.'

* * *

1963

My decision to retire from Formula One brought about a substantial reduction in the pressures of my motor racing life and racing income, but nevertheless I looked forward to the 1963 season with anticipation. I also reluctantly decided to part company with John Coombs who was – and still is – a great friend. I felt that Coombs had stretched himself preparing cars for both Graham Hill and myself, and I preferred to drive for a team that fielded cars just for me. There was a growing tendency for drivers to try to impose their will on a team, insisting on preferential treatment, and I felt that I had suffered from these pressures. I believed – and I was proved right – that I would be much happier driving only for 'Tommy' Atkins, whom I had known and trusted for many years.

During the year we achieved considerable success with the Jaguar 3.8 saloon, with the E-type and with the Cooper Monaco, despite problems with the sports car. This was a new T61M car powered by a 2.7-litre Coventry-Climax engine canted in the chassis, and fitted with the usual five-speed Cooper-Knight transaxle. It was built up by Harry Pearce and immaculately finished in Tommy's metallic green and white colours. Unfortunately it handled badly and we spent much of the season trying to sort it. Our best performances with the car were a win at Goodwood on Easter Monday, a really good victory over Ireland's Lotus 19 at Silverstone in May, and again at Silverstone at the British Grand Prix meeting, but I was beaten into second place by Roger Penske with the Zerex-Climax at Brands Hatch on August Bank Holiday Monday.

Above *Innes Ireland (Lotus 19) leads the pack at Silverstone in May 1963. I am in third place on the inside of the corner with Atkins' Cooper Monaco, but came through to win the race.* (Roy Salvadori collection).

Right *Another win with the Cooper Monaco was gained at Oulton Park in September 1963* (Roy Salvadori collection).

I scored another win with the Cooper and set a new class lap record at Oulton Park in September, the same meeting at which Jimmy Clark, World Champion to be, scored a win with his Formula One Lotus in the Gold Cup race. Tommy Atkins only came to the meeting on race day, and he had urged me to avoid the parties that were so much part of the pleasure of staying at the Chester Country Club and to get an early night on the Friday. Accordingly I booked a small room and after an early dinner went to bed at about 9:30 pm. An hour later there was a knock on the bedroom door; I opened it to find the manager, Denis Uren and a young lady who sometimes assisted in the pits. She explained that there was no accommodation and asked if she could share my room. I agreed with some reluctance and in due course went to sleep again.

After another hour or so there was again a knock on the door. This time it was Jimmy Clark, pleading to share my room because there was no accommodation at all in Chester. I finally agreed and opened the door to discover that Jimmy was accompanied by a young lady, and they were followed into the room by piles of extra bedding. Eventually the foursome settled down in the minute room, almost touching toes, and went to sleep. It was not long before Jimmy's snoring woke me and I was the only one to spend almost a completely sleepless night. I would have had far more sleep if I had spent half the night at one of the usual Oulton parties! The only consolation was that we both won our respective races.

At the end of the year Harry Pearce and I flew out to compete with the Cooper in the Riverside Grand Prix and, afterwards, hopefully to sell it. It was not one of our better races and I finished seventh after a pit stop to change plugs. I then lost the brakes completely. After the race I ran down poor Harry at about 15 mph – he was standing in front of the car, completely unaware that it was brakeless! Fortunately he was unhurt. We sold the Climax engine to Chuck Daigh, but we had to bring the Cooper chassis back to England.

Tommy had not raced a Jaguar 3.8 saloon before 1963 and the car, which was delivered by the factory as a body shell and a collection of bits and pieces and built up by Gordon Whitehead, was something of an unknown quantity. I drove the 3.8 to victory in the wet at Snetterton on March 30, leading home Graham Hill with the Coombs Jaguar, and this victory, which showed the car to be completely right, proved a marvellous boost for the team. Our outing at Oulton Park the following weekend proved far less successful. In the Touring Car race we ran the Jaguar on wider 6.5-in wheels (instead of the usual 6-in); these were supplied by the factory and we assumed that they were homologated. Despite the advice of the scrutineers, who queried whether the wider wheels were homologated, we used them in the race. I finished second to Graham Hill but was disqualified afterwards because these wheels were not in fact homologated. It was difficult to establish what was acceptable outside the standard Jaguar specification; for example, some of our competitors were running with MkX disc brakes which were or were not permitted according to individual interpretations of the regulations. Two of our competitors were running on lower than standard axle ratios – obvious when the cars accelerated away from the start-line – and these were certainly not homologated. Saloon car regulations badly needed redefining.

Shortly afterwards I was narrowly beaten into second place at Aintree by Graham Hill, my screen so badly covered with oil from Hill's car that I was forced to look out of the side window! By the Silverstone meeting a new force in saloon car racing was asserting itself. Although I finished second both at Silverstone and at the Crystal Palace a couple of weeks later, defeating Hill and the other Jaguar drivers, I had to give best to Sears' Ford Galaxie. It was only too clear that the reign of the Jaguars in short-distance saloon car racing was coming to an end. It was, however, a different story in longer races, when the Galaxie's drum brakes could let it down, and this was revealed in *The Motor* Six Hours race at Brands Hatch on July 6.

For this race the engines of our car, the Salmon/Sutcliffe car and the German-entered Lindner/Nöcker car were all prepared at the works and presumably all were prepared to the same specification. We decided to ask Denis Hulme to co-drive with me; he was easy to get on with, a very reliable and very quick driver and as he is near to my height, there would be no problem over seating positions.

There was a strong entry of three Ford Galaxies in this race. The drum-braked car of Dan Gurney/Jack Brabham was fastest in practice in 1 min 57.6 sec, Denny and I were second fastest in 1 min 58.6 sec and going really well with the Jaguar, but the other Galaxies were in trouble with the scrutineers over the eligibility of their disc brakes. Of the disc-braked Galaxies, one non-started, but Sir Gawaine Baillie/Peter Jopp (third fastest in 1 min 59.2 sec) decided to run on the basis that the eligibility of their disc brakes would have to be established within seven days if they finished in the results.

The race was run in torrential rain and I chased after Mike Salmon who led the race, driving superbly. After just over two hours Salmon, leading by about half-a-minute, handed over to Peter Sutcliffe. I made a pit stop but stayed at the wheel and took the lead just before half-distance. When I stopped for fuel, oil, brake pads and tyres and to hand over to Denny, the pit stop went disastrously wrong because the pads stuck and were difficult to remove and he joined the race in second place, three laps behind Salmon/Sutcliffe. Denny drove magnificently, gradually making up lost ground and he was on the same lap as the leaders at the finish.

That evening Tommy telephoned me to tell me that the Jaguar of Salmon and Sutcliffe had been disqualified because it had oversize valves (not, as I might have expected, because it was fitted with MkX disc brakes) and we had won the race. Tommy then received an urgent call to return the 3.8 to the factory – already the Lindner/Nöcker car which had finished third on the road had been taken back to Germany. Some days later Tommy received back our 3.8 with the engine rebuilt once more. I cannot help wondering what would have happened if our engine had been stripped by the scrutineers, because all three engines were apparently identical.

By Goodwood on Easter Monday Tommy had taken delivery of one of the newly homologated lightweight Jaguar E-types. The E-type was still not quite

Denis Hulme and I won The Motor *Six Hours saloon car race at Brands Hatch in 1963 after the disqualification of the similar Jaguar 3.8 driven by Salmon/Sutcliffe* (Temple Press).

as fast as the 250GTO, but it did achieve a good measure of success. I took a second place at Goodwood, second at Silverstone in May after a fantastic dice with Graham Hill's E-type and Parkes' GTO Ferrari (I lost the lead when I spun at Beckett's on the last lap, but set a new GT lap record of 102.90 mph) and third behind a brace of Ferrari 250GTOs in the Tourist Trophy at Goodwood.

I also drove a Cunningham-entered E-type at Le Mans for the second year in succession, but it proved a far less happy outing than in 1962. I was delighted to drive for Briggs Cunningham. This American millionaire was a really great enthusiast, charming, easy-going, but very professional and with a superb organisation. Cunningham had entered a team of three E-types and I was the fastest driver by quite a margin. Walt Hansgen, who was Cunningham's number one driver, was a little disconcerted about this, so the team manager, Alfred Momo, suggested that I tried the other team cars. I was still faster with both these cars than with my own and fastest of all with Hansgen's car, partly because of a 'tow' down the Mulsanne straight behind Sears' Ferrari Prototype. The last thing that I wanted was a dice with Hansgen in the opening laps and at my suggestion my co-driver Richards started the race. Richards drove very sensibly and when he handed the car over to me after three hours we were reasonably placed, but the Jaguar was already experiencing gearbox trouble which was plaguing all the Cunningham E-types. After a couple of pit stops to try to sort out the problem, I settled for lapping in fourth and fifth gears – and I was still matching my earlier lap times.

After my last pit stop I had been unable to get my seat harness done up as the shoulder strap would not clip into place. I was reluctant to make yet another pit stop and so I was driving with the harness loose round my waist because I had been unable to tighten it. Shortly afterwards, at the kink in the end of the Mulsanne straight which I normally 'straightened out' and took at about 165 mph, I saw a massive pool of oil on the road and a spinning car.

I knew that I could not avoid the oil and I thought that this was the end. I lifted my foot almost off the accelerator, leaving on just enough power to control the car, hit the oil, felt the car slide sideways, then the wheels bit again as I mounted the grass. I was sure that I had held the car and for a moment I felt immensely relieved. Then the Jaguar suddenly spun right round, I ducked, protecting my chest by keeping my hand over the gear-lever, and my bottom slipped out of the seat harness which was not tight unless the shoulder strap was done up. Then there was the most enormous bang as the car hit the opposite bank. It bounced back on the road and I was thrown through the perspex rear window on to the track, saturated in fuel from the ruptured fuel tank. My Jaguar careered forward into the bank again and caught fire.

I lay on the road, still very clear-headed, and could see just a few yards from me another driver, Jean-Pierre Manzon (the son of Robert Manzon), stretched out unconscious and obviously badly injured. I was petrified that the stream of fuel trailed by the Jaguar would burn its way back to me. I could not move my body because of the severe bruising (although, thankfully, I could feel no pain at this stage), so I stretched my fingers into the grass at the edge of the track and hauled myself up the bank. The marshalls quickly doused the burning Jaguar.

Manzon's René Bonnet had been the first to go off the road, Dewez' Aston Martin had ended up in the ditch, but, worst of all, Bino Heinz' Alpine had crashed on the other side of the circuit rolling end over end and bursting into flames. Poor Heinz was incinerated in the wreckage of his car without any of the marshalls crossing the road to try to get him out of the wreck. The incident had been caused by McLaren's works Aston Martin which had blown up in the biggest possible way, depositing the entire contents of its sump on the track. Although 1963 was the first year when electric illuminated warning signals were used, the marshalls had displayed no signals at all.

After a long delay I was taken to hospital, by then very shaken and racked by pain. I was supposed to stay in France because I was a witness to Heinz' fatal accident, but all I wanted to do was to go home. At 5:00 am on the Sunday morning a friend collected me from the hospital and drove me to Le Touquet in her Morris Minor convertible. Silver City would not allow me to stay in the car during the flight and, as I could not bend, I had to be carried into the aircraft like a stiff, dead body.

Although I had not broken any bones, I think that it was the worst shunt that I ever had; I was conscious throughout and remember every moment vividly. My bruising was agonising and I could barely move for a fortnight. Later the Automobile Club de l'Ouest issued a statement to the effect that the warning lights were on, that there was no oil on the circuit, and implying that the accident had been caused by drivers not taking enough care. I felt so badly about the mishandling of this accident and the white-washing by the organisers that in future Le Mans was a race that I could take or leave.

In September I had my first drive for Aston Martin for three years, and it was to prove the penultimate racing appearance of a David Brown entry. I had not been driving for Aston Martin over the last couple of years mainly because their racing programme had been so uncertain and I had committed myself to full seasons with Tommy Atkins and John Coombs. I was delighted when John Wyer asked me to drive one of the two Aston entries in the Coppa Inter-Europa, to be held at Monza just before the Italian Grand Prix. I liked Monza very much, I knew that the GT Aston Martin DB4GT with long-nose bodywork and 3,750 cc engine developing 312 bhp at 6,000 rpm was now well sorted and it was a great pleasure to race again for John Wyer and David Brown. The other DB4GT was driven by Lucien Bianchi and there was a strong Ferrari 250GTO entry. Mike Parkes with a 250GTO was fastest in practice on a damp track in 1 min 49.4 sec and although I did very little practice, so as to conserve my car, I was fourth fastest in 1 min 54.6 sec. The Aston was handling superbly, it was very fast and the gear ratios, thanks to inspired guesswork by the team manager John Horsman, were just right.

In the race Parkes led, but I kept him firmly glued in my sights. Driving really hard, I closed up on him and I knew that I was putting him under pressure. At half-distance Parkes made his routine refuelling stop; he was stationary long enough for me to pull out a lead of about 1 min 12 sec, and then I made my stop. The Aston Martin pit-work was very slick, partly because the team was using a pressurised refuelling system, and I rejoined the race just behind the Ferrari.

The remainder of the race turned into the closest possible duel; I was leaving my braking to the last possible moment, far later than I would have thought conceivable with a heavy GT car, and both Parkes and I were right on the limit. I found that I had the edge on the straight and could just nose past the Ferrari. But the 250GTO, thanks to its five-speed gearbox (the Aston had a four-speed 'box), was quicker out of the corners and the vital corner was the corner before the pits, the last before the finishing line. So if Mike was on my tail on the last lap of the race, he would win because he could out-accelerate me to the line. As the cars were only feet apart, we were both concerned about the possibility of a collision and I made a practice of giving Mike signals all round the circuit. If we were about to lap a car on the approach to a corner, I made my intentions clear by holding my hand right up as if to say, 'I'm going through'. If I thought that Mike had a chance of passing, I would wave as if to say, 'Go ahead if you can' and hold my car to one side of the circuit to give him room to pass if he could. With the benefit of hindsight I suspect that my co-operation lulled him into believing that I was not right on the limit and had the race under control.

I knew if I was to win the race I had to break the tow and pull out a couple of seconds over the Ferrari so that Mike could not repass me before the finishing line. The chance did not come until a couple of laps from the end when we caught two slower cars on the approach to Lesmo. They obviously had not seen us and I thought if I could scramble past them just before the apex of the corner, then Mike would be forced to hold back and take them on the exit. It was a very risky manoeuvre, I eased off a fraction giving Mike the impression that I was going to follow the two cars through the corner, got my timing to absolute perfection and dived through on the inside. This caught Mike off balance and he was forced to follow the two cars through the corner. On the exit to the corner he got on to the grass and this gave me the chance to pull out several cars' lengths. Mike chased me hard to the finish, but I still led by a second or two as we crossed the line. For me it had been a fantastic race, not least because Mike was great to race against and completely trustworthy. Throughout the race I had been conscious of the atmosphere amongst the crowd and for much of the race I felt their support; in fact they had been told that an Italian was driving the Aston. Later in the race I felt that the support had switched to Parkes and afterwards I learned that the announcer had corrected his original statement and told the crowd that the Aston was driven by an Englishman, albeit with an Italian name.

My winning speed was 120.28 mph (higher than the previous GT lap record) and I set a new lap record speed of 124.27 mph. Bianchi finished third. It was a great finale to John Wyer's career with Aston Martin, for at the end of September he left to join the Ford GT40 project. For my performance at Monza I was awarded the ERA Trophy for the best performance of 1963 by a British driver in a foreign race. Works drivers, of course, have to hand back trophies to the team, but John gave me the two trophies for the win at Monza, magnificent momentoes of my many years with Aston Martin. The greatest satisfaction after the race came when Juan Fangio said of Jimmy Clark (who won the Italian Grand Prix), 'Clark drives with his head. He is very good, and Salvadori was fantastic, a great Sports car driver.'

The Ford GT40

When John Wyer joined the Ford GT40 programme, I was delighted to accept his invitation to join him. Apart from our close friendship, he was a superb team manager and a brilliant development engineer. Roy Lunn appeared to have overall responsibility from an engineering and development standpoint, and whilst I knew very little about him he seemed very knowledgeable and capable. Eric Broadley, as good a designer as they come and with whom I had worked well in the past was in charge of design, building and testing the cars prior to the actual racing. Part of my role would be to test the cars and I believed that I could make a contribution to the team's success. An important factor was that Bruce McLaren, a very good test driver, was also in the team.

What I had not realised was that John Wyer was not in overall charge of the project. He was in fact responsible for administration, the drivers and preparing the cars, and his real role would not be fulfilled until the cars were raced. Because of this division of responsibility, the odds were really stacked against us. Lunn, who seemed to have more influence with Ford than anyone else, and Broadley were both well capable of designing a car on their own, but teamed together they seemed to be working against each other. John ended up as referee!

The background of the Ford GT40 project is too familiar to describe here and I was not involved until the first car, still basically a Lola, was ready for testing. I had anticipated that the car would be competitive and largely sorted and that the purpose of testing would be to make minor improvements and refinements. I was to be sadly disappointed.

When I first tested the Lola-based car at Monza in October 1963 I found that there was virtually nothing about it that I liked. The car was unstable on the approach to the Curva Grande and the faster parts of the circuit, it needed a great deal of concentration to drive and there was no opportunity to relax at all. My initial reaction was not to blame the car and I was wondering whether I was at fault – perhaps my driving was getting rusty and I ought to give up competition driving. This was a mistake and I should have stuck to my initial, instinctive reaction. I found that it was difficult to hold a smooth drift with the GT40 and that inhibited my driving. The car felt very light on the steering at speed and aerodynamically unstable. Because I had been assured that the aerodynamics had been carefully developed through wind-tunnel testing, I initially attributed the trouble to the suspension or rear shock absorbers over-responding and throwing the car in the air. At one stage I persuaded Eric Broadley and Roy Lunn to lie on their stomachs on the ground in front of the pits to see to what extent the car was airborne as it passed!

The car handled quite well on the slower corners, it was immensely powerful and it was undoubtedly the fastest car that I had ever driven; this made its high-speed handling problems even worse. In addition every time I applied the brakes, a shuddering set up through the car and this proved to be a fault in the car's alloy wheels, which for some reason could not be balanced properly. The gear change was a hit-and-miss affair with a tricky cable operation that sometimes left the car in neutral even when the gear-lever was in the right place. In short it was not my idea of a raceworthy car.

Neither Bruce nor I was able to lap the car quickly – we could not even approach the GT lap record that I had set with the Aston Martin the previous month – but Bruce was more favourably disposed towards the car than I. I was adamant that there was something seriously wrong with it, but Bruce was saying that he was reasonably happy with the car. The difference of opinion caused such an embarrassing situation that I made an excuse to return to England.

When the team had completed its testing at Monza, it was announced that Bruce had unofficially broken the Prototype lap record. It was only long afterwards that I discovered that this was a phoney claim, made purely to satisfy the people at Dearborne that progress was being made. John Wyer was very unhappy about the deception and took no part in it. The truth came out following a report that appeared in an American magazine. During three days' testing the Lola covered 250 miles – the sort of mileage that we were used to covering in a morning's testing with an Aston Martin at Goodwood.

I later drove the GT40 in its more definitive form at the Motor Industry Research Association track near Rugby, at Silverstone in March 1964 and at Goodwood. The car had been marginally improved, especially the brakes, although I was still far from happy with the handling. We then took the GT40 to the Le Mans Test Weekend in April and it was wet both days. Our experiences on the Sarthe circuit confirmed my worst suspicions. The car was handling appallingly and lifting badly on the Mulsanne straight, even though we were not gunning the cars but had revs in hand and were feathering the throttle. The GT40 was well capable of over 200 mph on the Mulsanne straight but we were frightening ourselves at around 165–170 mph! I had a very nasty experience when a door blew open on the Mulsanne straight at about 165 mph and I travelled a considerable distance sideways before I got everything back under control again. It was discovered that the wind was getting under the doors and lifting them open. Gusting winds, especially where there was a break in the trees, gave particular problems, and in these conditions the car seemed to want to take off. I was soon back in the pits, explaining the problems and telling John that I did not want to drive the car any more, but in the meanwhile Schlesser lost the other GT40 at around 170 mph on the Mulsanne straight, crashed heavily and was extremely lucky to escape without serious injuries. I suspect that his accident occurred because he had tried to gun the car flat out down the straight.

On the second test day the other Ford drivers, including Phil Hill and Richie Ginther, arrived at the circuit. It was obvious from Schlesser's accident that there was a lot wrong with the cars and John suggested to me that if I took out the surviving car for a few cautious laps, it would encourage the other drivers by showing them that I was happy to drive the GT40. The fact was that I was far from happy about driving it, but it did seem a sensible idea.

I covered the first lap steadily but, thinking to myself that I really ought to go much faster, I sped up considerably and accelerated very hard down the Mulsanne straight. I took the kink just before the end of the straight very fast – not quite flat out but with a trailing throttle – and then, as the road dipped down to the Mulsanne corner, the car lifted and seemed to hang in the air before landing crabwise. I eventually got the car straight and then braked very hard. In fact I braked much too hard because I now knew that the car's behaviour was proving everything that I had said about it and all I wanted to do was to get to the pits as quickly as possible to say, 'I bloody well told you so!' In my haste I locked a wheel on the damp track, the car went sideways and I wrote off the front against the concrete barrier. With all my experience, I should have known better. I had no need to brake so hard and I should have taken the escape road. It meant the end of Ford's Le Mans testing session.

Now I knew that I had reached the end of the road with the GT40 project. I told John Wyer that I had lost confidence in the GT40 and in fact I wrote several reports, setting out my views on the cars. I sent back my retainer, but Ford's Frank Zimmerman thought that because of all the testing I had done I should keep the money. John asked me to continue with the testing and as I had learned that Frank Zimmerman had made John completely responsible for the project, I felt that this was the least I could do.

It seemed to me that there were immense problems in sorting out the GT40. The car had many inherent defects; Bruce McLaren, who was basically a very good test driver, had talked himself into believing that the car was better than it was and was really not much help to John; and the team seemed to have too many chiefs so that John, torn between the conflicting views of Eric Broadley and Roy Lunn, lacked the authority to achieve what he wanted. It was only now with John in overall charge of the project that real progress was made, but it was not until 1965 that the GT40 began to win races.

My last drive with the GT40 was at MIRA and here John gave Roy Lunn and Eric Broadley the chance to make whatever modifications they wanted and so Bruce and I kept trying it again and again after a large number of suspension modifications. Bruce seemed to think that the car was getting better, but I believed that he was simply getting more used to it. I was taking a very gloomy view and always looking for trouble. During one of my spells at the wheel I noticed that I could see the sky through a gap between the gull-wing doors and the surround and I found that I could put my fingers in the gap. Shortly afterwards I noticed that the bonnet was beginning to swell, presumably because air was getting under it. When I got back to the pits I reported this to Lunn, Broadley and John, but I felt that even John was viewing what I said sceptically so I suggested that he came out with me in the car. I worked the Ford up to about 170 mph and said, 'Look, John, you can see the sky through the top of the doors.' Just as I said, 'Now look at that bonnet swelling', there was a tremendous explosion and we lost our vision momentarily as the complete nose section disintegrated. I looked at John, who seemed to have lost a lot of his colour, laughed and said, 'You will believe me next time John, won't you!'

Towards the end of the day's testing John decided to try the car with a spoiler, even though Roy Lunn thought that this would only make the car worse, possibly dangerous. I tried the car in this form with strict instructions from Roy Lunn not to exceed 100 mph. As soon as I started, I knew immediately that the car was right and on the first straight I took the GT40 up to 170 mph without problem. The handling was transformed and it seemed that a real breakthrough had been achieved at last.

I got on enormously well with Frank Zimmerman and I had the greatest respect and liking for John. I knew and had worked with Eric Broadley previously and I had formed a good working relationship with Roy Lunn. We could have made a superb team if only we had started out on the right lines.

1964

In February the Hon John Dawnay, now Lord Downe, entered myself and Mike Salmon with the Aston Martin Project 214 car in the Daytona 2,000 Km race. Part of the deal included the flight from New York to Daytona and along with other British drivers we left Kennedy airport in an ancient piston engined-aircraft which, we later learned, had only just been repossessed in Cuba. It was a horrific flight during which the Captain was forced to feather one engine five times altogether because it was losing oil and hastily seek an airfield at which to land. From the first time that this happened, the passengers became more and more disenchanted with the flight and it was only through copious quantities of free booze that the crew managed to keep us aboard. The race proved little more successful for us and I retired the Aston Martin with engine trouble even before Mike Salmon had a turn at the wheel.

I continued to drive for Tommy Atkins in 1964. We retained the lightweight E-type and acquired a very exciting Cooper Monaco-based sports/racing car with strengthened chassis and powered by a 4,941 cc (94×89 mm) Maserati V-8 engine. This engine was claimed to develop 420 bhp at 6,200 rpm on four twin-choke Weber carburettors and was used with a Colotti Type 37 four-speed gearbox. With a weight of only 14 cwt the straight-line performance should have been tremendous and we believed that we would be able to clean up British sports car races. We expected to be able to run away from the opposition on the straights and it would not matter too much if the cornering power was not of the highest.

The car proved to be a mistake and we should have stuck with the Climax 2.7-litre engine. The Maserati factory had set a rev limit of 7,000 rpm and the power did not come in until about 4,800 rpm. Then the power came in with a tremendous rush, but the engine started to misfire at over 6,000 rpm. As a result there was either too much power or the engine was spluttering; apart from the fact that it was only too easy to spin the car in the dry, it was undrivable in the

At the wheel of the 5-litre Cooper-Maserati in 1964 (T. C. March).

wet and the only way that I could keep it under control in these conditions was to turn off one of the magneto switches so that I was running on single plugs only, substantially reducing the power. Later in the year we took the engine to Coventry-Climax and tried it on their dynamometer. It was soon discovered that the power was way below the figures quoted by Maserati and valve bounce was setting in at 6,100/6,200 rpm; until then we had been convinced that the misfire was caused by carburation problems.

The Cooper-Maserati was not ready to race until the May Silverstone meeting where I took second place on a damp track to McLaren's Zerex-Climax. We won the Sports Car race at the Whitsun Goodwood meeting and at the British Grand Prix Meeting at Brands Hatch I finished third in the Sports Car race. Bernie Ecclestone, who had been out of racing for some while, helped us out in the pits at Brands Hatch. After my retirement Bernie told me that he did not really think that we were tackling our racing the right way and suggested that he should enter a sports/racing car for me in 1965. I was already thinking of retiring from racing and did not follow up the proposal – I have often wondered whether I missed out on one of the best opportunities in my racing career! I retired in the heavily contested Guards Trophy at Brands Hatch on August Bank Holiday Monday while holding a strong second place. At the end of the year rather optimistically we ran the Cooper in the *Autosport* Three Hours' race at Snetterton, but I had brake trouble right from the start and retired after the first hour's racing.

By the July Brands Hatch meeting we had just put together our long-awaited Cobra. It was completely new and untested but I managed to finish third in the GT race behind Sears (Cobra) and Jackie Stewart (E-type). We entered the Cobra in the GT category of the Tourist Trophy at Goodwood on August 29.

Because of lack of time we had still not got the car properly sorted and we were hoping to do this in practice. We struggled to get the balance of the Cobra right and to get it oversteering like other Cobras – we had a bad understeer, but could not see any difference between our Cobra and the others entered. Towards the end of practice we tried two small front spoilers and this made a tremendous difference. Even if the car was still far from perfect, at least we were keeping the front end glued to the road! Just before the end of practice I lapped in 1 min 28.0 sec, matching the time of Jack Sears, the most successful British Cobra driver, and only slightly slower than the works Daytona Cobras of Phil Hill and Dan Gurney.

I went really well in the race, pulling ahead of Gurney's and Phil Hill's Daytonas and Jack Sears' open Cobra to lead the GT category and hold sixth place overall. I was driving really hard and confident of holding my lead in the GT category. I knew that my tyres would be wearing rapidly, but it seemed that everyone would be in the same situation. Because of the tyre wear I lost the Cobra at Lavant, but carried straight on and shortly afterwards made my routine pit stop for fuel, oil and tyres. I rejoined the race still going very well, but what had been a slight engine misfire on the straights before my pit stop was now getting worse and worse. I came into the pits again and Harry Pearce found that the points had closed up; I had lost a lot of time and rejoined the race well down the field, but lapping very quickly again. I returned to the pits and after a short discussion with Tommy we withdrew the car.

In the old days I would never give up, however far behind I was, but my attitude had changed for the worse. It was becoming only too clear that I ought to retire from racing! In fact so many cars retired in this race that if I had kept going, I would still have finished well up the field. The official reason for my retirement was 'clutch trouble'. Graham Hill won the race outright with Ronnie

Left *With the Cobra in the 1964 Tourist Trophy. Note the two small spoilers which had been added during practice* (B. F. E. Clarke).

Right *At Snetterton in 1964 I drove this Maranello Concessionaires-entered Ferrari 250LM to win the Archie Scott-Brown Memorial Trophy race* (Roy Salvadori collection).

Hoare's Ferrari 330P and Gurney, in third place overall, won the GT category. I set a new GT lap record, later equalled by Gurney. Despite my exit from the race I got a good press and *Motoring News* commented, 'Salvadori was in great form, hurling his Cobra through the corners in a style highly reminiscent of his wild, young days. . . .'

On two occasions in 1964 I was asked by Colonel Ronnie Hoare to drive the Maranello Concessionaires Ferrari 250LM. The first race was the Archie Scott-Brown Memorial Trophy for Prototypes and GT cars at Snetterton. Although built as a GT car the very fast rear-engined 3.3-litre Ferrari coupé had not been homologated and ran as a Prototype. Apart from its speed I was not impressed with the 250LM. Its handling was such that you could not throw it around in the way you could with a 250GTO which drifted very nicely. The cockpit was cramped and I did not like the layout of the controls. The opposition at Snetterton included Salmon with one of the ex-works Aston Martin DB4GTs and Coundley with an Ecurie Ecosse-entered Tojeiro-Ford. I was fastest in practice, made a fairly gentle start, took the lead on the second lap and by the finish had pulled out an enormous advantage – only Salmon was on the same lap.

I had no plans for entering the Coppa Inter-Europa at Monza, but I received a telephone call from the organisers asking if I would be running and this was followed by a call from Ronnie Hoare asking me to drive the 250LM there. Although the 250LM was not homologated, the Italians were only too willing to let it run as a GT car. The entry was nearly all Ferraris with other 250LMs driven by Nino Vaccarella and David Piper and a strong supporting cast of 250GTOs. Vaccarella and I duelled throughout this one-hour race; his 250LM seemed to have better acceleration (I think that he had a lower axle ratio), but my car was slightly faster at the top end. He was driving rather wildly, trying on an early lap to take me on braking, locking his wheels, bumping over the grass and bouncing back on to the road again to resume his pursuit. I also found that if I took my car up to the permitted 7,600 rpm, a lot of smoke entered the cockpit, so I had to restrict the revs. I managed to stay in front until the last lap but one when I was held up passing a slower car and Vaccarella was able to pass me at the end of the straight. I expected to repass him on the approach to the Curva Grande. As I moved out to pass, Vaccarella zig-zagged in front of me in full view of the spectators, pushing me off on to the grass. I had to lift my foot and I lost a couple of seconds and all prospects of overtaking him before the finish.

The combination of business commitments and the fact that I had been racing since 1946 made me decide that it was time to hang up my helmet at the end of 1964. In fact things did not quite work out like that. I became involved in another project for 1965 and I was to drive in two more races before finally retiring.

1965

For 1965 Carroll Shelby, John Wyer and I put together a deal whereby Ford Advanced Vehicles with John at the helm would build and race a King Cobra. This consisted of a Cooper Monaco chassis powered by the Ford 4.7-litre engine. Shelby was to supply a really good Ford engine. I was to drive the car and I received a very substantial retainer from Shell who were backing the project. The King Cobra had already achieved considerable success in the United States, British short-distance Sports Car events were very much my speciality and we thought that we should be able to beat the Lotus 30s, McLaren-Oldsmobiles and Lola T70s that were likely to be the most serious opposition. Because the European regulations were different, there were a lot of changes to be made to the chassis, including finding somewhere to put the spare wheel; these problems were to a certain extent resolved when the European regulations were relaxed. Matters were not helped by late delivery of both the chassis and the engine. The car was built up by Ermanno Cuoghi who worked for Wyer and later became his chief mechanic; some years later he moved on to be Niki Lauda's mechanic at Ferrari.

Cuoghi was terribly overworked and was still trying to get the car ready after it arrived at Silverstone for the Senior Service '200' race at the end of March. There was no undershield, the race was run on a soaking wet track and as water was getting everywhere, under my visor and soaking me completely, I pulled out of the race. At Goodwood on Easter Monday I was unable to engage gears in the ZF 'box in practice and when the same thing happened as I went to the line for the start of the Sports Car race, I had no alternative but to pull out.

Ford Advanced Vehicles did not have the time to complete and develop the King Cobra, so there was no alternative but to abandon the project. I explained all this to Keith Ballisat, the Competitions Manager of Shell, and told him that I would not be continuing with motor racing. I offered to return my retainer, but

Keith took the view that I had fulfilled my part of the bargain and that I should keep the retainer.

I did, however, compete with success in one last race in 1965. Ronnie Hoare asked me to drive his Ford GT40 at Goodwood on Whit Monday. The GT40 went very well in practice for the Sports and GT race and in the race I finished second to John Coundley with a Sports Mclaren-Oldsmobile, having moved up a place when Nathan retired his Brabham-Oldsmobile, and I won the GT category. It was ironic that my last race should be with a car that caused me so many problems and so much heartache.

My retirement from racing was not too much of a blow, and to a certain extent was brought about by my involvement as Cooper racing manager and I did much of the Cooper-Maserati testing in 1965–66. My one regret was giving up long-distance sports car racing.

Chapter 14

Racing manager, 1965–67

In 1960 I had sold Elmbridge Motors to the Chipstead Group of Companies, run by Jonathan Sieff, Peter Hodge and Mario Tozzi-Condivi. It proved a very successful deal, for I enjoyed excellent relations with Jonathan and Mario, a very able and persuasive Italian who had once worked with me, and Chipstead gave me a service contract which left me free to run the business.

I still used to see the Coopers frequently and it was a sad blow when Charles Cooper died in October 1964. It was clear that John Cooper felt his father's death very deeply, both at a personal level and in connection with the Cooper Car business. Charles had been an astute but cautious businessman who had believed in carefully costed and steady development of the business. John realised that he was no real businessman himself – his only interest was racing – and he saw the possibility that Cooper Cars might run into business difficulties. John and I discussed the situation at length and I suggested that the Chipstead Group might be interested in buying the business. A meeting was set up with Jonathan Sieff and Mario Tozzi-Condivi and before long a deal was concluded whereby John kept the freehold properties as a long-term investment and Chipstead bought the Cooper Car business for something over £200,000.

Chipstead asked me to act as racing manager to the Cooper team and I was also appointed a director of the Cooper Car Company. The deal was concluded in April 1965 and this was the last year of the 1,500 cc Grand Prix Formula. Cooper had two excellent drivers but a very indifferent space-frame car powered by the Coventry-Climax V-8 engine used by every other British constructor except BRM. Cooper had been in a steady decline and had not won a Grand Prix since Monaco in 1962.

Cooper's number one driver was Bruce McLaren, a very experienced, very able driver who was keen to be involved in the development of the cars, although at this time there was very little development going on. The other member of the team was Jochen Rindt, in his first year of Formula One racing, very fast but rather wild, and tied to the team by a three-year contract which was less than generous and simply gave him a drive – if Coopers wanted him! Neither driver was happy with the cars and Jochen was in constant conflict with both John Cooper and the mechanics. All in all there was a very unhappy atmosphere in the team.

John Cooper believed that the cars were competitive and that the drivers were not giving of their best. I strongly disagreed and I was very keen to have an outside driver test the cars. I had in mind John Surtees who was then at the peak of his career (he had just won the 1964 Drivers' Championship). I was sure that this would clearly pinpoint whether the problems were with the cars – as I believed and as hindsight has shown to be correct – or with the drivers. John strongly opposed the idea of an outsider testing the cars because, I suspect, he was not willing to face up to the fact that his cars might not be competitive. It was stalemate, with an unhappy team and what was to prove an unsuccessful season's racing.

There was no alternative but to struggle through the year with the existing cars, while planning a completely new and, hopefully, much more successful design for the new 3,000 cc Grand Prix Formula that was coming into force at the start of 1966. While Formula One was dominated by Jim Clark with the monocoque Lotus 33, and the BRMs of Graham Hill and Jackie Stewart achieved a fair measure of success, we were battling for places well down the field behind the Brabhams and Ferraris. Our best results were a fourth place by Rindt at the Nürburgring and fifth places by McLaren at Monaco and Monza.

Monaco is the one race in that year etched vividly on my memory because of the failure of Jochen Rindt to qualify as a starter. In practice he seemed to be trying really hard, but despite stopping at the pits for minor changes to be made to the car by the mechanics, he was unable to achieve a good time. Jochen was very despondent, I was unhappy too and the atmosphere in the team was even frostier than usual. As practice began to draw to a close Jochen complained to John that his Climax engine was no good. John, like everyone else frustrated by our poor showing, exploded. It was only too clear that John, so used to working with Jack Brabham who was so full of constructive ideas and happy to work on the cars himself, lacked the patience to deal with Jochen who could not put his finger on the precise problem. After the final practice session it was discovered that one of the mechanics had carried out a private modification to the car hacking off a lug supporting the throttle cable to make tank installation easier. He replaced the lug with tape which allowed the cable outer and inner core to move together and thus prevented full throttle being used. Jochen was understandably furious and so I suggested that I tell the press that his failure to qualify was the team's fault and the team would recompense him with the starting money. Jochen was not the easiest driver to get on with, but this was the start of an improved relationship in which we could understand each other and work better together.

Throughout 1965 we planned our new 3,000 cc Grand Prix car. Our first task was to find a suitable engine to power the new Cooper. Because of Mario's close connections with Adolfo Orsi, the Chipstead Group were British concessionaires for Maserati, and it seemed logical that we should ask Maserati to supply engines for the new car. Mario, Jonathan, John and myself made several trips to Modena during 1965 to negotiate the supply of engines. We talked to engineer Giulio Alfieri, who was then working on the production side but was enthusiastic to get back into racing, and we won his support. The Orsis were not so keen, but Mario traded on his friendship with them and was his usual persuasive self. Soon they agreed to go along with our ideas and we won over the Bertocchis, father and son. Guerrino Bertocchi was nominally only chief mechanic, but his influence at Maserati was far more powerful than his title suggested and it was vital to win him over to our side.

Eventually a deal was struck and Cooper paid an advance against the supply of engines and service of them on a fixed price basis. It was a wonderful deal for Cooper, but unfortunately the engines were never quite as good as we had hoped. Heaped in a corner of the Maserati workshops were a number of the old 1957 Formula One 2.5-litre V-12 engines with twin overhead camshafts per bank of cylinders, and these formed the basis for Alfieri's development work. The result was a 2,989 cc (70.4 × 64 mm) engine still safe up to 10,000 rpm. Initially the engines were not producing much over 300 bhp, but by the middle of 1966 Maserati were claiming 360 bhp at 9,200 rpm.

These engines proved reasonably reliable during two seasons' racing, but not only were they down on power compared with rivals such as the V-12 Ferrari, they were substantially down on Maserati's own quoted figures. Bertocchi did the testing at Modena on a Heenan and Froude dynamometer and I am convinced that he relied on flash, as opposed to consistent, readings on the dynamometer. In 1966 we loaned one of the Maserati engines to Coventry-Climax who were always interested in what other manufacturers were doing. Alfieri was in the country and we took him to see the engine on test. The most that was achieved on the Climax brake was 330 bhp – 30 less bhp than claimed by Maserati. Alfieri made one or two comments about the temperature in the test room and suggested that this was affecting the engine's performance, but he was struggling and I believe he knew it.

There were constant strikes at the Maserati factory. Only too often the Maserati mechanics wanted to work on the engines, but were deterred from going to the factory by the threat of being beaten up. Coopers employed a brilliant Swiss mechanic, Heini Mader, to supervise engine rebuilds at Modena and to collect and deliver the engines. Heini used to spend hours working on the engines himself and trying to persuade the Maserati mechanics to get on with the job in the face of threats from their striking workmates. In later years Mader ran his own business tuning BMW Formula Two engines and is now responsible for maintaining the turbocharged BMW engines powering the Arrows Formula One cars.

We brought in Derrick White, formerly of Jaguar, as Chief Designer and he was responsible for the chassis of the new car. He was ably assisted by Tony Robinson, whose motor racing experience had started with the Moss Cooper-Alta in 1953 and who latterly had gained a lot of experience of monocoque cars while working for the British Racing Partnership.

Derrick produced an open-topped 'bath-tub' type monocoque based on Lotus practice, with two stressed-skin booms linked by a stressed floor and three bulkheads. In each boom there was a 25-gallon fuel bag. At the front, suspension was by inboard coil spring/damper units, while at the rear there

Above *With Jochen Rindt. Ours was a reasonably successful, but not always easy relationship* (Roy Salvadori collection).

Above *I did most of the testing with the prototype Cooper-Maserati. This is the original space-frame car seen at Silverstone in late 1965* (Roy Salvadori collection).

were reversed lower wishbones, single lateral top links, twin radius rods and outboard coil spring / damper units. Although completely new in detail, the rear suspension followed existing Cooper design practice. At the front White adopted the unusual feature of mounting the disc brakes inboard of the hub carriers and driven by stub axles. This was a bulky arrangement, but facilitated brake cooling and allowed wider front wheels to be fitted if needed. Spoked alloy 13-in or 15-in wheels were fitted. Transmission was by a 7¼-in Lockheed dry-plate clutch to a ZF 5DS25 gearbox/final drive unit as used on the Ford GT40. The new car, typed the T81, was heavier and bulkier than we had hoped and the engine bay seemed to be crammed with complicated machinery.

While the new cars were under construction we were testing at Goodwood with a V-12 engine fitted into the space-frame chassis built to accommodate the flat-16 1,500 cc Coventry-Climax engine that was never fully developed. I did most of the testing and was fastest with the car until it was driven by Denis Hulme who was about half-a-second a lap faster. By the end of 1965 we were reasonably happy with the performance of the car.

We frequently drove to Goodwood for test sessions with the Cooper-Maserati and on one occasion I drove my BMW there with Jochen Rindt and Derrick White as passengers. Jochen was a dreadful passenger, complaining all the time, whereas Derrick usually proved to be a good passenger. This day it was raining and I was driving quite hard, sliding through the corners to a chorus of complaints, on this occasion from both passengers, that I should let Jochen drive. One thing was for sure and that was that I was not going to be driven by the likes of Jochen. Eventually it was suggested that we should stop for a cup of tea – I should have been suspicious. Afterwards neither Jochen nor Derrick would get back in the car if I drove and eventually we reached the compromise that Derrick should take the wheel. Although Derrick was a very good, safe driver, Jochen and I criticised everything he did. When we caught up the team transporter, Derrick stopped and both he and Jochen got out of the car to continue the journey to Goodwood by transporter! I was left to drive to the circuit on my own.

In a year when most teams were running on Firestone or Goodyear tyres, I negotiated a contract with Dunlop who paid substantial sponsorship. We carried out comparative tests between Dunlop and Firestone tyres and there was nothing to choose between them in lap times. However, the use of Dunlop tyres was to prove our undoing, as I shall recount a little later on. I negotiated all the team's sponsorship and we had a special deal with Dunlop whereby if their tyres proved uncompetitive we could change to another maker's tyres without any refund of the sponsorship monies. Altogether I had arranged a very good sponsorship package for the team, helped by the fact that I had known so many people in motor racing for such a long time. I was fully occupied with the Formula One team and the Formula Three team was John Cooper's responsibility. Unfortunately he was not really interested in Formula Three and these cars were largely unsuccessful.

I was also negotiating the sale of Formula One cars to private owners and I agreed that we should sell the third car to be completed to Rob Walker. The deal was negotiated at a special price because with such a good driver as Siffert and Rob's close relations with the works it was almost a third works car. John Cooper disapproved, as he thought that we should keep the third car built as a spare team car and let Rob Walker have the fourth car. I saw the situation rather differently. Rob Walker ran a very well organised team. If he was supplied with an early car his development testing would have a useful spin-off for the works and there were prospects that Siffert would achieve considerable success. John and I always discussed these differences on a friendly basis and, sooner or later, one or other of us would accept the situation. On this occasion John gave in and Rob was supplied with the third car as I had wanted. Other T81s were sold to Joakim Bonnier and Guy Ligier. John Cooper later sold one to Mitsubishi.

For 1966 Bruce McLaren left Cooper to set up his own racing team and our drivers were Jochen Rindt, in his second season with Cooper, and American Richie Ginther. Ginther was only available until the new V-12 Honda was raceworthy, so I was on constant look-out for a replacement driver. I signed on the young New Zealander, Chris Amon, who had driven in Formula One with Tim Parnell's team in 1965; Amon was due to drive for us at Reims and if he went well we would retain him for the rest of the season. Chris was a very relaxed, undemanding, but extremely quick driver; if there had been more drivers like Chris around, life would have been much easier. There was, however, a major development on the driver front before Reims and so we ran Chris in the one race only.

Not long before the Reims race Mario received a telephone call from Modena in the early hours of the morning informing him that John Surtees had left Ferrari following a dispute over team arrangements at Le Mans. Although John was reputedly not the easiest person to deal with, he was a brilliant driver and just the man we needed in the Cooper team. The Cooper directors met the same day and it was decided to prepare another chassis and hope that John would contact us. Within a matter of days John and I were discussing terms and once the fuel contracts were sorted out (Cooper were on BP and John was contracted to Shell), I was pleased to welcome him into the team. In fact John proved extremely easy to deal with and his main aim seemed to be to get back into racing and beat the Ferraris!

We were anxious to avoid any clash between Jochen and John so we set up what were virtually two teams. Each driver had his own chassis, engines and mechanics. John had two ex-Aston Martin mechanics, Jim Potten and Jerry Holmes, whom he knew when he was racing for the Bowmaker team and whom he liked and trusted. Jochen had by this time chosen one of our team mechanics, Ron Dennis (now head of the McLaren team), whom he trusted implicitly. The arrangement was cumbersome, but operated well and prevented either driver from complaining that the other was receiving preferential treatment. Whilst I was in overall control of the team, John Cooper was responsible for the preparation of the cars and this worked well until the Monza race where things went badly wrong.

The 1966 racing season

The Cooper T81 made its first public appearance at the Racing Car Show in January 1966. The following month the team moved to new premises at Canada Road, Byfleet and the racing début of the 3-litre cars was at the *Daily Express* Trophy at Silverstone on May 14. It proved a disappointing race for Cooper. The engine of Rob Walker's car broke in practice so we loaned our space-frame 'hack' car to him for Siffert to drive in the race. Neither of the works cars handled well in practice and we tried changing the rear dampers and varying the suspension settings without any real improvement. Jack Brabham led throughout the race to win from Surtees (Ferrari). Rindt held third place for a while, but the handling deteriorated for reasons that at the time we did not understand, and he dropped back to finish fifth. Ginther retired because of overheating and the clutch failed on Siffert's borrowed car. The best Cooper performance – on Firestone tyres – was third place by Bonnier.

The Monaco Grand Prix was held the following weekend and we believed that we were in with a chance. Overheating was our real problem, we kept making the air intake bigger and bigger and although we ran the cars with cut-off noses at Monaco, they were still running close to the temperature limit. Jochen, trying very hard, was seventh fastest in practice in 1 min 32.2 sec (Jim Clark with the 2-litre Lotus 33-Climax was fastest in 1 min 29.9 sec) and in the race he barged through to second place before falling back to retire with engine trouble. Ginther was in fifth place on lap 80 after a pit stop for a drive-shaft to be changed and when another drive-shaft broke, he retired.

At the Belgian Grand Prix at Spa Cooper fortunes showed a dramatic improvement. In practice Jochen was second fastest in 3 min 41.2 sec – fastest was Surtees with the rather more powerful Ferrari in 3 min 38.0 sec – but it was in the race, run in the most dreadful conditions, that Jochen displayed fantastic ability. Rain was threatening at the start and the drivers ran into heavy rain and appallingly slippery circuit conditions by the time they had reached Malmedy. On the first lap Bonnier, Spence, Siffert, Stewart, Hill and Bondurant all went off the circuit.

In torrential rain Jochen forced his way through into the lead, driving, I thought, courageously fast for the conditions, throwing up great clouds of spray, with Surtees (Ferrari) some three seconds behind and reasonably clear of the Cooper's spray. Jochen's driving was superb, sure-footed and confident, and although at one stage he spun at 150 mph, he collected it all together again and carried on without losing the lead. But it terrified me and I thought that I really ought to slow him down. Ginther was going well too, driving rather more cautiously and holding fifth place. As the race progressed and the rain eased, we became convinced that Jochen must win.

During the last quarter of the race the track began to dry and Jochen's lap times slowed noticeably. Surtees surged past the Cooper to win the race, Jochen finished second and Ginther fifth. It was a great disappointment, but our best performance to date. After the race Jochen told me, 'As the track dried out, the car became almost uncontrollable.' We knew that we had a major problem, but we had not yet analysed it. As we realised later, Jochen's trouble was attributable to the Dunlop tyres which were causing handling problems on oily surfaces. There were no problems in practice, when there was little or no oil on the track, and there were no problems on a really wet track, but on a drying, oily track the cars' handling deteriorated substantially. Ferrari were the only other team running on Dunlop tyres and I believe that Surtees, with his vast racing experience, had instinctively grasped the situation. As Spa dried out, Surtees was avoiding the oiliest parts and slowing down where absolutely necessary only, while Jochen was slowing all round the course. Jochen suspected that the self-locking mechanism of the ZF final drive was at fault and we gave the ZF factory a terrible time, as they tried to trace a fault that did not exist.

We fielded three cars for Surtees, Rindt and Amon in the French Grand Prix at Reims. Ferrari power came into its own on this very fast circuit and it looked as though the Maranello V-12s would dominate practice. John Surtees, however, was very bitter about the way he had been treated by Ferrari and he was trying really hard, although he could not match the Ferrari lap times. When the opportunity arose Surtees pulled into the slip-stream of Ferrari driver Bandini and turned in a really fast lap before the Italian could do anything about it. John lapped in 2 min 8.4 sec which for a while stood as fastest practice time. During the final session Bandini recorded 2 min 7.8 sec to take pole position, but John

Jochen leads John through Druids in the 1966 British Grand Prix at Brands Hatch (Roy Salvadori collection).

was still second fastest ahead of Parkes. Jochen was fifth fastest in 2 min 10.9 sec. Chris Amon drove a new car and spent much of practice sorting out the braking and a sticking throttle.

We were in trouble from the start of the race which was run in extremely hot weather. All three Coopers were plagued by fuel vaporisation. As the race progressed, the handling of the cars deteriorated, especially through the Thillois hairpin which had a very thick coating of oil. Surtees made a long pit stop because of fuel vaporisation and eventually retired; Jochen finished fourth, two laps behind race-winner Brabham, and Amon was eighth and last after a pit stop to fix a loose wheel nut.

In practice for the British Grand Prix at Brands Hatch, the cars went reasonably well with Surtees recording sixth fastest time in 1 min 36.4 sec and Rindt seventh fastest in 1 min 36.6 sec. Jack Brabham led throughout the race and although Surtees and Rindt worked their way up into second and third places while the circuit was wet, they fell back once it began to dry out and the circuit became very oily. In these conditions the cars became almost uncontrollable and through Paddock Bend Surtees was all over the road. Jochen finished fifth but John retired because of what we believed to be differential problems, later diagnosed as tyre problems.

We had another miserable time at the Dutch Grand Prix at Zandvoort. Neither car ran well in practice (Jochen was sixth fastest in 1 min 29.2 sec) and neither survived the race. Jochen spun off on the second lap and John was eliminated by electrical problems after a slow race battling with his car's dreadful handling, again the result of the oil on the circuit, although we still believed that the ZF differentials were at fault.

The Cooper team showed much better form in the German Grand Prix at the Nürburgring. John Surtees was brilliantly swift and smooth in practice, lapping second fastest in 8 min 18.0 sec. It was raining at the start of the race and John took the lead ahead of Jack Brabham, but then fell back to hold second place with Jochen third. As the race progressed, John lost the use of the clutch and was making clutchless gear changes, whilst a drying track coated in parts with oil brought on the usual handling problems and ensured that neither Cooper driver could catch the leader. So Cooper had to settle for second and third places, but it was a very good showing.

By the Italian Grand Prix I had realised the cause of our handling problems and I persuaded the drivers that we should run on Firestone tyres. I think that John Surtees had been aware of the problem even before me, and supported my decision completely using the escape clause in his personal contract with Dunlop. Of course the Firestones were no faster than the Dunlops in practice, but I was expecting a real advantage in the race. I should explain that whilst cars obviously do drop oil in practice, this is far less of a problem than in a race. Marshalls quickly cement down oil patches in practice – the cars will slow right down while this is being done – and any car dropping oil will come into the pits for attention. Furthermore no driver would attempt a really fast practice lap while there is oil on the circuit

For Monza the Maserati company produced an improved engine with the inlet ports inclined inwards and this made the engine more compact. Jochen used one of the new engines in the race, but John retained one of the original V-12s. All the Orsi family, Alfieri and the Maserati mechanics turned up to support the Cooper team at Monza and were hoping to see us defeat Ferrari.

In practice John was very fast, fourth overall in 1 min 31.9 sec behind the Ferraris of Parkes and Scarfiotti and Clark's rather fragile H-16 BRM-powered Lotus. Jochen was not much slower, sixth fastest in 1 min 32.7 sec. On the eve of the race I had wanted to fill the rubber bag fuel tanks of the Coopers because the fuel tended to settle after fuelling and it was literally possible to massage the tanks to make the fuel settle well down. My idea was to leave the tanks overnight and top them up in the morning to get in as much fuel as possible. John Cooper did not agree to this, as he did not want the fuel to be left in the tanks overnight, and so he left refuelling until midday on race day. Shortly before the race we found that one of the tanks on Surtees' car was seeping and there was no time to change it.

On the first lap Surtees was in third place behind two of the Ferraris and he moved up a slot when Bandini stopped at the pits. Brabham came through to take the lead, then stopped at the pits, and then Hulme with the second Brabham entry went ahead. John was still going magnificently in third place and he jockeyed for position with the leading bunch until lap 32 when he came into the pits. There was fuel everywhere, in the cockpit and over the back tyres, and we could do nothing but retire our faster runner. The Ferraris of Scarfiotti and Parkes took the first two places ahead of Hulme's Brabham; Jochen finished fourth, crossing the line with a front tyre punctured and off the rim. All in all it was a very unhappy day when hopes of success had been high. The sole consolation was that both cars, on their Firestone tyres, had handled well throughout the race.

After the race there was a heated discussion between Mario Tozzi-Condivi and John Cooper about the leaking fuel tank and fortunately Derrick and I were able to keep out of the dispute. Mario changed the management of the team and my overall control now included responsibility for the preparation of the cars. Apart from anything else this resolved a conflict between John Cooper and Derrick White. John had believed that Derrick's development work was slow and unsatisfactory, while I was convinced that Derrick could and would develop a really competitive car. For the rest of 1966 and throughout 1967 we ran on Firestone tyres.

At the United States Grand Prix at Watkins Glen the cars went well in practice and we were particularly pleased with Surtees who was fourth fastest in 1 min 8.73 sec (Hulme was fastest of all with a time of 1 min 8.42 sec). We thought that we were in with a chance. In the race Surtees was in fourth place, moved up to third ahead of Clark's Lotus-BRM H-16 and was going really well. When he came up to lap Arundell's works Lotus, the Lotus veered across the front of the Cooper and the two cars collided wheel to wheel. Both drivers came into the pits for their cars to be checked over and John spent so long sounding off about Arundell and about drivers who did not use their mirrors that by the time he was back in the race he was in 13th place and three laps in arrears. John was of course very upset, but it had been an unnecessarily long, time-wasting pit stop and it was to cost Cooper and Surtees the race.

Once he was back in the race, John drove brilliantly, tearing through the field, gaining two laps on the leader (who was now Clark with the Lotus) and finishing third behind Jochen who ran out of fuel on his last lap. If you take into account the time wasted by John in the pits and the distance he was behind Clark at the finish, then if he had gone straight off when the car had been checked, he would easily have won the race.

Pedro contemplates his Cooper, while the mechanics get on with the preparation. To the right of the picture is Ron Dennis, now McLaren team chief (Richard Garrett).

For the Mexican Grand Prix the Maserati engines had been carefully tuned to suit the high altitude of the Mexico City circuit (7,300 ft) and they ran with the air intakes opened right up to give the appearance of a very broad snout. At this race we entered a third car, just newly completed, for local driver Moises Solana whose drive was being paid for by the organising club. It proved a repetition of 1962 when I was racing for the Bowmaker team and they had made available a car for Solana at Mexico City. Throughout practice Solana was in and out of the pits complaining that the car was no good, but the truth of the matter was that the fault lay with his driving and not the car. In practice both Surtees and Rindt displayed superb form. John was fastest, albeit in the absence of the Ferraris which missed this race, with a time of 1 min 53.18 sec and Jochen was fifth fastest in 1 min 54.19 sec.

Surtees started the race with a rough-running engine, but as the engine got really hot this cleared. After holding fifth place on the first lap, he was soon picking up places and he took the lead from Jack Brabham on lap 6. Solana was the first Cooper retirement, stopping at the pits with an overheated engine and retiring a lap later because of sagging oil pressure. As the race progressed there were two further Cooper retirements in quick succession. On lap 32 Jochen, in third place, pulled on to the grass with the left front wheel leaning drunkenly and a lap later Siffert retired because of the same problem. In both cases a ball joint in the suspension had broken and it seemed clear that the failure was caused by the loading of the banked 180-degree turn before the pits.

We were most concerned in case Surtees should have the same trouble and considered whether we should call him in to retire for safety reasons. Pat Surtees, who was running John's pit, was well aware of the problem and must have been frantically worried. As both breakages had occurred as the cars came out of the banked turn with a wide run-off area, and the drivers had controlled the cars without real difficulty, I decided to let John carry on. I am not sure even now that it was the right decision, but I am quite certain that if I had been able to discuss the problem with John he would have wanted to carry on. John was a tough nut and had taken the breakages on the Lolas we raced in 1962 in his stride. John looked a winner all the way and went on to take the chequered flag from Jack Brabham by a margin of 8 seconds.

After a poor start to the year Cooper fortunes had steadily improved, especially since John Surtees had joined the team. With the points gained at the wheel of both Ferrari and Cooper cars John took second place to Jack Brabham in the Drivers' Championship and Jochen was third. In addition Cooper had finished third in the Constructors' Championship, 12 points behind the winning Brabham team but a mere point behind Ferrari in second place.

The 1967 racing season

Although the Coopers were large and heavy compared with some of their rivals, we believed that development was on the right lines and our aim was to shed weight and increase power. We lost Surtees to Honda, which was almost inevitable, and we decided that Pedro Rodriguez, who had some Formula One experience and immense talent, was a good prospect to replace him.

In practice for the South African Grand Prix at Kyalami Pedro did exactly what was asked of him. He never complained, he said that he was completely satisfied with the car and he was lapping very quickly. I suspect that if I had asked whether the car was understeering or oversteering, he would not have understood what I meant. Fastest in practice were the Brabham-Repcos of Brabham (1 min 28.3 sec) and Hulme (1 min 28.9 sec), Clark with his Lotus recorded 1 min 29.0 sec and Pedro was fourth fastest in 1 min 29.1 sec. For some reason Jochen Rindt took an instant dislike to Pedro and was terribly rude to him all the time. The situation was not helped by the fact that we were having problems with Jochen's car which we did our damnedest to cure. But all Jochen wanted to do was to get into Rodriguez' car. I said to Rindt, 'Jochen, you have just finished a season with John Surtees and at no stage did he ask for your car and at no time would I have given your car to Surtees. Why are things so different now that we have got Rodriguez in the team?' Jochen's retort was that Rodriguez was not an established Formula One driver.

During practice we had problems with Jochen's car because it was 'fluffing' at maximum revs and it became obvious that Jochen was using up his tyres at such a furious rate that they would not last the race. In contrast there were no problems with Pedro's tyre wear and I urged Jochen to temper his driving. I was still being pressured by Jochen and other drivers, including Denis Hulme who came to me and said that some of the drivers thought that I should let Jochen have Pedro's car. This rather upset me, as it was purely an internal team matter and a decision for me to make. Eventually Jochen recorded 1 min 30.2 sec which was joint seventh fastest.

Pedro tries to explain his problems, while I listen with my good ear. With some other drivers I thought it better to listen with my deaf ear! (Richard Garrett).

With Jochen and Pedro at the 1967 South African Grand Prix (Errol Higgins).

In the race Pedro was superb and both he and Jochen were well up with the leaders. With 30 laps of this 80-lap race completed Jochen and Pedro were in third and fourth places, but Jochen, who was so very hard on his cars at this stage in his career, was soon out of the race because of gearbox trouble. When we inspected the car after the race we saw that his tyres were very badly worn and it was obvious that they could not have lasted the race distance. Pedro was still lapping steadily, but as he lost the use of third and fourth gears his lap times became slower; he kept on going steadily although losing some ground.

Because there were so many retirements in this race, Pedro found himself in second place behind local driver John Love (2.7-litre Cooper-Climax). Love's Tasman car had limited fuel capacity and when he stopped to refuel, Pedro took a lead that he never lost, winning from Love by a margin of 26 seconds. There was a lot of press comment about Pedro's supposedly lucky win, but in fact he had driven a superb and intelligent race, nursing his car and conserving his tyres. I was very glad that I had stuck to my guns and not given his car to Jochen – although I think that Pedro might still have won with Jochen's car!

While we had been in South Africa both Bernie Ecclestone, who had accompanied us, and I had played gin rummy a lot, both with each other and with drivers from other teams. Jochen had become interested in the game and had got in a few hands, but was not having a good run and had lost a fair amount of money. On the flight back to England we all travelled together and we now had another keen entrant in the gin rummy stakes – Pedro Rodriguez. In fact we did not want to play with him because we thought that he was going to be the original sucker and would lose all down the line. Pedro, however, insisted on playing and did not do very well, losing a few dollars. Jochen, still hostile to Pedro, was fighting to play him, but we were not too keen on this as there was already enough trouble between them. In the end we had no alternative but to let them play and when Jochen picked up his cards, his eyes were alight at the thought of taking Pedro to the 'cleaners'. Jochen had had a bad time so far; he had lost with me, he had lost with Bernie and now was his chance to get his money back from the guy who did not really understand the game. Pedro, however, who had been so lucky in the race, was even luckier at cards and he slaughtered Jochen. Jochen was so furious that he left the aircraft at Nairobi, although he had a through ticket to London!

Our main aim in the early part of 1967 was to concentrate on developing the cars before the start of the European season. As a result we sent cars for Jochen and Pedro to the Race of Champions at Brands Hatch on March 12, but gave a miss to the Spring Cup race at Oulton Park and the *Daily Express* International Trophy at Silverstone. As Denis Jenkinson wrote in *Motor Sport*, 'The works Coopers were just not fast enough', and in the final Pedro finished fourth behind Gurney (Eagle), Bandini (Ferrari) and Siffert (with Walker's Cooper). Jochen was eliminated by clutch trouble.

By the Monaco race on May 7 we had a number of new developments ready. Alfieri had produced a revised V-12 Maserati engine which combined the 1966 bottom end with new cylinder heads having three valves per cylinder, and this we tried out in the spare car. Derrick had also produced new fabricated magnesium-alloy wheels made in two parts with a collar in between so that they could be used for any width we chose. Neither these nor a new smaller and lighter radiator were used at Monaco, but all the cars had new one-piece half-shafts with rubber doughnut couplings.

Neither Jochen nor Pedro went well in practice at Monaco, they were slower than Jo Siffert with the Walker car and they both started from the back row of the grid. Jochen had been bouncing his car over the kerbs in practice, finishing practice with a broken wheel and damaged suspension. Poor Ron Dennis had to work overnight to rebuild the car virtually in time for the race, and was so exhausted that he spent the race sleeping under the pit counter. At least Jochen had confidence in Ron and it was only through his untiring devotion to the car that we were able to keep Jochen happy. Jochen's race did not last long – he retired with gearbox trouble on lap 15 – and by this time he had again virtually wrecked the Cooper by bouncing over the kerbs, but he had kept up with the leading bunch.

Just before the start of the race Alfieri carried out some adjustments to the engine of Pedro's car; the Maserati engine went on to ten cylinders and there was no time to do anything about it. He ran through the race with his engine sounding as rough as hell and was classified fifth, four laps behind Hulme's winning Brabham when the results were announced. Tony Rudd of BRM complained to me that his team's H-16 driven by Mike Spence was in reality fifth and the Cooper sixth. I agreed with him but the organisers did not change the results. After the race I drove Jochen to Nice Airport and we had a furious argument about the way he treated his cars. I told Jochen that he would never be World Champion – his stated ambition – unless he drove his cars more sympathetically. He began to drive his cars with consideration after he joined Lotus in 1969 and he eventually became World Champion, albeit posthumously.

At the Dutch Grand Prix at Zandvoort Jochen was entered with the new and lighter T81B car with Hewland gearbox and the new wheels. We were still using the 24-valve engines, as we were not satisfied as to the reliability of the new 36-valve unit. Despite the presence of the new Cosworth-powered Lotus 49s which were to transform the face of Grand Prix racing, both the Cooper drivers went well in practice and were on the second row of the starting grid. The track was damp and slippery at the start of the race and Jochen held a strong third place until about lap 15 when the track started to dry out, the handling of his car deteriorated (it was nothing to do with tyres) and he retired on lap 40. Pedro was eliminated by gearbox trouble.

We had quite a good race at Spa on June 18. Jochen was fourth fastest in practice with the T81B and in the race Pedro and he worked their way through to third and fourth places. Amon (Ferrari) then passed both Coopers. Pedro's engine blew up three laps from the finish (he was classified ninth although not running) and Jochen finished fourth behind Gurney (Eagle), Stewart (H-16 BRM) and Amon.

In 1967 the French Grand Prix was run on the silly little Bugatti circuit at Le Mans, a short, tortuous course constructed through the pits and car park of the famous Sarthe circuit and incorporating the usual straight in front of the pits

Jochen and the Cooper-Maserati on their way to fourth place in the 1967 Belgian Grand Prix at Spa (Nigel Snowdon).

and grandstands. It was a pretty miserable race for the Cooper team, neither of our drivers was happy on this circuit, Jochen was ninth fastest in practice and Pedro fifteenth; Jochen had a bad spin and retired with piston failure, while Pedro was sixth after a pit stop to repair a leak in the fuel pressure system.

By the British Grand Prix at Silverstone there were substantial developments. For Jochen we entered the new T86 car, built on the same general lines as the T81 but much lower, narrower and squatter, with flat scuttle, a very ugly nose and magnesium-elektron skinning. It was powered by the 36-valve Maserati engine used in conjunction with the Hewland gearbox. The new car was driven by Jochen and ordinary cars were entered for Pedro and Alan Rees who had carried out a great deal of testing for us and was having a one-off drive. The changing and more competitive face of Grand Prix racing was emphasised by the performance of the Lotus 49s which dominated the race: Jimmy Clark (1 min 25.3 sec) and Graham Hill (1 min 26.0 sec) were fastest in practice and Clark scored an easy win in the race. Our new Cooper did not go as well as we had hoped and Jochen's best lap was 1 min 27.4 sec, eighth fastest, compared with Pedro's 1 min 27.9 sec. Jochen had a poor race, stopping twice at the pits because his car was putting out oil smoke (it was the catch-tank overflow getting on to the exhausts) and retiring with engine trouble. Pedro plugged on steadily to finish fifth and Alan Rees, driving a cautious race as instructed, took a distant ninth place, four laps behind the winner.

Although the new T86 was displaying a tendency to lift at speed and was not showing the form we had expected, we still pinned our hopes on it and again entered this car for Jochen at the Nürburgring and sent along a T81B with Hewland gearbox for Pedro. Jochen had a really nasty moment in practice when the flywheel on his spare T81B disintegrated, damaging the crankcase, cutting a gash in the chassis and damaging the cockpit area; he was very lucky to escape without injury. Both our drivers were back on the third row of the grid, Jochen retired on lap 5 when the steering rack worked loose and Pedro finished eighth after a pit stop to replace a broken rear suspension ball-joint.

A new addition to the World Championship calendar in 1967 was the Canadian Grand Prix at Mosport. It was a pleasant circuit, with lap speeds around the 105 mph mark and with good organisation. I always enjoyed competing in North America, I liked the hospitality and the atmosphere, but the race was a major headache in that we had to fly the cars over for the race on August 27, fly them back to compete at Monza on September 10 and fly them across the Atlantic again for the United States Grand Prix on October 1. We also had a driver problem as Pedro had been injured in an accident in a Formula Two race at Enna, and so we brought Dickie Attwood into the team. Both drivers used T81B cars (we were saving the T86 for Monza). Throughout practice the Coopers (including the private cars) were plagued by breaking starter rings and on Jochen's car in practice a starter ring shattered with such force that it pierced the monocoque, went through the fuel bag and came out the other side of the car. The problem was caused by a faulty batch of starter rings and there was nothing much we could do about it until we got home again.

Neither car went particularly well in practice – Jochen was eighth fastest – and in the race, run in torrential rain and thoroughly miserable conditions, the Coopers were handling badly and were completely uncompetitive. Jochen retired early in the race because of water-soaked electrics and Attwood just kept going steadily to finish tenth, six laps in arrears.

Before the Italian Grand Prix I made one of my frequent visits to the Maserati factory at Modena to see how Giulio Alfieri was progressing with development work on the latest version of the V-12 engine. Initially Bertocchi used to meet me at Milan airport and would drive me to the factory at speeds of up to 150 mph on the Autostrada to Modena. After a couple of these suicidal drives I decided always to take the train. Although Bertocchi was killed recently in a road accident, ironically he was not driving at the time.

Alfieri was always full of enthusiasm and friendly co-operation, completely dedicated to his work and prepared to talk about his engines at any time, even if I telephoned him in the middle of the night. He now had ready a new version of the 36-valve engine with combustion chambers of improved shape and this engine was fitted to both our entries at Monza. We had now – more by luck than by design – cured the handling problems of the T86. During the German Grand Prix Jochen had nudged another competitor and bent the lower tip of the nose cowl; this improved the roadholding and so we adopted a front spoiler.

Pedro was still out of action at the Monza race, so whilst Jochen drove the T86 as usual, we brought Jacky Ickx into the team to drive the T81B. Jacky, at this time very much a coming man, had been recommended to us unreservedly by Ken Tyrrell for whom he drove Formula Two Matras. We were down on power compared with many of our rivals, but Jochen drove a wonderful, flat-out race to finish fourth and Ickx, doing everything that was asked of him, exactly as Tyrrell said he would, drove a steady, disciplined race to finish sixth. It was one of our better results in the latter part of 1967 and it cheered the Maserati boys who were at the race because we beat the sole Ferrari entry driven by Chris Amon into seventh and last place.

We again entered Jochen with the T86 and Jacky Ickx with the T81B in the United States Grand Prix at Watkins Glen. Ickx' car was fitted with the usual 24-plug engine, but in Jochen's car we installed Alfieri's latest development, a 36-plug engine with the extra plug for each cylinder on the inside of the vee. Again I quote from *Motor Sport*, 'A successful engine designer [it was Keith Duckworth] who was looking at the engine commented that if you need more than one plug per cylinder there is something wrong with the design.' It proved a disastrous race for us: both cars blew their engines. After the race Jochen boasted that feeling that his engine was about to blow he had deliberately booted it as hard as possible so that it would blow up spectacularly and could never be used again. This rather upset me, but Jochen no longer had his heart in racing for Cooper; he had only one more race for the team and when he said that he did not want to drive at Mexico City, I was quite relieved to field only a single car.

Pedro, although still in considerable pain, was just about fit enough to drive in Mexico and very keen to put up a good performance on home territory. On Alfieri's recommendation we again used a 36-plug engine, but Pedro preferred the T81B chassis and we faced quite a struggle installing the engine with its profusion of coils and wires in the older chassis. Although Pedro started from well back on the grid, he drove a fine race to finish sixth, two laps in arrears. In the Drivers' World Championship Pedro took joint sixth place with 15 points, thanks to his steady driving throughout the year, and Jochen's 6 points (which made him joint 11th) reflected his charging, press-on driving style and how hard he had been on his cars.

There had of course been negotiations with Jochen for the 1968 season, but the problem was that to compensate for the three years when he had had terrible terms, Jochen was seeking a retainer of £25,000. I had already lined up good sponsorship for 1968, but I knew that if Jochen was to be in the team (or another top-line driver) then we could cover the cost in additional sponsorship. John Cooper resented the idea of paying a driver so much money and the Chipstead directors supported John, so Rindt left the team. It was only after Jochen left Coopers and during his years with Brabham and Lotus that he matured as a Champion driver. Once he started to score points regularly with the rather fragile Lotus 49, he had obviously arrived as a driver. There has been much comment over the years about the friction between Jochen and myself. I think that it has all been rather exaggerated. Obviously we had flare-ups from time to time, but I believe that Jochen had confidence in me and Derrick White, the Cooper team were doing the best we could to make the cars race winners and we were on good and friendly terms most of the time.

I must say that I always believed Pedro Rodriguez to have as great a potential as Jochen. He was quick and reliable, he did not overdrive his cars and he had tremendous stamina. At the end of a race most drivers were completely exhausted and had almost to be dragged out of the cars, but Pedro would jump out, still fresh and looking as though he had only done a couple of laps. I would always speak highly of Pedro and perhaps I said too much, for although Pedro's contract with Cooper lasted until the end of 1968, he broke it to join BRM for the coming year.

For 1968 Cooper also opted to use the new V-12 BRM engine and were even less successful than BRM themselves. I wanted Cooper to use the Cosworth engine, but John Cooper was very much in favour of the BRM. John was very anxious because he thought that the team would lose its sponsorship from the British Motor Corporation if we used the Ford engine. In fact the money was not substantial and amounted to only a small proportion of our total sponsorship money. We were likely to lose the BMC money in any case because the days of the Mini-Cooper were numbered and I did not believe that the choice of the Ford engine would influence BMC's decision.

There was considerable dissension between the Cooper directors and two new directors who had joined the board supported John. Unfortunately we had lost our anchor-man Mario Tozzi-Condivi, who had left Cooper, and without Mario I reckoned that the cards were stacked against us. I resigned my directorship and so had no involvement in either the cars or the choice of drivers for 1968. I had expected that we would have a meeting when I would hand over the reins to my successor, but this never happened. Cooper lost much of the sponsorship that I had arranged for 1968 and the cars were so uncompetitive that the team withdrew from racing at the end of the season. Derrick White left when I did. I had great confidence in Derrick and I believed that he would make the grade even if rather slowly. He was so thorough, reliable, cautious and dependable.

Together with Robert Perry I bought Thomson & Taylor (Brooklands) Ltd from the Chipstead Group. We expanded and developed this old and established Alfa Romeo distributors and acquired the nearby Central Garage Ltd which became BMW dealers. I missed motor racing very much, but the business took more and more time. In 1971 we decided to sell out to a public company, William Jacks Ltd, and three years later I fulfilled my long ambition of going to live in Monaco.

Postscript

There have been momentous changes in International motor racing since I quit the scene in 1968. Many of these have been technical and we have seen the transformation in the handling and performance of Formula One cars as a result of suspension and tyre developments, ground effect and turbocharging. Equally significant has been the revolution in the organisation of the sport; I know there are many critics of the FISA and FOCA, but the sport is now correctly regulated, excellently organised and, thanks mainly to the efforts of drivers in the late 1960s and early 1970s, circuits are very much safer. With today's safety standards I am fairly certain we would not have lost Archie Scott-Brown at Spa in 1958 or Collins, Schell and Jimmy Clark, amongst many others, from their accidents, and I would not have had my near-fatal accident at Silverstone in 1951.

Scrutineering for today's Formula One races is by appointment at your own garage and not after hours of queueing, sometimes in the rain, only to find the scrutineering bay closed for a two-hour lunch break. The bargaining for starting money, not knowing whether your entry has been accepted until only weeks before the event, the queueing for pit passes, practice sessions frequently shortened at will, the long wait the day after the race to collect one's starting money – all these things I remember with very little pleasure, and these problems no longer exist. Today the circuits are maintained to an exacting standard and marshalling is very professional throughout the motor racing world, not just in England as was the case. After all, drivers are not gladiators but competitors in a dangerous sport in which they wish to minimise the risks.

Whilst the FISA and FOCA have no doubt created areas of dispute, I am quite sure these can eventually be sensibly resolved. In my racing days the sponsorship came from within the motor industry and with only limited outside backing, but today, the appearance of multi-national sponsors has ensured that entrants are fully financed and that drivers receive more than adequate rewards for their efforts.

I made a commercial success of my motor racing mainly because I combined the role of manager and racing driver, and in my good years I could average £25,000 a year. However, to do this I had to race in almost every category of motor racing, and it was fortunate that I did not consider it necessary to have a racing manager or any form of racing organisation, which would have greatly

Top *With Bernie Ecclestone at Monza* (Roy Salvadori collection).

Above *On the grid at Monza with the Marsh Plant Aston Martin DBR4* (Roy Salvadori collection).

reduced that income. Mike Hawthorn and Peter Collins, who drove for Ferrari, had to obtain permission from Enzo Ferrari for their other drives and were fairly restricted because of this, with the net result that their earning capacity suffered accordingly.

Whilst one might envy the earnings of the present day drivers one has to remember that we were participating in a sport of our own choice and, for that era, being highly paid for it; I am fairly certain that if the money had not been there, we would still have raced for the sheer pleasure.

In some ways I regret giving up motor racing when I did. I seemed to have

Stirling and myself at Goodwood for a test session prior to the launch of the John Wyer Aston Martin book (Roger P. Stowers).

mastered long-distance racing and I was still very competitive with GT and sports cars, so I feel I could have continued with reasonable success. My interest in motor racing has not diminished with the passing of the years or because of moving to Monaco. Apart from the fact that the Monaco Grand Prix takes place literally on my doorstep (the apartment block where I live is situated just above the start/finish line), I am not far from the Paul Ricard circuit, only three hours' drive from Monza, and many retired and active racing drivers settle in Monaco so I am surrounded by friends with the same interests. Indeed my entrants and friends for so many years, Sir David Brown and John Coombs, also live here.

I have had the opportunity of driving historic Aston Martins from time to time. I have driven Neil Corner's DBR4, Lord Downe's DBR1 and the similar cars owned by Geoffrey Marsh's Marsh Plant Company in historic events at Goodwood, Silverstone, Monza and Dubai. I have raced in Celebrity races at Brands Hatch and Macau. On three occasions I have driven in the pre-Motor Show Cavalcade through the streets of Birmingham superbly organised by Martin Hone.

Appendix

Racing successes, 1946–65

Because of the large numbers of events entered, results have been limited to first three places in British National races and first six places in major International events.

1946

June 15	**Gransden Lodge**		
	Racing cars up to 750 cc, 6 miles	MG R-type	2nd

1947

May 25	**Chimay**		
	Grand Prix des Frontières, Formule Libre, 81 miles	Alfa Romeo Monoposto	5th
July 13	**Gransden Lodge**		
	Gransden Trophy, 44 miles	Alfa Romeo Monoposto	3rd

1951

August 9	**Boreham**		
	W. Lyons Trophy, Jaguar XK120s, 30 miles	Jaguar XK120	3rd
	Unlimited sports cars, 21 miles	Jaguar XK120	3rd
October 6	**Castle Combe**		
	Sports cars over 1,500 cc, 18 miles	Frazer Nash Le Mans Replica	3rd

1952

April 12	**Castle Combe**		
	1,500–2,500 cc sports cars, 11 miles	Frazer Nash Le Mans Replica	2nd
	Unlimited sports cars, 11 miles	Frazer Nash Le Mans Replica	3rd
April 19	**Ibsley**		
	3,000 cc sports cars, 15 miles	Frazer Nash Le Mans Replica	2nd
May 10	**Silverstone**		
	Production sports cars, 50 miles	Frazer Nash Le Mans Replica	6th (1st in 2-litre class)
May 17	**Goodwood**		
	3,000 cc sports cars, 12 miles	Frazer Nash Le Mans Replica	1st, 76.59 mph (and fastest lap of 78.98 mph)

May 24	**Silverstone**		
	Unlimited sports cars, 11 miles	Jaguar XK120	2nd
May 29	**Douglas**		
	British Empire Trophy, sports car handicap, 200 miles	Frazer Nash Le Mans Replica	4th
June 21	**Boreham**		
	W. Lyons Trophy, Jaguar XK120s, 30 miles	Jaguar XK120	2nd
	Unlimited sports cars, 15 miles	Jaguar XK120	2nd
June 28	**Snetterton**		
	Sports cars, 1,501–2500 cc, 14 miles	Frazer Nash Le Mans Replica	1st, 75.77 mph (and fastest lap of 77.43 mph)
	Sports car handicap, 14 miles	Frazer Nash Le Mans Replica	2nd (and fastest lap of 78.05 mph)
August 2	**Boreham**		
	Sports cars up to 2,0000 cc, 100 miles	Frazer Nash Le Mans Replica	2nd
	Sports cars over 2,000 cc, 100 miles	Ferrari Tipo 225	4th (2nd in 3,000 cc class)
August 4	**Thruxton**		
	Sports cars up to 2,500 cc, 17 miles	Frazer Nash Le Mans Replica	1st, 67.58 mph
	Unlimited sports cars, 28 miles	Frazer Nash Le Mans Replica	1st, 72.16 mph (and fastest lap of 76.08 mph)
	Invitation race, 17 miles	Frazer Nash Le Mans Replica	1st, 75.02 mph
August 16	**Goodwood**		
	Nine Hours race	Ferrari Tipo 225 (with R. Baird)	3rd
October 4	**Castle Combe**		
	Formula Two, 37 miles	Ferrari Tipo 500	1st, 83.20 mph (and new class lap record of 85.38 mph)
October 11	**Charterhall**		
	Unlimited sports cars, 40 miles	Ferrari Tipo 225	3rd

1953

April 6	**Goodwood**		
	Lavant Cup, Formula Two, 17 miles	Connaught A-series	2nd (and fastest lap of 89.44 mph)
April 18	**Snetterton**		
	Sports car handicap, 27 miles	Frazer Nash Le Mans Replica	3rd
	Formule Libre, 27 miles	Ferrari Tipo 500	2nd
	Invitation race, 27 miles	Frazer Nash Le Mans Replica	2nd
May 9	**Silverstone**		
	Daily Express International Trophy, 102 miles	Connaught A-series	2nd (and 3rd in heat 2)

May 25	**Crystal Palace**		
	1,500 cc supercharged cars, 14 miles	ERA-Delage	2nd
June 27	**Snetterton**		
	Sports car handicap, 14 miles	Frazer Nash Le Mans Replica	3rd (and fastest lap of 80.60 mph)
	Formule Libre, 27 miles	Connaught A-series	1st, 86.34 mph (and new lap record of 88.04 mph)
July 11	**Crystal Palace**		
	Crystal Trophy, Formula Two, 21 miles	Connaught A-series	2nd
July 18	**Silverstone**		
	Sports cars, 102 miles	Aston Martin DB3S	2nd
July 25	**Snetterton**		
	Sports cars under 2,000 cc, 41 miles	Frazer Nash Le Mans Replica Mk II	1st, 78.85 mph (and fastest lap of 80.60 mph
August 15	**Charterhall**		
	Formula Two, 100 miles	Connaught A-series	2nd
	Formule Libre, 100 miles	Connaught A-series	3rd (took over Fairman's car)
August 30	**Nürburgring**		
	1,000 Kms race	Jaguar C-type (with I. M. Stewart)	2nd (and 1st in Production Sports Car class)
September 26	**Goodwood**		
	Madgwick Cup, Formula Two, 12 miles	Connaught A-series	1st, 89.63 mph (and new Formula Two lap record of 90.95 mph
October 3	**Castle Combe**		
	Sports cars over 1,500 cc, 28 miles	Maserati A6GCS	2nd
December 20	**Casablanca**		
	12 Hours race	Aston Martin DB3 (with M. Sparken)	4th

1954

April 3	**Castle Combe**		
	Sports cars up to 2,500 cc, 13 miles	Maserati A6GCS	1st, 79.42 mph
	Unlimited sports cars, 18 miles	Maserati A6GCS	1st, 80.29 mph (and joint fastest lap of 81.78 mph)
April 10	**Oulton Park**		
	British Empire Trophy, sports handicap, 71 miles	Maserati A6GCS	2nd (class record of 74.33 mph and 1st in heat)
April 19	**Goodwood**		
	Lavant Cup, Formula One, 17 miles	Maserati 250F	2nd (and joint fastest lap of 89.81 mph)
	Chichester Cup, Formule Libre, 12 miles	Maserati 250F	2nd (and joint fastest lap of 90.38 mph)
April 24	**Snetterton**		
	Sports cars up to 3,000 cc, 13 miles	Maserati A6GCS	2nd (and fastest lap of 84.37 mph)

	Invitation race, 27 miles	Maserati A6GCS	2nd (and fastest lap of 84.52 mph)
May 8	**Ibsley**		
	Closed cars, 10 miles	Aston Martin DB2	1st, 72.21 mph
	Sports cars over 1,500 cc, 15 miles	Maserati A6GCS	3rd (1st in class)
May 15	**Silverstone**		
	Sports cars, 73 miles	Aston Martin DB3S	7th (1st in class)
June 5	**Snetterton**		
	W. Lyons Trophy, Jaguar handicap, 27 miles	Jaguar C-type	3rd (and fastest lap of 84.82 mph)
	Sports cars up to 2,000 cc, 13 miles	Maserati A6GCS	2nd (and joint fastest lap of 83.08 mph)
	Formula One, 27 miles	Maserati 250F	1st, 87.85 mph (and fastest lap of 89.34 mph)
	Unlimited sports cars, 13 miles	Jaguar C-type	1st, 84.26 mph (and fastest lap of 85.56 mph)
	Unlimited sports cars, handicap, 13 miles	Jaguar C-type	1st, 85.29 mph (and fastest lap of 86.79 mph)
	Formule Libre, 27 miles	Maserati 250F	1st, 87.63 mph (and fastest lap of 90.19 mph)
June 7	**Goodwood**		
	Racing cars up to 2,500 cc, 12 miles	Maserati 250F	2nd (and fastest lap of 90.95 mph)
	Whitsun Trophy, Formule Libre, 36 miles	Maserati 250F	3rd
June 19	**Crystal Palace**		
	2,000 cc sports cars, 14 miles	Maserati A6GCS	1st, 67.44 mph
July 11	**Rouen**		
	Grand Prix, 301 miles	Maserati 250F	3rd
July 17	**Silverstone**		
	Sports cars, 73 miles	Aston Martin DB3S	2nd (and fastest lap of 89.30 mph)
August 2	**Crystal Palace**		
	August Trophy, Formula One, 14 miles	Maserati 250F	2nd (and 2nd in heat)
August 14	**Snetterton**		
	Sports cars up to 2,000 cc, 54 miles	Maserati A6GCS	2nd
August 28	**Castle Combe**		
	Unlimited sports cars, 18 miles	Maserati A6GCS	1st, 80.72 mph (and joint fastest lap of 81.98 mph)
September 4	**Charterhall**		
	Unlimited sports cars, 20 miles	Jaguar C-type	1st, 78.94 mph
September 25	**Goodwood**		
	Sports cars up to 2,000 cc, 12 miles	Maserati A6GCS	1st, 82.13 mph
	Goodwood Trophy, Formula One, 50 miles	Maserati 250F	3rd
	Sports cars over 2,000 cc, 12 miles	Jaguar C-type	1st, 83.88 mph

October 9	**Snetterton**		
	Sports cars over 2,000 cc, 14 miles	Aston Martin DB2	2nd (1st in class and fastest lap of 79.16 mph)
	Sports cars over 1,500 cc, 27 miles	Maserati A6GCS	3rd (1st in class)
	Formule Libre, 27 miles	Maserati 250F	1st, 89.37 mph (and fastest lap of 91.26 mph)
	Sports car handicap, 14 miles	Maserati A6GCS	2nd
October 23	**Pedralbes**		
	Barcelona Cup race, 157 miles	Jaguar C-type	2nd

1955

March 26	**Snetterton**		
	Formule Libre, 41 miles	Maserati 250F	1st, 76.19 mph
April 11	**Goodwood**		
	Lavant Cup, racing cars up to 2,000 cc, 45 miles	Connaught A-series	1st, 86.57 mph (and fastest lap of 88.16 mph)
	Chichester Cup, Formule Libre, 17 miles	Maserati 250F	2nd
	Sports cars over 2,000 cc, 12 miles	Aston Martin DB3S	1st, 83,40 mph
	Richmond Trophy, Formula One, 50 miles	Maserati 250F	1st, 89.26 mph (and fastest lap of 92.11 mph)
	Easter Handicap, 12 miles	Maserati 250F	2nd
April 16	**Charterhall**		
	Formule Libre, 40 miles	Connaught A-series	1st, 82.08 mph
April 30	**Ibsley**		
	Formule Libre, 31 miles	Maserati 250F	1st, 86.60 mph (and lap record of 88.04 mph)
	Sports cars over 2,750 cc, 31 miles	Aston Martin DB3S	1st, 80.95 mph (and class lap record of 84.30 mph)
May 7	**Silverstone**		
	Sports cars, 117 miles	Aston Martin DB3S	2nd
	Daily Express International Trophy, 176 miles	Maserati 250F	2nd (and lap record of 98.48 mph jointly with P. J. Collins)
May 28	**Snetterton**		
	Curtis Trophy, Formula One, 27 miles	Maserati 250F	1st, 89.03 mph (and fastest lap of 90.00 mph)
	Formule Libre, 27 miles	Maserati 250F	1st, 90.72 mph
May 30	**Crystal Palace**		
	Norbury Trophy, unlimited sports cars, 14 miles	Aston Martin DB3S	2nd (and fastest lap of 71.00 mph)
June 25	**Snetterton**		
	Eastern Counties '100' Trophy, unlimited sports cars, 100 miles	Aston Martin DB3S	1st, 86.30 mph
July 10	**Brands Hatch**		
	Sports cars over 1,900 cc, 12 miles	Cooper-Maserati	2nd

July 16	**Aintree**		
	Sports cars, 51 miles	Aston Martin DB3S	1st, 81.32 mph
July 30	**Crystal Palace**		
	International Trophy, Formula One, 14 miles	Maserati 250F	3rd (2nd in heat)
	Unlimited sports cars, 14 miles	Aston Martin DB3S	1st, 73.16 mph (and sports car lap record of of 74.49 mph)
August 1	**Brands Hatch**		
	Rochester Cup, Formule Libre, aggregate of two 19-mile heats	Maserati 250F	3rd on aggregate
August 13	**Snetterton**		
	Sports cars up to 1,300 cc, 54 miles	Cooper-Climax	1st, 74.27 mph
	Sports cars up to 2,750 cc, 54 miles	Cooper-Maserati	1st, 81.19 mph
	Formule Libre, 68 miles	Maserati 250F	2nd
September 3	**Aintree**		
	Sports cars up to 1,500 cc, 51 miles	Cooper-Climax 1,100 cc	4th (1st in class)
	Daily Telegraph Trophy, Formula One, 51 miles	Maserati 250F	1st, 83.72 mph (and fastest lap of 86.26 mph)
	Unlimited sports cars, 51 miles	Aston Martin DB3S	3rd
	Formule Libre, 51 miles	Maserati 250F	2nd
October 1	**Castle Combe**		
	Sports cars up to 2,000 cc, 37 miles	Lister-Bristol	3rd

1956

March 24	**Sebring**		
	12 Hours race	Aston Martin DB3S (with C. Shelby)	4th (1st in class)
April 2	**Goodwood**		
	Lavant Cup, racing cars up to 2,000 cc, 17 miles	Cooper-Climax Sports 1,500 cc	1st, 87.17 mph
	1,500 cc Sports cars, 17 miles	Cooper-Climax 1,500 cc	1st, 86.30 mph (and joint fastest lap of 87.45 mph)
	Richmond Trophy, Formula One, 77 miles	Maserati 250F	2nd
April 14	**Oulton Park**		
	British Empire Trophy, sports handicap, 71 miles	Cooper-Climax 1,500 cc	3rd (2nd in heat)
April 21	**Aintree**		
	2,000 cc sports cars, 24 miles	Cooper-Climax 1,500 cc	2nd
	Unlimited sports cars, 30 miles	Aston Martin DB3S	1st, 83.20 mph (and class lap record of 84.38 mph)
May 5	**Silverstone**		
	1,500 cc sports cars, 73 miles	Cooper-Climax 1,500 cc	1st, 95.13 mph (and class lap record of 96.67 mph)
	Unlimited sports cars, 73 miles	Aston Martin DB3S	1st, 94.79 mph

June 17	**Oporto**		
	City Cup, 1,500 cc sports cars, 148 miles	Cooper-Climax 1,500 cc	1st, 92.96 mph
June 23	**Aintree**		
	Unlimited sports cars, 30 miles	Aston Martin DB3S	1st, 81.33 mph and fastest lap of 82.70 mph)
July 8	**Rouen**		
	Grand Prix, 3,000 cc sports cars, 203 miles	Aston Martin DB3S	5th
July 14	**Silverstone**		
	Formula Two, 73 miles	Cooper-Climax F2	1st, 96.00 mph
	Sports cars, 73 miles	Aston Martin DB3S	2nd
July 22	**Snetterton**		
	1,500 cc sports cars, 27 miles	Lotus-Climax 1,500 cc	1st, 88.01 mph
	Vanwall Trophy, Formula One, 41 miles	Maserati 250F	1st, 92.00 mph
	H. W. Sear Trophy, Formule Libre, 27 miles	Maserati 250F	1st, 89.57 mph (and fastest lap of 93.46 mph)
August 5	**Nürburgring**		
	Rheinland Cup, 1,500 cc sports cars, 99 miles	Cooper-Climax 1,500 cc	3rd
August 6	**Brands Hatch**		
	Formula Two, 20 miles	Cooper-Climax F2	1st, 70.87 mph
August 26	**Caen**		
	Grand Prix, 153 miles	Maserati 250F	3rd (and lap record of 91.35 mph)
September 8	**Goodwood**		
	Woodcote Cup, 2,000 cc racing cars, 24 miles	Cooper-Climax F2	1st, 88.34 mph (and fastest lap of 89.81 mph)
	Sussex Trophy, Formula Two, 24 miles	Cooper-Climax F2	1st, 89.07 mph (and lap record of 90.57 mph)
	Goodwood Trophy, sports cars over 1,500 cc, 50 miles	Aston Martin DB3S	2nd
September 22	**Oulton Park**		
	Gold Cup, Formula Two, 110 miles	Cooper-Climax F2	1st, 83.84 mph (and lap record of 84.95 mph)
October 14	**Brands Hatch**		
	Formula One, 19 miles	Maserati 250F	3rd

1957

April 6	**Oulton Park**		
	British Empire Trophy, unlimited race, 69 miles	Aston Martin DBR1 (2.5-litre engine)	2nd
April 22	**Goodwood**		
	Sussex Trophy, unlimited sports cars, 50 miles	Aston Martin DBR1 (2.5-litre engine)	2nd
May 12	**Spa-Francorchamps**		
	Belgian National Sports Car race, 132 miles	Aston Martin DBR1	2nd

May 26	**Nürburgring**		
	1,000 Kms race	Aston Martin DBR1 (with L. Leston)	6th
June 9	**Brands Hatch**		
	2,000 cc sports cars, 12 miles	Cooper-Climax 1,500 cc	2nd
June 10	**Crystal Palace**		
	London Trophy, Formula Two, aggregate of two 14-mile heats	Cooper-Climax F2	2nd on aggregate
	Norbury Trophy, 2,000 cc sports cars, 14 miles	Cooper-Climax 1,500 cc	2nd (and fastest lap of 74.02 mph)
July 14	**Reims**		
	Coupe Internationale de Vitesse, Formula Two, 191 miles	Cooper-Climax F2	4th
	Reims Grand Prix, 315 miles	Vanwall	5th
July 20	**Aintree**		
	Sports cars, 51 miles	Aston Martin DBR1	2nd (and joint fastest lap of 81.94 mph)
	British Grand Prix, 270 miles	Cooper-Climax 2-litre	5th
July 28	**Caen**		
	Grand Prix, 188 miles	Cooper-Climax 2-litre	2nd
August 25	**Spa-Francorchamps**		
	RACB Sports car Grand Prix, 3 hours	Aston Martin DBR1	4th
September 14	**Silverstone**		
	Daily Express International Trophy, 102 miles	Cooper-Climax F2	8th (1st Formula Two car, Formula Two lap record of 99.41 mph, 12th in heat)
	Unlimited sports cars, 73 miles	Aston Martin DBR2	1st, 96.08 mph (and new class record of 98.48 mph)
September 28	**Goodwood**		
	Woodcote Cup, Formula Two, 24 miles	Cooper-Climax F2	1st, 94.43 mph
	Goodwood Trophy, unlimited sports cars, 50 miles	Lotus-Climax 1,500 cc	4th (1st in 2,000 cc class, class lap record of 90.00 mph)

1958

April 7	**Goodwood**		
	International '100', Formula One, 101 miles	Cooper-Climax 2-litre	3rd
	Chichester Cup, 1,100 cc sports cars, 24 miles	Lotus-Climax 1,100 cc	3rd
April 19	**Aintree**		
	Over 1,100 cc sports cars, 45 miles	Aston Martin DBR2	2nd (and sports car lap record of 87.38 mph)

May 3	**Silverstone** *Daily Express International Trophy*, 146 miles	Cooper-Climax 2-litre	2nd
May 26	**Zandvoort** *Dutch Grand Prix*, 195 miles	Cooper-Climax 2.2-litre	4th
July 19	**Silverstone** *Sports cars*, 73 miles	Lotus-Climax 2-litre	2nd (1st in 2,000 cc class)
	British Grand Prix, 220 miles	Cooper-Climax 2.2-litre	3rd
August 3	**Nürburgring** *German Grand Prix*, 213 miles	Cooper-Climax 2.2-litre	2nd
September 7	**Monza** *Italian Grand Prix*, 250 miles	Cooper-Climax 2-litre	4th
September 13	**Goodwood** *Tourist Trophy*, 4 hours	Aston Martin DBR1 (with J. Brabham)	2nd
September 20	**Oulton Park** *Unlimited sports cars*, 124 miles	Lotus-Climax 2-litre	1st, 84.99 mph (and sports car lap record of 86.28 mph)

1959

March 30	**Goodwood** *Lavant Cup*, Formula Two, 36 miles	Cooper-Climax F2	2nd (and lap record of 95.79 mph)
	Fordwater Trophy, saloon cars, 24 miles	Jaguar 3.4	2nd
April 11	**Oulton Park** *Unlimited sports cars*, 55 miles	Cooper Monaco-Maserati 2.5-litre	2nd
April 18	**Aintree** *Saloon cars*, 30 miles	Jaguar 3.4	2nd (and class lap record of 76.70 mph)
	Unlimited sports cars, 51 miles	Cooper Monaco-Maserati 2.5-litre	1st, 85.22 mph (and fastest lap of 86.12 mph)
May 2	**Silverstone** *Grand Touring cars*, 35 miles	Jaguar 3.4	2nd
	Daily Express International Trophy, 146 miles	Aston Martin DBR4	2nd (and fastest lap of 105.37 mph)
	Sports cars up to 3,000 cc, 73 miles	Cooper Monaco-Maserati 2.5-litre	1st, 98.40 mph
	Production Touring cars, 35 miles	Jaguar 3.4	2nd
May 10	**Monaco** *Grand Prix*, 195 miles	Cooper-Maserati	6th

May 18	**Crystal Palace**		
	Anerley Trophy, sports cars up to 1,500 cc, 14 miles	Cooper Monaco-Climax 1.5-litre	2nd (and 2nd in heat)
	London Trophy, Formula Two, 50 miles	Cooper-Climax F2	1st, 80.78 mph (and fastest lap of 82.30 mph)
	Norbury Trophy, sports cars over 1,500 cc, 21 miles	Cooper Monaco-Maserati 2.5-litre	1st, 81.37 mph
June 20/21	**Le Mans**		
	24 Hours race	Aston Martin DBR1 (with C. Shelby)	1st, 112.57 mph
July 18	**Aintree**		
	British Grand Prix 225 miles	Aston Martin DBR4	6th
August 3	**Brands Hatch**		
	John Davy Trophy, Formula Two, aggregate of two 31-mile heats	Cooper-Climax F2	2nd
August 23	**Lisbon**		
	Portuguese Grand Prix, 209 miles	Aston Martin DBR4	6th
September 26	**Oulton Park**		
	Gold Cup race, Formula One, 152 miles	Cooper-Maserati	4th
	Closed cars, 52 miles	Jaguar 3.4	1st, 76.68 mph

1960

April 2	**Oulton Park**		
	Oulton Park Trophy, Formula Two, 69 miles	Cooper-Climax F2	3rd
April 18	**Goodwood**		
	Lavant Cup, Formula Two, 36 miles	Cooper-Climax F2	3rd
	Sussex Trophy, sports cars, 50 miles	Cooper Monaco-Climax 2.5-litre	1st, 89.96 mph (and class lap record of 96.43 mph)
	Fordwater Trophy, closed cars, 24 miles	Jaguar 3.8	2nd
April 30	**Aintree**		
	Sports cars, 51 miles 51 miles	Cooper Monaco-Climax 2.5-litre	1st, 85.96 mph
May 7	**Oulton Park**		
	Sports cars over 1,100 cc, 41 miles	Cooper Monaco-Climax 2.5-litre	1st, 89.24 mph (and class lap record of 91.52 mph)
	Formula Two, 55 miles	Cooper-Climax F2	1st, 89.98 mph
May 14	**Silverstone**		
	Sports cars, 73 miles	Cooper Monaco-Climax 2.5-litre	1st, 100.73 mph (and class lap record of 102.90 mph)
	Production touring cars, 35 miles	Jaguar 3.8	1st, 87.55 mph (and class lap record of 89.00 mph)
June 25/26	**Le Mans**		
	24 Hours race	Aston Martin DBR1 (with J. Clark)	3rd

August 1	**Brands Hatch**		
	Raffles Club Trophy, unlimited sports cars, 53 miles	Cooper Monaco-Climax 2.5-litre	1st, 78.23 mph
	Kingsdown Trophy, saloon cars, 27 miles	Jaguar 3.8	1st, 75.98 mph
August 20	**Goodwood**		
	Tourist Trophy, GT cars, 3 hours	Aston Martin DB3GT	2nd (and GT lap record of 89.81 mph)
September 17	**Snetterton**		
	Lombank Trophy, Formula One, 100 miles	Cooper-Climax	4th
October 9	**Watkins Glen**		
	International Grand Prix, Formule Libre, 230 miles	Cooper Monaco-Climax 2.5-litre	3rd
October 23	**Montlhéry**	Aston Martin DB4GT (with I. Ireland)	6th
	Paris 1,000 Kms race		

1961

February 4	**Teretonga**		
	Invercargill Trophy, Formule Libre, 75 miles	Louts 18-Climax	2nd (and 1st in the Invitation race)
March 6	**Longford**		
	International Gold Star race, Formule Libre, 108 miles	Cooper-Climax	1st, 104.50 mph
March 25	**Snetterton**		
	Lombank Trophy, Formula One and Inter-Continental Formula, 100 miles	Cooper-Climax	5th (3rd in Formula One class and class lap record of 99.55 mph)
	Grand Touring cars, 33 miles	Aston Martin DB4GT	3rd
April 3	**Goodwood**		
	International '100', Formula One, 101 miles	Cooper-Climax	3rd
April 15	**Oulton Park**		
	Oulton Park Trophy, GT cars, 69 miles	Jaguar E-type	3rd (and joint GT lap record of 84.69 mph)
April 22	**Aintree**		
	Saloon cars, 30 miles	Jaguar 3.8	1st, 76.14 mph
April 25	**Siracusa**		
	Grand Prix, Formula One, 191 miles	Cooper-Climax	5th
May 6	**Silverstone**		
	Sports cars, 73 miles	Cooper Monaco-Climax 2.5-litre	2nd
	International Trophy, Inter-Continental Formula, 234 miles	Cooper-Climax	3rd
May 22	**Crystal Palace**		
	Norbury Trophy, GT cars,	Jaguar E-type	1st, 76.40 mph (joint

	21 miles		class lap record of 77.00 mph)
	Green Helmet Trophy, sports cars, 21 miles	Cooper Monaco-Climax 2.5-litre	1st, 79.87 mph
	London Trophy, Formula One, 51 miles	Cooper-Climax	1st, 82.55 mph (joint fastest lap of 83.96 mph)
	Touring cars, 21 miles	Jaguar 3.8	1st, 70.44 mph
June 3	**Brands Hatch**		
	Peco Trophy, GT cars, 27 miles	Jaguar E-type	2nd
	Silver City Trophy, Formula One, 201 miles	Cooper-Climax	4th
July 15	**Aintree**		
	British Grand Prix, 225 miles	Cooper-Climax	6th
July 23	**Snetterton**		
	Scott-Brown Memorial Trophy, GT cars, 54 miles	Jaguar E-type	2nd
August 7	**Brands Hatch**		
	Peco Trophy, GT cars, 53 miles	Jaguar E-type	3rd
	Guards Trophy, Inter-Continental Formula, 201 miles	Cooper-Climax	5th
	Redex Trophy, saloon cars, 53 miles	Jaguar 3.8	2nd (and class lap record of 78.97 mph)
August 19	**Goodwood**		
	Tourist Trophy, GT cars, 3 hours	Aston Martin DB4GT	3rd
August 20	**Karlskoga**		
	Cannon race, Formula One, 56 miles	Cooper-Climax	4th
August 26/27	**Copenhagen**		
	Grand Prix, Formula One, aggregate of three heats totalling 80 miles	Cooper-Climax	3rd on aggregate
September 10	**Monza**		
	Italian Grand Prix, 267 miles	Cooper-Climax	6th
September 23	**Oulton Park**		
	Saloon cars, 52 miles	Jaguar 3.8	1st, 79.44 mph
September 30	**Snetterton**		
	Saloon cars, 33 miles	Jaguar 3.8	2nd
	Molyslip Trophy, GT cars,	Jaguar E-type	2nd

1962

January 6	**New Zealand** *Grand Prix*, Ardmore, 100 miles	Cooper-Climax	4th
April 23	**Goodwood**		
	St Mary's Trophy, saloon cars, 24 miles	Jaguar 3.8	2nd (and fastest lap of 88.34 mph)

	Lavant Cup, Formula One 4-cyl cars, 50 miles	Lola-Climax	2nd
	International '100', Formula One, 101 miles	Lola-Climax	4th
April 28	**Aintree**		
	Saloon cars, 30 miles	Jaguar 3.8	2nd
May 27	**Brands Hatch**		
	Peco Trophy, GT cars, 27 miles	Aston Martin DB4GT	2nd (and class lap record of 80.30 mph)
	Touring cars, 27 miles	Jaguar 3.8	2nd
June 11	**Crystal Palace**		
	Saloon cars, 21 miles	Jaguar 3.8	1st, 74.51 mph (and joint fastest lap of 75.59 mph)
	Crystal Palace Trophy, Formula One, 50 miles	Lola-Climax V-8	2nd
June 22/23	**Le Mans**		
	24 Hours race	Jaguar E-type (with B. Cunningham)	4th
July 1	**Reims**		
	Grand Prix, 258 miles	Lola-Climax V-8	6th
August 6	**Brands Hatch**		
	Peco Trophy, GT cars, 66 miles	Ferrari 250GTO	2nd
	Molyslip Trophy, saloon cars, 80 miles	Jaguar 3.8	3rd
August 12	**Karlskoga**		
	Formula One, 56 miles	Lola-Climax V-8	2nd
August 18	**Goodwood**		
	Tourist Trophy, GT cars, 240 miles	Jaguar E-type	4th

1963

March 30	**Snetterton**		
	Sports and Prototype GT cars, 68 miles	Cooper Monaco-Climax 2.7-litre	2nd
	Touring cars, 60 miles	Jaguar 3.8	1st, 83.41 mph
April 15	**Goodwood**		
	St Mary's Trophy, saloon cars, 24 miles	Jaguar 3.8	2nd
	Sussex Trophy, GT cars, 36 miles	Jaguar E-type	3rd
	Lavant Cup, sports cars, 50 miles	Cooper Monaco-Climax 2.7-litre	1st, 84.14 mph
April 27	**Aintree**		
	Unlimited sports cars, 51 miles	Cooper Monaco-Climax 2.7-litre	1st, 85.39 mph (and class lap record of 86.82 mph)
	Touring cars, 30 miles	Jaguar 3.8	2nd
May 11	**Silverstone**		
	GT cars, 73 miles	Jaguar E-type	2nd (and class lap record of 102.90 mph)
	Production touring cars, 73 miles	Jaguar 3.8	2nd

	Sports cars, 35 miles	Cooper Monaco-Climax 2.7-litre	1st, 106.20 mph (and class lap record of 107.96 mph)
June 3	**Crystal Palace**		
	Saloon cars, 21 miles	Jaguar 3.8	2nd
July 6	**Brands Hatch**		
	Motor Six Hours saloon car race	Jaguar 3.8 (with D. C. Hulme)	1st, 72.62 mph
July 13	**Mallory Park**		
	Grovewood Trophy, GT cars, 41 miles	Jaguar E-type	3rd
July 20	**Silverstone**		
	Sports and GT cars, 73 miles	Cooper Monaco-Climax 2.7-litre	1st, 102.99 mph (and fastest lap of 105.58 mph)
August 5	**Brands Hatch**		
	Molyslip Trophy, saloon cars, 53 miles	Jaguar 3.8	3rd
	Guards International Trophy, sports and GT cars, 133 miles	Cooper Monaco-Climax 2.7-litre	2nd (and fastest lap of 91.73 mph)
August 24	**Goodwood**		
	Tourist Trophy, GT cars, 312 miles	Jaguar E-type	3rd
September 8	**Monza**		
	Coppa Inter-Europa, GT cars, 3 hours	Aston Martin DB4GT	1st, 120.23 mph (and class lap record of 124.27 mph)
September 21	**Oulton Park**		
	Sports cars, 52 miles	Cooper Monaco-Climax 2.7-litre	1st, 93.80 mph (and class lap record of 95.76 mph)

1964

May 2	**Silverstone**		
	Sports cars, 73 miles	Cooper-Maserati 4.5-litre	2nd (and fastest lap of 100.16 mph)
May 18	**Goodwood**		
	Sports and GT cars, 50 miles	Cooper-Maserati 4.5-litre	1st, 96.15 mph (and fastest lap of 99.31 mph)
July 11	**Brands Hatch**		
	Ilford Films Trophy, GT cars, 53 miles	Cobra-Ford	3rd
	Guards Trophy, sports cars, 53 miles	Cooper-Maserati 4.5-litre	3rd
July 19	**Snetterton**		
	Archie Scott-Brown Memorial Trophy, prototypes and GT cars, 100 miles	Ferrari 250LM	1st, 95.30 mph (and fastest lap of 98.35 mph)
September 6	**Monza**		
	Coppa Inter-Europa, GT cars and Prototypes over 2 litres, one hour	Ferrari 250LM	2nd

1965

June 7	**Goodwood** *Sports and GT cars,* 50 miles	Ford GT40	2nd (and 1st in GT class)

Index